Different Cultures
Same School

Different Cultures
Same School

ethnic minority children in europe

Edited by
Lotty Eldering
Leiden University
Jo Kloprogge
Institute for Educational Research in The Netherlands

SWETS & ZEITLINGER B.V. AMSTERDAM / LISSE   PUBLISHERS

SWETS NORTH AMERICA INC. BERWYN, PA   1989

Library of Congress Cataloging in Publication Data
Different cultures same school : ethnic minority children in Europe /
   Lotty Eldering, Jo Kloprogge, editors
         p.   cm.
   Bibliography: p.
   ISBN 90 265 0989 8
   1. Children of minorities–Europe–Education–Cross-cultural studies.
   2. Education, Bilingual–Europe–Cross-cultural studies.
   I. Eldering, Lotty.   II. Kloprogge, Jo, 1948-
   LC3736.A2D54 1989
   371.91–dc20   89-33797
                                                                                  CIP

CIP-gegevens Koninklijke Bibliotheek, Den Haag

Different

Different cultures same school : ethnic minority children in Europe /
Lotty Eldering, Jo Kloprogge (eds.) -
Amsterdam [etc.] : Swets & Zeitlinger ; Berwyn : Swets North America
ISBN 90-265-0989-8 geb.
SISO eu 452.9 UDC 376.6/.7-052-053.5-054.62(4) NUGI 724
Trefw.: onderwijs ; ethnische minderheden ; Europa

Cover design and layout: Rob Molthoff
Cover printed in the Netherlands by Casparie, IJsselstein
Printed in the Netherlands by Offsetdrukkerij Kanters B.V., Alblasserdam

ISBN 90 265 0989 8
NUGI 724

Foreword

In most Western European countries the number of children of ethnic minority groups is growing. Some of these children come to Western Europe during their childhood, others are born here. All need good schooling and educational qualifications to have a chance of finding a place in the sophisticated labour markets of the industrialized countries. Accomplishing this is not easy, neither for the children and their parents nor for the schools and teachers. Differences in language and culture, the often low socio-economic status of the parents and the inadequate responses of schools to these factors contribute to the educational disadvantages of the children.

Clearly, this situation is socially and economically undesirable, both for the minority groups and for the societies in which they live.

Much research has been done on this situation, and our understanding of the problems and of possible solutions is slowly improving. The differences in approach between scientists from different disciplins and the variation in national policies and social constraints, however, make it difficult to analyse the situation correctly.

This book may help to overcome these limitations. It is a collection of essays by experts from various scientific fields and countries, who explored the issue of the education of ethnic minority children during a conference held in the Netherlands in September 1988. At this conference, organized by the Dutch *Ministry of Education and Science* in collaboration with the Dutch *Ministry of Welfare, Health and Cultural Affairs*, the foundation for an integrated European research programme in this field was laid. The *Institute for Educational Resarch in the Netherlands* will stimulate the further development of such a programme. This book shows that much can be gained by international cooperation. It is important for the researchers and policy-makers in the countries described, but is of equal interest to other countries in which similar problems are encountered.

I would like to thank the authors and editors for the work they have done. They show us that cooperation across the borders of scientific disciplines and countries is possible and fruitful. We need this kind of cooperation to be able to solve the many problems involved in providing adequate policies and adequate education for ethnic minority children.

This book would not have been possible without the contribution of Mrs. J. Burrough, who revised the English text, and of the support team from the Dutch Ministry of Education and Science (Messrs. P. Kooiman, H. Knol and J.W.T. Mayvis, Mrs. W. Toetenel and Mrs. J. Lely), who organized the International Workshop.

W.J. Deetman,
Minister of Education and Science

Contents

1

Lotty Eldering & Jo Kloprogge

Leiden University & Institute for Educational
Research in the Netherlands

Introduction

This book presents an overall picture of the educational situation of ethnic minority children in Northwest European countries. It is the first publication in this field. In it, experts in pedagogy, psychology, sociology, cultural anthropology and linguistics give their views on issues concerning the education of immigrant children in their countries and indicate priorities for further research.

The equality of ethnic minority children in education is a topic of major concern for educationalists, policy-makers and researchers in Northwest European countries, which in the last thirty years have experienced a massive influx of migrant workers and their families from former colonies and from Mediterranean countries.

In 1981 the *Council of Europe*, which has long been concerned with the cultural and educational needs of migrant workers and their families, launched a project on *The education and cultural development of migrants* (CDCCs Project No. 7). One of the recommendations made by member states of the *Council of Europe* at the end of the Project was to prepare and implement a coordinated European research programme, in which one of the central topics would be the school success and failure of migrant children and its relationship to socio-cultural factors, language development and the position of migrant women and girls (Report of the Final Conference, 1987).

In 1987 the Dutch Ministry of Education and Sciences took the initiative of organizing an International European Workshop to prepare a
research programme in the aforementioned field.
This book is based on the papers presented at the workshop in Kerkrade, Netherlands, 12-14 September 1988. It has three parts, which
correspond closely to the three themes discussed at the workshop:
1. Ethnic-cultural and socio-economic factors influencing the school
   careers of ethnic minority children (chapters 2-7);
2. Second language acquisition (chapters 8 and 9);
3. School organization and school effectivity (chapter 10).

Departing from a given, common framework, the authors have elaborated *theme 1* from different perspectives, according to their own
discipline and with a varying accentuation.
Tomlinson (chapter 2) depicts the educational policy towards minority pupils in Britain, moving through three stages from assimilation,
through integration to cultural pluralism. The Education Reform
Act, which became law in 1988, will probably intensify racial and
religious segregation in schools. She further points out that whereas
in pre-1980 research it was concluded that pupils from ethnic minority backgrounds generally underachieved at school, research in the
1980s showed that these pupils are gradually improving their educational performance. The differences between the various ethnic
groups as well as between the sexes, however, remain considerable.
In their review of the situation in Federal Germany, *Boos-Nünning
and Hohmann* (chapter 3) emphasize the contradictions between official policy, issued by the Federal Government or its constituent states
('Bundesländer') and educational practice. An important issue under
discussion is whether the stay of migrant workers ('Gastarbeiter')
and their families should be seen as temporary, or their settlement in
Germany be accepted as a basis for educational policy. Whereas in
some respects the educational situation of migrant children has
improved in recent years, in other fields educational performance
has worsened. A comprehensive theory to explain this diversity is
still lacking. The authors also dwell extensively on the orientation
and aspirations of Turkish parents with regard to the schooling of
their children.
Costa-Lascoux (chapter 4) gives an historical overview of foreign
children in French schools from the 1920s and the way the educational system responded to their presence. The central issue in this
chapter is how the philosophy of equality is to be translated in edu-

cational policy and practice, without producing non-anticipated, adverse effects. She discusses the dilemma between equality of opportunity in the sense of uniformity of schooling independent of ethnic and class origins, and differentiation, or even positive discrimination in the educational system.

Roosens (chapter 5) depicts the situation of ethnic minority children in Belgium from a cultural anthropological perspective. After describing the major immigrant groups, he discusses the cultural position of second generation children in the family and society at large and their ethnic identity. Future research should, in his opinion, place more emphasis on how ethnic minority pupils and parents themselves view education and school success or failure. This research needs a holistic approach.

Eldering (chapter 6) sketches the history of immigration in the Netherlands and Dutch educational policy regarding immigrant children moving through three successive stages based on varying assumptions. The assumption underlying the 1985 Educational Priority Policy that ethnic minority children are comparable with Dutch children from disadvantaged groups in terms of their educational arrears at the beginning of their school careers, needs to be questioned. An important issue for further research is the explanation of differences in school performance between the various ethnic groups. European theorists might learn from the current discussion on this topic by educational anthropologists in the US.

The contribution of *Kağıtçıbaşı* (chapter 7) is the only one by an expert from a country of emigration. She deals with the question of whether cultural backgrounds or social class differences account for the disparity between the educational attainment of ethnic minority children and that of the majority population. Several studies on the child rearing environment in Turkey have shown that there is a strong connection between the socio-economic position of parents in society and the way they value and stimulate their children. In the second part of her chapter she discusses the effects of an early enrichment programme, carried out in Istanbul, on the child rearing practices of mothers and the development of their four-year-old children.

The two chapters on *theme 2*, second language acquisition, are complementary to each other, since they have a different theoretical as well as geographical emphasis.

Extra and Vallen (chapter 8) focus on second language acquisition by ethnic minority children in three neighbouring countries: the Netherlands, Belgium and the Federal Republic of Germany. They give an overall picture of legislation and facilities as well as of studies on second language acquisition in these three countries. Most West European countries have hardly begun to develop a consistent policy and legislation for first and second language teaching. Extra and Vallen also discuss two basic questions in this field: how the properties of the target language are acquired and how much time it takes to acquire these properties. Attention is further paid to didactic approaches and models of language teaching in multilingual settings.

Strömqvist (chapter 9) spells out some theoretical points of departure concerning the nature of the language acquisition process and the perspectives from which first and second language acquisition might be viewed: the developmental or the deviation perspective. He gives a brief review of how views on second language acquisition have influenced the debate, research and educational policy in Scandinavia. In Sweden, research in the 1970s was much inspired by the method of error analysis, whereas the focus in the 1980s research shifted to developmental processes rather than normative target states and to spoken language and interaction rather than written text. In discussing suggestions for further research he points out the great potential of communication- and ecology-oriented studies, from both a theoretical and a practical point of view. This kind of research needs multidisciplinary cooperation between linguists, cultural anthropologists, sociologists and psychologists.

Theme 3, school organization and school effectiveness, has been elaborated by *Sammons* (chapter 10). After an overview of research on the effectiveness of schools in general, she presents the findings from a recent study of junior education in the United Kingdom. This longitudinal study followed a complete age group of pupils (about 2000 seven-year-olds from 50 schools in inner London, entering their junior classes) and examined their progress and development throughout the whole period they received junior education. Relationships between ethnic background, pupils' fluency in English and their attainment and progress in the various cognitive and non-cognitive areas were also investigated. Ethnic background as well as sex proved to affect children's attainment and progress. As to the school effects on different groups, it was found that schools that were effective in promoting the progress of one group of pupils, were also effective for other groups, regardless of sex, social class or ethnic backgrounds. In the final section of this chapter she gives a survey of key factors for effective schooling.

Although the various authors viewed the issues in question from the perspective of their own discipline and focused on different geographical areas, several topics of common interest regarding the nature and the specific themes of future research were identified in the papers and in the discussions at the workshop. First of all, research should have a longitudinal character and be holistic in approach and it should include qualitative, more specifically cultural-anthropological, as well as quantitative methods of research. Chapter 11 outlines a possible programme for international, multidisciplinary research.

In the degree in which they make use of empirical facts or theoretical/philosophical concepts, the chapters also reflect to some extent the scientific cultures of the countries of the authors. This suggests that not only do differences between cultures in one country deserve attention, but also that what is a minority culture trait in one country may well be a dominating culture trait in another.

REFERENCE

Final Conference, Rotterdam 7-11 April 1986. General Report by Lotty van den Berg-Eldering. Council of Europe. Strasbourg 1987.

2

Sally Tomlinson
University of Lancaster

Ethnicity and Educational Achievement in Britain

1. INTRODUCTION

The issue of the educational achievement of ethnic minority pupils
has provided a focus of concern in Britain[1] for minority parents, and
communities, and for educational practitioners for over twenty-five
years and continues to cause anxiety. Parents are acutely aware that
without educational credentials their children may be denied access
to higher levels of education and training and may thus remain in
unskilled employment or unemployed. The provision of equal educational opportunity for ethnic minority groups has become an important political issue.

Although up to the 1980s research studies demonstrated that minority pupils on the whole, did not achieve educational credentials on a
par with white pupils, the situation in the 1980s may be changing.
Taking a long-term view – first generation immigrant minority
parents did not improve much on their own educational or vocational qualifications, but their children appear to be catching up with the
white majority in acquiring such credentials and there is marked improvement in the *progress* of minority pupils, particularly those of
Afro-Caribbean origin, as they move through school. The desire of
minority pupils to stay on in education and acquire some qualifications far exceeds that of white pupils. A whole set of explanations

for 'underachievement' by minorities has been put forward over the years. In particular, social disadvantage, home and family background, and lack of fluency in English were popular explanations in the 1960s and 1970s. Now, educational research is focusing on those factors in schools and in the education system itself which might hinder the progress of minority pupils. Research in the 1980s certainly distinguishes more carefully between various minority groups and avoids simplistic explanations, recognizing that the reasons for any educational underachievement are likely to be complex.

This chapter outlines the history of migration and some characteristics of minority groups in Britain, overviews educational policies towards the education of minority children and reviews research evidence and explanations offered for minority educational achievements up to and after 1980. The chapter concludes with some suggestions about the possible effects of the 1988 Education Reform Act on ethnic minority pupils.

2. ETHNIC MINORITIES AND THEIR CHILDREN

In Britain, post-war migration from Commonwealth countries and from Cyprus, Malta and other European countries, resulted in a range of pupils whose backgrounds were racially and culturally different arriving in British schools. Although it is the migration of 'non-white' people from the New Commonwealth and Pakistan which has attracted most attention in terms of social and educational policy, migration and cultural mixing are a part of British history. The Irish, who formed 3 per cent of the British population by 1851, are the largest minority group in the United Kingdom, and the number of Jewish people is estimated at over half a million. Small communities of black people had developed in parts of Cardiff and Liverpool by the early twentieth century. Under the 1948 British Nationality Act, migrants from the Commonwealth had the right of free entry and during the 1950s and 1960s came from the Caribbean, the Asian sub-continent, East and West Africa and the Far East. Migration from Poland, the Ukraine, Yugoslavia, Italy and the Baltic countries was encouraged in the immediate post-war period and migrants also came from Germany and Spain. The purpose of migration was to provide labour, and the British government and employers encouraged this. The British Transport Commission, London Transport and the National Health Service recruited directly from the Caribbean, particularly Jamaica. Restrictions on immigration were, however, imposed by the Commonwealth Immigration Acts of 1962 and 1968, the Immigration White Paper 1965, the Immigration Act 1971 and by the British Nationality Act of 1981.

The Census conducted in Britain every ten years has not to date included an 'ethnic' question, although in the 1991 Census people will be asked about their ethnic origin. The 1981 Census relied on 'Birthplace of Head of Household' to enumerate minority groups and the resulting figures are probably an underestimation.

Table 1: *Characteristics of Heads of Household Born in the 'Non-European' Commonwealth*

Birthplace of Head of Household	Number	Percentage with Three or more Children	Percentage Single Parent
India	673 704	19.5	1.4
Caribbean	545 744	11.5	10.4
Pakistan	295 461	40.1	1.8
Bangladesh	64 561	35.2	1.3
East Africa	181 321	11.4	1.8
Far East	120 123	10.1	2.0
Cyprus/Malta	170 078	9.1	2.5
Other Non-European	156 253		
Total	2 207 245		

Source: Adapted from 1981 Census Tables. London. Office of Population, Census and Surveys (OPCS).

Table 1, adapted from census tables, indicates that the most numerous minority groups are Indian, followed by Caribbean, Pakistani, East African (Asians mainly), Mediterranean groups (mainly Greek and Turkish Cypriot and Maltese), Far East (including Hong Kong), Bangladeshis – the most recently arrived immigrant group – and a variety of smaller groups, including West Africans, with a further 16000 Vietnamese settling in 1982. European groups include Italian, Polish and Ukrainian settlement, and the number of gypsy children is estimated between 30000 – 50000 (Taylor 1988). Although 'non-white' ethnic minorities make up just over 4 per cent of the UK population, 6.8 per cent of children under four belong to these groups and most ethnic minority children under fifteen were born in Britain and are British citizens.

Country of origin and place of settlement are factors which have never been fully taken into account when explaining minority pupils' educational achievements. For example, the city of Leicester was the place of settlement for numbers of Indians and East African Asians with relatively high educational and skill levels. It is to be expected that their children would achieve better at school than, say, the children of Pakistani rural unskilled workers who migrated to small towns in the north-west of England.

The family size of minority groups remained larger than that of the majority population in 1981. In particular, Pakistani and Bangladeshi groups were far more likely to have more than three children in their households, and Caribbean homes were more likely to be headed by a single parent.

There are no national statistics collected on the numbers of ethnic minority pupils in British schools. Statistics on 'immigrant' pupils were collected between 1965-1972, on the assumption that after ten years a child would cease to be counted as an immigrant. Collection of statistics was discontinued in 1972, mainly because of objections from teachers' unions, but in the late 1980s a committee set up by the Department of Education and Science has recommended that national statistics on numbers of ethnic minority pupils should be collected from 1990. It has been strongly argued that it is difficult to monitor the achievement of minority pupils unless such statistical data are available.

It is well established that ethnic minorities in Britain face greater difficulties and disadvantages than white people and the circumstances of their lives tend to be poorer. The rate of unemployment is twice as high among people of Afro-Caribbean and South-Asian origin than among whites and it is nearly 50 per cent among Afro-Caribbeans aged 16-19 (Brown, 1984). Ethnic minorities tend to be concentrated in urban areas, and occupy poorer housing, although this situation is slowly improving. Despite attempts to oppose racial discrimination by law, there is still a substantial amount of discrimination by employers. For example, although some unemployment can be explained by lower educational or job qualifications and lack of fluent English, if comparisons are made between ethnic minority men and white men with similar qualifications, differences in rates of unemployment and job levels remain the same (Smith, 1981).

Much research had indicated that minority parents have always had higher aspirations for their children to acquire the credentials which would allow for social and occupational mobility (Tomlinson, 1984;

Bhachu, 1987) and many parents remained in low-skilled, low-wage jobs, hoping the education system would provide better chances for their children. To some extent these aspirations are now being realized.

Table 2, extracted from data gathered by Brown (1984) for a national survey of 'Black and White Britain', illustrates how the younger generation of 'West Indians' and 'Asians' are now far more likely to have educational and vocational qualifications than the older generation, although they often have to remain longer in full-time education to acquire these qualifications than young white people.

Table 2: Percentage of Males with an Academic or Vocational Qualification by Ethnic Origin

	White	West Indian	Asian
No qualification aged 44+	64	87	74
No qualification aged 16-24	27	35	35
No academic but vocational qualification aged 16-24	5	3	1
No vocational but an academic qualification aged 16-24	50	48	56
Age 17 or over at completion of full-time education 16-24	29	41	58

Source: Adapted from C. Brown (1984). Black and White Britain London. Policy Studies Institute. pp. 145-7.

3. EDUCATIONAL POLICIES

Educational policy towards minority pupils in Britain has moved through three stages – usually described as assimilation, integration and cultural pluralism. In the 1960s, the assimilationist position attempted to minimize cultural and ethnic differences and to preserve a monolingual, monocultural society. A report in 1964 was concerned that immigrant children should culturally assimilate into British life and considered that "the education system cannot be expected to perpetuate the different values of immigrant groups" (Commonwealth Immigrants Advisory Council 1964, 10). Much emphasis was placed on English language teaching, in a Ministry of Education pamphlet on *English for Immigrants*, appearing in 1963. Special language centres withdrawing children from neighbourhood schools were set up and peripatetic language teachers were trained. It was considered undesirable at this time to have a high concentration of immigrant children in any school and the CIAC report also recommended dispersing children by bus to suburban schools. A *Government White Paper* in 1965 suggested that no school should have more than 30 per cent immigrant children. There was no two-way bussing, it was only immigrant, usually Asian, children who were bussed until the practice was ruled to be racially discriminatory in 1971. Demographic settlement meant that the '30 per cent rule' could not be enforced and many schools in urban areas eventually took in large numbers of Asian and Afro-Caribbean pupils.

By the 1970s, crude assimilationist policy had given way to ideas of integration, which amounted to a greater recognition of cultural differences, but the absorption of minorities remained a major issue. In 1966, Roy Jenkins, the then Home Secretary, had offered a classic definition of integration as "not a flattening process of assimilation but .... equal opportunity accompanied by cultural diversity, in an atmosphere of mutual tolerance". The desire of ethnic minorities to retain their own languages, religions and other cultural attributes was accorded some recognition, although schools still resisted Asian languages being taught in school time. The majority society remained unwilling to change and the government made an attempt to subsume the problems of minorities under those of the poor and disadvantaged, claiming that policies aimed at the disadvantaged would help minorities. The major extra source of funding for children of 'New Commonwealth' origin was, and still remains, grants given to local authorities under the 1966 Local Government Act (section 11) by which a proportion of teachers' salaries is paid by central government in areas of high minority settlement. During the 1970s, Afro-Caribbean parents became particularly worried about the underachievement of their children in schools, and a network of voluntary supplementary schools, to improve basic skills, began to emerge. Asian parents began to demand single-sex schools, and also voluntary-aided Muslim schools on a par with other aided religious schools. The government has so far resisted this demand.

By the 1980s, policies designed to give greater recognition to minority cultures were beginning to emerge and there was a good deal of rhetoric about encouraging equal opportunities. A government committee of enquiry into the education of ethnic minority pupils was set up in 1979 and reported in 1985. (DES 1985, The Swann Report). This report recommended a range of policies to deal with poorer school achievement of ethnic minority pupils, curriculum change to help white pupils appreciate that they now lived in a multicultural society and an interdependent world, improved teacher training, better advisory services and resourcing of urban schools and recommendations on language and religious education. A movement for the provision of Asian languages as part of the modern language curriculum in secondary schools, and for bilingual programmes for young children began to make some impact (Tansley & Craft, 1984), and all teacher training courses were required, by 1984, to offer intending teachers some training for a multicultural society. From 1985, central government gave educational support grants to selected local education authorities to support curriculum developments and other initiatives appropriate for the education of all children in a multi-ethnic society. During the 1980s Local Education Authorities continued to produce guidelines or written policies concerning multicultural developments in their areas. By 1987, 77 of the 115 authorities in England, Wales and Scotland had produced some sort of policy statement (Commission for Racial Equality, 1987). However, the production of local policies and central government rhetoric is no guarantee that changes are actually taking place in schools, and it is questionable whether policy and developments along multicultural and anti-racist lines will be assisted by the 1988 Education Act.

4. ACHIEVEMENT PRE-1980

There are now thorough reviews of the literature on the family backgrounds and educational achievements of Caribbean pupils (Taylor, 1981; Tomlinson, 1983), Asian pupils (Tomlinson, 1983; Taylor & Hegarty, 1985), Chinese, Cypriot, Italian, Ukrainian, Vietnamese and other minority pupils (Taylor, 1987, 1988). Pre-1980 research on the achievement of minorities should now be treated with caution, as much of it was small-scale and used problematic methodology. Also, the use of the blanket category 'Asians' obscured differences between pupils of different Asian origin and often, explanations for underachievement reflected the prejudices of the researchers.

However, from 1960 to the early 1980s there was a general consensus among researchers, practitioners and minority parents that pupils from minority groups, particularly of Afro-Caribbean, Turkish-

Cypriot and Bangladeshi origin, 'underachieved' at school. These concepts of underachievement came to mean anything from a low reading age at infant school, to failure to acquire a university place. It was most generally taken to mean that when comparisons were made between majority and minority pupils on standardized group tests of ability and attainment (usually in reading and mathematics) and on individual IQ tests, and in school examinations, minority pupils performed less well than their white peers. Minority pupils tended to be allocated to lower 'streams' or bands, to attain less well all through school and to leave with fewer or lower-level examination passes. Afro-Caribbean pupils were also four times more likely to be allocated to schools for what were then described as the educationally subnormal (Tomlinson, 1982). In retrospect, all this should not be too surprising, given that many pupils were moving into an unfamiliar education system which, apart from providing some English as a second language subject for pupils with no English, did little to accommodate the pupils.

The most influential large-scale studies carried out in the 1960s and 1970s were the 1968 Inner London Education Authority (ILEA) studies of pupils' transfer at eleven to secondary school, which indicated that Indian and Pakistani pupils performed less well at 11+ than white pupils, and Afro-Caribbean and Cypriots least well (Little, 1975). An ILEA literacy survey which tested 32 000 pupils at eight, eleven and fifteen years (the pupils being fifteen in 1975) has also been much quoted as evidence of the under-achievement of Afro-Caribbean pupils, because their reading age had fallen behind all other groups at fifteen (Mabey, 1981). However, Mabey followed all these young people past school-leaving age and found the Afro-Caribbean pupils were more likely to stay in education, and achieve more examination passes than would have been predicted from their earlier reading scores (Mabey, 1986).

Educational priority area studies carried out in London and Birmingham in the 1970s, showed Asian children scoring lower than white or Afro-Caribbean on reading and literacy tests, which was considered by the researcher to be due to language and cultural factors (Payne, 1974). Data from the National Child Development study, which followed a cohort of children from 1958, adding 'immigrant' children as the study progressed, also showed Asian and Afro-Caribbean pupils achieving less well than white pupils, but school achievement improved considerably with length of residence in Britain, particularly for Asian pupils (Essen & Ghodsian, 1979). A retrospective study of children in an East Midlands area (Scarr et al., 1983) comparing the progress of white, Indian, Pakistani and Afro-Caribbean pupils, also found Asian performance improved with length of stay in Britain and Afro-Caribbean pupils performed least well. However, several studies over this period presented a more optimistic picture for Afro-Caribbean pupils – particularly when social class background was taken into account (Bagley et al., 1979). Certainly, research studies between 1965 and 1980 demonstrated that the longer all minority pupils had been in education in Britain and the more efforts local authorities and schools had made to accommodate them, the better their educational performance. Researchers offered varied explanations for minority underachievement, and as Parekh (in DES, 1985, p. 69) pointed out, they often "searched for a single factor" to explain complex situations.

4.1 The Rampton-Swann evidence
Anxiety about the education of Afro-Caribbean pupils led a House of Commons Select Committee to urge the government to set up an independent inquiry into the possible causes of under-achievement of these children and in 1979 a committee chaired by Anthony Rampton was created. The interim report of this committee (DES, 1981) provided statistics on the examination performance of all school-leavers in six local authorities in 1979 and indicated that Afro-Caribbean pupils achieved fewer examination passes at CSE, 'O' and 'A' level[2] than white or Asian pupils and only 1 per cent went on to full-time higher education degree courses. The committee was chaired by Lord Swann from 1981 and a further report was produced in 1985 (DES, 1985). Statistics were collected in the same Local Education Authorities for school-leavers in 1982. The figures showed that although Afro-Caribbean pupils were still achieving fewer examinations than white or Asian pupils there had been a considerable improvement in their educational performance between 1979 and 1981, whereas Asian performance had remained static. Thus in CSE and 'O' level the percentage of Afro-Caribbean pupils obtaining five or more higher-grade examination passes increased from 3 to 6 per cent between 1979 and 1982 and in English Language increased from 9 to 15 per cent over this period. Also, their performance at 'A' level improved considerably between 1979 and 1982.

In some respects the Swann Report presented a misleading picture of Asian and Afro-Caribbean educational performance. 'Asian' pupils were not differentiated, social class was not taken into account and the data were not analysed by gender. Unfortunately, the report was taken to reflect minority educational achievement in Britain in the 1980s. An OECD report for the Centre for Educational Research and Innovation (Organization for Economic Co-operation and Development, 1987) accepted without question that "the average performance of Asian pupils is undoubtedly comparable on the whole with that of white majority pupils" (p. 255) and went on to suggest explanations for poor Caribbean achievement. This is misleading, because research in fact indicates that some Asian pupils, particularly recently arrived Bangladeshi pupils and some pupils of Pakistani origin, do not achieve well in school and are more likely to be regarded as having special educational needs. Research has also indicated that children of Turkish-Cypriot origin have consistently underachieved at school, but there has been little focus on this group. It is now becoming clearer that the sterotype of "all Asians doing well" and "all Afro-Caribbeans underachieving" is unhelpful and misleading.

4.2 *Special education*
It is also the case that, in common with other European countries, there is an over-representation of migrant and minority children in various kinds of special education. A study for the Organization for Economic Co-operation and Development (OECD, 1987) showed that in seven European countries, minority pupils, particularly bilingual and Muslim pupils, were over-represented in special education. This study noted that the original purpose of special education had been steadily expanded to such an extent that many children having difficulty in mainstream schools for a variety of reasons, tended to be placed in special schools or classes. The OECD study warned that by using special education rather than providing good bilingual policies and a good basic general education Western countries may be relegating many migrant and minority children "to the fringes of advanced industrial society" (OECD, 1987, p. 33). In Britain in the 1960s and 1970s there was an over-representation of Afro-Caribbean pupils in schools for what was then termed the "mildly educational sub-normal" and in the 1980s these pupils are more likely than any other group to be found in provision for behaviourally disturbed pupils. Pupils of Asian origin appear to be over-represented in provision for more severe mental and physical handicaps. However, serious debate about the assessment and placement of minority and bilingual pupils thought to have learning difficulties has only recently begun, and England is still far behind some European countries in

offering adequate bilingual programmes to second language learners.

4.3 Explanations for minority educational performance

Explanations for the levels of educational achievement currently lack a conceptual framework for understanding which factors, inside and outside the education system, affect the educational performance of ethnic minority pupils in ways which are different from those factors which affect white pupils. This has created confusion and parental anxiety, as competing explanations have been put forward by different interest groups.

Outdated beliefs that different races have different intellectual capacities still persist in Britain, and some teachers still believe that black children have a natural lower ability. The Swann Committe (DES 1985, p. 148) commissioned a rigorous review of evidence on "race and IQ" and were able to dispose of this proposition. The review concluded that ethnic differences in IQ are caused by the same factors that are responsible for IQ differences in the white population. The importance of home and family background for success in education is well-documented and a number of research studies in the 1960s and 1970s attributed poorer ethnic minority school performance to family structures and cultural differences. This led to unhelpful stereotyping of many families. For example, single-parent Afro-Caribbean families were presented as disorganized and disadvantaging to their children, and Asian cultural segregation and language differences were presented as problems in the education of the children. Ethnic minority parents' organizations have been active in repudiating stereotyped views and making it clear that they are interested in their children's education and success, despite the differences in family structure and culture.

The difficulties of second language speakers in acquiring enough English for educational success have always been regarded as a possible explanation for the underachievement of some bilingual and bidialectical pupils. The situation described by Strömqvist (see chapter 9 in this volume) by which bilingualism is regarded as a 'deviation', still applies in Britain. However, the belief that bilingualism implies a language deficit and creates educational difficulties was challenged in 1977 by the EEC Directive (European Economic Community, 1977), which suggested that the teaching of mother tongue improves rather than impairs the performance of bilingual children. Schools in Britain have been slow to concede that bilingualism might be an asset rather than a deficit, and the monolingual tradition has ensured that pupils who speak English as a second language are regarded as potential underachievers.

As most studies of educational achievement have related success to higher socio-economic position and a good material environment, it is not surprising that explanations for minority pupils' underachievement have also been sought in terms of social class and social disadvantage. Certainly, studies into the 1980s have indicated that some Pakistani, Bangladeshi, Afro-Caribbean and Vietnamese families are particularly disadvantaged and are more likely to have unemployed parents. However, researchers have also pointed out that stressing social and economic disadvantage as a major cause of educational underachievement can seem to absolve educators from their professional duty to educate all pupils effectively.

In the 1980s, researchers in Britain are stressing factors relating to the structure and processes of schooling, appropriate curriculum material, and teacher attitudes, expectations and behaviour as important factors affecting the educational success of ethnic minority pupils. Several studies have indicated that placement in higher level examination groups in the third year of secondary schooling is related to ethnicity and to social class, as well as to actual attainment (Eggleston, 1986; Smith & Tomlinson, 1989).

During the 1980s, the whole notion of white racism, in individual or institutional forms, and the way racism can affect the educational performance of ethnic minority pupils, has been the topic of a heated debate. A study by the Commission for Racial Equality (1987) documented the racial harassment of some minority pupils and pointed out that it is not possible to "Learn in Terror". However, it is not easy to document empirically any assertion that poor educational performance is the result of racism.

Debate and discussion on the achievements of ethnic minority pupils offer explanations in terms of all the causal factors noted above, but there is an increasing acceptance that changing the school processes and structures, and improving home and school contacts and understandings may have the greatest effects in terms of improving educational performance.

4.4 Minority parental expectations
The limited research enquiring into the expectations of all groups of minority parents about their children's education indicates that parents are becoming increasingly anxious that schools are not equip-

ping the children with the skills and credentials necessary to compe-
te for jobs with white pupils (Tomlinson, 1984; Taylor & Hegarty,
1985). The anxiety has deepened as unemployment has risen in Britain, and *more* qualifications are demanded for entry to job training
and to go on to higher education. Most immigrant minority parents
are, in crude socio-economic terms, 'working class', but in their positive views and high expectations of education, they hold what can be
described as 'middle class' values. Many took low-skilled, low-wage
jobs in the expectation that, through education, their children would
be socially and economically mobile and they have been bitterly dis-
appointed that this has not happened. They have, however, lacked
the detailed knowledge of the education system and in some cases
the necessary command of English, to question what has been happening to their children in schools.

There is, in the 1980s, evidence of a mismatch of expectations between what minority parents expect of education, and what schools
and teachers think they can offer the children. Caribbean parents
have become increasingly angry at attempts to blame the home rather than schools for their children's lower educational performance,
and there has been a sustained increase in the number of black supplementary schools. Some black parents are choosing to send their
children to all-black religious schools set up by the Seventh Day
Adventists.

Muslim parents are increasingly in conflict with a secularized coedu-
cational Western system and have become more assertive in demanding state-aided Muslim schools within the system, in addition to setting up private Islamic schools. The 1988 Education Act, which
specifies that the daily act of worship in schools be mainly Christian,
has created further anxiety for them (Muslim Educational Trust,
1988). There is currently a need for research into the relations between schools and minority homes, and the production of more appropriate policies, both to restore the confidence of the parents in the
system and to help teachers see how they can work more produc-
tively *with* the parents.

5. ACHIEVEMENTS IN THE 1980s

Although evidence about the educational achievements of ethnic
minority pupils in the 1980s from pre-school to higher education levels, is still relatively sparse and occasionally conflicting, and expla-

nations offered by researchers still speculative, some patterns are
emerging:

1. Afro-Caribbean pupils, particularly girls, are improving their
   educational performance at all levels – there is evidence that
   black and white working class pupils enter infant school with
   similar skill levels.
2. There are considerable differences in the educational attainments
   of pupils of different 'Asian' origins. It seems likely that it is pupils of East African and Indian origin who are more likely to 'do
   best' and move into higher education more. The attainments of
   Bangladeshi and Turkish Cypriot pupils remain low.
3. Afro-Caribbean and Asian pupils have high aspirations and are
   far more likely than white pupils to stay in education beyond the
   school-leaving age, usually in colleges of further education, and
   they eventually obtain more lower-level credentials than white
   pupils. However, Afro-Caribbean are least likely to enter higher
   education.
4. Research is demonstrating the importance of school effects as an
   explanation for minority school performance and is showing that
   some school processes can disadvantage ethnic minority pupils
   who do not necessarily enter schools with educational disadvantages, but who fall behind because of the way schools interact
   with them.
5. There is still a need for improved teaching of English as a second
   language, as many Asian pupils are still disadvantaged by poor
   English.
6. More information is now available about the educational performance of other minority group pupils, notably Chinese, Cypriot,
   Vietnamese and gypsy children.
7. Explanations for differential educational performance now try to
   take into account the interaction of complex variables such as
   school and teacher practices, socio-economic background, gender,
   linguistic skills, country of origin, region of settlement in Britain
   and a continued climate of hostility to racial and ethnic groups in
   the country.

It is not possible here to expand properly on all these points, but a
brief discussion of relevant research should provide some indication
of the situation. Evidence that the Afro-Caribbean pupils are improving their educational performance over time comes from statistics
provided by the Inner London Education Authority (ILEA, 1987). In
an analysis of examination performance at 'O' and 'CSE' level be-

tween 1976 and 1985, improvement "has been most marked for the Caribbean group" (p. 8) and in 1986 the examination score for Afro-Caribbean pupils was only slightly below that for English, Scottish and Welsh pupils. Table 3 illustrates this, and also the differences in examination achievements for different 'Asian' and other groups.

Table 3: Average Performance Score* in 'O' level and 'CSE' level Exams by Ethnic Group

African	17.6
Arab	14.1
Bangladeshi	9.3
Caribbean	13.5
English/Scottish/Welsh	14.7
Greek	19.5
Indian	22.0
Irish	16.6
Pakistani	20.9
S.E. Asian	19.5
Turkish	12.2
Other Black	14.7
Other White	17.5
Other European	21.0
All	15.2

* The average score was obtained by weighting grades achieved at CSE and O level by numbers.

Source: Adapted from ILEA Report No. RS 1120/87. London, ILEA. 1987, (part 2, page 7).

Further evidence comes from a longitudinal study of black pupils in a London borough which showed that between the ages of 10-14 years black girls' (but not boys') reading progress was equal to that of whites and there was no widening of the gap between black and white pupils' reading progress between 8-16 years (Maughan & Rutter, 1986). In secondary school, black pupils were less likely to leave school without examination passes than white pupils and stayed on into the sixth form more than whites – this was especially true for black girls. The study found no evidence that black children were falling behind their white peers during the early years of secondary schooling, and were able to make up for earlier educational disadvantages by persistence in education (Maughan & Rutter, 1986). A further longitudinal study of secondary school pupils between 1981-

1986 showed that Afro-Caribbean pupils progressively 'caught up' in all school subjects except maths and finally achieved slightly higher examination passes in English (but not in other subjects) than white or Asian groups (Smith & Tomlinson, 1989).

At the infant end of schooling, a study by Blatchford et al. (1985) demonstrated that the literacy and numeracy skills of a group of black and white London pupils aged nearly five were similar, with girls achieving better than boys. Black mothers were found to have higher education levels than white, and black parents were more likely to help their children with reading. These children were followed through their infant schools in a study of children in thirty-three schools carried out by Tizard et al. (1988). At age seven, it was black girls who had made more progress in reading and writing than any other group, although white and black boys progressed better in maths.

Research in the 1980s is now demonstrating more clearly differences in levels of achievement between pupils of Indian, Pakistani, East African Asian, Bangladeshi and other origins, between Sikhs, Muslim and Hindu pupils and between 'Asian' boys and girls.

Table 3 taken from ILEA statistics demonstrates this clearly. Bangladeshi pupils in London are least likely to achieve examination passes, but they are the most recently arrived 'immigrant' group, and have least fluency in English. A study recently begun by MacIntosh et al. (1988) in three Midlands towns, suggests that Pakistani children in these towns are achieving less well than Indian or Caribbean pupils. Also, in the longitudinal study carried out by Smith and Tomlinson in four local authorities (1989), Indian and East African Asian pupils made more progress than Pakistani or Bangladeshi pupils, and a study by Tanna (1987) suggested that Indian and East African Asians were more likely to achieve university places than other Asians. There is now, however, accumulating evidence that pupils of both Afro-Caribbean and Asian origin have more educational aspirations than white pupils and are more likely to stay in education to acquire credentials (Rutter et al., 1982; Murray & Dawson, 1983; Eggleston et al., 1985; Tanna, 1987).

There is still no national collection of ethnic statistics of students applying for and entering higher education although discussion is currently taking place and it is likely that ethnic monitoring policies will be required by 1990. Such evidence as is available suggests that 'Asian' students in urban areas go into higher education at a later age, but on a par with white urban students, whereas Afro-Caribbean do not generally achieve higher education places. Some do arrive in higher education via access courses, which black women in particular use more than other groups.

There is in the 1980s increasing evidence that schools can affect the progress and achievements of ethnic minority pupils and that some school processes can disadvantage pupils. Mortimore et al. (1988) in a study of pupils progressing through 50 London junior schools, found that when pupils were allocated to various 'bands' for their secondary schooling, on the basis of test scores, Caribbean children were far more likely to be allocated by their teachers to a band lower than that predicted by their test score. Similarly, Wright (1987) found that in the third year of secondary schooling, teachers were more likely to allocate pupils of Afro-Caribbean origin to CSE rather than 'O' level examination groups even when their test scores would suggest they should be in 'O' level groups. A similar finding is reported in the research carried out by Smith and Tomlinson (Tomlinson, 1987). This longitudinal research, which set out to be a study of school effects, concluded that the school a child attends makes far more difference than the ethnic group it belongs to and also found that school differences affect all ethnic groups in similar manner: schools which provided a poor education for ethnic minority pupils also provided a poor education for white pupils.

Studies of ethnic minority achievements all testify to the continuing importance of a good command of English to achieve well in education. However, although the only consistent national policy to help ethnic minority pupils has been the provision of services to teach English as a second language (ESL), these services have been inadequate and their methods outdated. An investigation into the ESL teaching of Mirpuri pupils in Calderdale, Yorkshire, found that practices established in the mid-1960s were still in use 20 years later, and by segregating non-English speakers from mainstream schooling, Calderdale was actually in breach of the 1976 Race Relations Act (Commission for Racial Equality, 1986). Also, whereas in most countries in Europe it is considered an asset to be bi- or multilingual, in Britain it is still considered to be a liability, and there are few bilingual education programmes. There is no doubt that the educational achievement of many Asian children born in Britain continues to be affected by the lack of suitable language teaching.

Socio-economic background continues to be an important variable in explaining the educational performance of all pupils, whatever their ethnic origin. A recent study published by Bradford council which examined school-leaving qualifications by ethnic origin in 1983-1987, found that 'black' (mainly Asian) children at advantaged schools in wealthier catchment areas achieved school-leaving credentials on a par with their white classmates and concluded that social class has a greater influence on examination results than race (Archer, 1988). This research also indicated that minority pupils were less likely than white pupils to leave school without a single educational qualification. 19 per cent of whites left without an educational qualification compared with 7 per cent of minority pupils; however, more white pupils left with higher level qualifications.

5.1 *Other minorities*
Information on the home background, family circumstances and educational achievements of the other minority groups in Britain has been gathered together by Monica Taylor, a researcher at the National Foundation for Educational Research. She has published reviews of research on Chinese pupils in Britain (Taylor, 1987) and of Cypriot, Italian, Ukrainian, Vietnamese, gypsy and Liverpool black children (Taylor, 1988). Chinese pupils in Britain, who are mainly from Hong Kong and the New Territories, do not appear to achieve their potential at school, although a few do outstandingly well. It is estimated that the Cypriot population in Britain equals one-third of the total population of Cyprus, with most Cypriot pupils now at school being UK-born. Research from the 1960s has noted that Greek Cypriot pupils tend to achieve higher scores than Turkish Cypriot pupils on tests of cognitive ability and attainment. Indeed, Turkish Cypriot pupils have usually performed at a lower level than those of Afro-Caribbean origin, but this has never generated the same concern or political debate that has been accorded to Afro-Caribbean school achievement (Taylor, 1988).

Taylor estimated that in the early 1980s, some 25000 children of Italian origin were in school in Britain and that such pupils had never been the subject of much research. A majority of Italian pupils live in the Bedford area, which was involved in a Mother Tongue and Culture project sponsored by the European Community between 1976-1980. The Italian government has been involved in the provision of language classes for Italians in Britain since 1971 (Taylor, 1988).

Between 1979-1982 some 16000 Vietnamese were accepted into Britain as refugees rather than migrants. Most of the children arrived with little knowledge of English and received little specialized language tuition. Unsurprisingly, the progress of Vietnamese pupils is slow at the moment and some able pupils have been placed in classes for slow learners.

Research literature on the education of gypsy children is sparse but Taylor remarks that "it is clear that there has been a substantial failure to meet the educational needs of gypsy children" (1988, p. 364). Some local education authorities provide mobile classrooms and schools on camp sites, but schooling is often disrupted as families move on, and gypsy culture has traditionally relied on the family for all educative functions.

5.2 *The effect of new policies*
An Education Reform Act became law in 1988 and will considerably change the structure and organization of the English education system. It is likely that the position of ethnic minorities will be affected by the Act, and that moves towards racial and religious segregation in schools will intensify. The parts of the Act which will particularly affect minorities are:
- the 'opting-out' of local authority control by some schools to become grant-maintained by central government
- the new requirement that religious education in state schools be 'mainly Christian'
- a national curriculum
- regular testing at seven, eleven and fourteen years
- open enrolment of pupils at schools chosen by parents
- increased powers for school governors

In addition, the Act allows for the creation of City Technology Colleges, which were originally to be located in disadvantaged urban areas, and for the abolition of the Inner London Education Authority, the largest authority in England and Wales, which contains the largest number of ethnic minority pupils in the country. The stated intentions of the Act are to increase parental choice by allowing schools (by parental vote) to opt out of local authority control and become grant-maintained by central government. Both open enrolment and opting-out are likely to increase segregation by racial and religious characteristics. Parents at Dewsbury, Yorkshire, recently won the right to send their children to predominantly white schools, rather than the 85 per cent Asian school their children had been allocated to. It is likely that white parents will increasingly choose to enrol their children in white schools and refuse to send them to ethnically mixed schools. Schools which have opted-out could become more selective in their intake, and could choose not to use local authority multicultural or minority group support services. A number of private fundamentalist Muslim and Christian schools and two all-black Seventh Day Adventist schools, have given notice that they wish to become grant-maintained schools, and an Evangelical Christian group has announced that they are sponsoring a City Technology College.

The Dewsbury parents based part of their case on their desire to have their children educated in the Christian religion, and the new Act restricts adequate consideration of other world religions, apart from Christianity, in schools. The primacy given to Christianity rather than a multi-faith approach will certainly undermine previous moves to offer all children a multicultural education, and will encourage non-Christian groups towards segregated education.

The Act ushers in, for the first time in Britain, a national curriculum with specified subjects. This provision could actually benefit ethnic minority pupils and help ensure equal opportunities. Research quoted previously in this chapter (Wright, 1987; Tomlinson, 1987) showed that schools can allocate ethnic minority pupils to different subject areas or to lower level examination classes. With a national curriculum, minority parents will have the opportunity to ensure that the curricular experiences their children receive is not second best. In addition, the Act requires that all pupils are tested at seven, eleven and fourteen years. Whereas many local education authorities have regularly tested pupils at seven and eleven, there was no requirement that parents should know about this. Although there is, as yet, little indication that new testing processes will take account of linguistic and cultural factors, minority parents and pupils will be better informed of their educational strengths and weaknesses. The expansion of the power of school governors and parents could also allow minority parents to play a more active role in the management of their children's schools and could ensure more opportunities for parents to check that their children were being offered a sound education.

There is no doubt that the education system is about to become more diverse[3] and possibly more ethnically divisive in Britain. It is crucially important that in future the place of ethnic minority pupils in the various selective and allocative mechanisms of British schooling is checked and monitored. It will then be possible to collect accurate information on the achievements of ethnic minorities, to assess reasons for low achievements and to implement effective school policies which will overcome this. In addition, as so many of the problems of educational achievements of minorities are common to all European countries, comparative and joint research between countries would seem to be crucial as Europe moves towards closer links in 1992.

NOTES

1 Much of this paper refers to the education system in England and Wales. Different legislation applies to Scotland and N. Ireland.

2 CSE = Certificate of Secondary Education.
'O' level = Ordinary level, General Certificate of Education
'A' level = Advanced level, General Certificate of Education
CSE and 'O' level have now been combined into the General Certificate of Secondary Education (GCSE) taken by pupils at 16+ in a variety of subjects at different 'levels'.

3 Pupils in Britain will in the future be attending one of the following types of schools:
Independent − fee-paying schools (7 per cent of the school population)
Local Authority Controlled
− Comprehensive School
− Grammar School
− Primary School
Centrally-Funded Grant-Maintained
− Comprehensive School
− Grammar School
− Primary School with over 300 pupils.
Part Centrally-Funded Part Industry-Funded
− City Technology Colleges

REFERENCES

ARCHER, C. (1988). *Examination Results in School Leavers 1983-87*, Bradford City Council.
BAGLEY, C., BART, M., & WONG, J. (1979). Antecedents of Scholastic Success in West Indian Ten-Year Olds in London. In G.K. Verma and C. Bagley (Eds.) *Race, Education and Identity*. London: MacMillan.
BHACHU, P. (1985). *Twice Migrants*. London: Tavistock.
BLATCHFORD, P., BURKE, J., FARGUHAR, C., PLEWIS, I. & TIZARD, B. (1985). Educational Achievements in the Infant. Origin, Gender and Home on Entry Skills. *Educational Research*, 27(1), pp. 52-60.
BROWN, C. (1984). *Black and White Britain*. London: Policy Studies Institute.
COMMISSION FOR RACIAL EQUALITY (1986). *Teaching English as a Second Language*. London.

COMMISSION FOR RACIAL EQUALITY (1987). *Learning in Terror*. London.

COMMONWEALTH IMMIGRANTS ADVISORY COMMITTEE (1964). *Second Report*. London: HMSO.

DEPARTMENT OF EDUCATION AND SCIENCE (1981). *West Indian Children in Our Schools*. London: H.M.S.O. (Rampton Report).

EDUCATION REFORM ACT (1988). London.

EGGLESTON, J., Ounn, D. & Anjal, M. (1986). *Education for Some – the educational and vocational experience of 15-18 year old members of ethnic minority groups*. Stoke-on-Trent: Trentham Books.

ESSEN, J. & GHODSIAN, M. (1979). The Children of Immigrants – school performance. *New Community, 1*(3), 422-429.

EUROPEAN ECONOMIC COMMUNITY (1977). *Council Directive on the Education of the children of Migrant workers. 77/486*. Brussels.

INNER LONDON EDUCATION AUTHORITY (1987). *Research and Statistics Report*. London.

LITTLE, A. (1975). Performance of Children from Ethnic Minority Backgrounds in Primary Schools. *Oxford Review of Education, 1*(2), pp 117-135.

MABEY, C. (1981). Black British Literacy – a study of London black children from 8-15 years. *Educational Research, 23*, 83-95.

MABEY, C. (1986). Black Pupils Achievements in Inner London. *Educational Research, 28*, 163-173.

MACINTOSH, N., MASCIE-TAYLOR, C.G. & WEST, A.M. (1988). West Indian and Asian Children's Educational Achievement. In G.K. Verma & P. Pumfrey (Eds.), *Educational Attainments*. Lewes: Falmer Press.

MAUGHAN, B., DUNN, G. & RUTTER, M. (1985). Black pupils' progress in secondary school: I. – Reading Attainment between 10-14. *British Journal of Development Psychology, 3*, 113-121.

MAUGHAN, B. & RUTTER, M. (1985). Black pupils' progress in secondary school: II. – Examination Attainment. *British Journal of Development Psychology, 4*(11), 19-29.

MAUGHAN, B. & DUNN, G. (1988). Black Pupils' Progress in Secondary Schools. In G.K. Verma & P. Pumfrey (Eds.), *Educational Attainments*. Lewes: Falmer Press.

MORTIMORE, P., SAMMONS, P., STOLL, L., LEWIS, D., ECOB, R. (1988). *School Matters – The Junior Years*. London: Open Books.

MULLARD, C. (1982). Multi-Racial Education in Britain – From Assimilation to Culture Pluralism. In J. Tierney (Ed.) *Race, Migration and Schooling*. London: Holt Educational.

MURRAY, C. & DAWSON, A. (1984). *Five Thousand Adolescents*. Manchester: Manchester University Press.

MUSLIM EDUCATIONAL TRUST (1988). *What Should Muslims Do?* London.

ORGANIZATION FOR ECONOMIC CO-OPERATION AND DEVELOPMENT (1987). *Immigrants' Children at School*. Paris: O.E.C.D.

PAYNE, J. (1974). *Educational Priority Areas, Surveys and Statistics*. London: H.M.S.O.

SCARR, S., CAPARULO, B., FRERDMAN, B., TOWERS, B., CAPLAN, B. (1983). Development, Status and School Achievements of Minority and Non-Minority Children from Birth to 18 in a British Midlands Town. *British Journal of Developmental Psychology. 1*(1), pp. 31-48.

SMITH, D. (1981). *Unemployment and Racial Minorities*. London: Policy Studies Institute.

SMITH, D. & TOMLINSON, S. (1989). *School Effects – A Study of Multi-Racial Seconda-ry Schools*. London: Policy Studies Institute.

STRÖMQVIST, S. (1988). *Perspectives on Second Language Acquisition in Scandinavia*. Paper presented at the International Workshop on "Education and the Cultur-al Development of Ethnic Minority Children". Kerkrade, The Netherlands, 12-14 September.

TANNA, K. (1987). *The Experiences of South Asian University Students in the British Education System*. (Unpublished). Ph.D. thesis. Birmingham: University of As-ton.

TANSLEY, P. & CRAFT, M., (1984). Mother Tongue Teaching and Support. *Journal of Multilingual and Multicultural Matters, 5*, 367-384.

TAYLOR, M. (1981). *Caught Between a Review of Research into the Education of Pupils of West Indian Origin*. Slough: NFER-Nelson.

TAYLOR, M. & HEGARTY, S. (1985). *The Best of Both Worlds? A Review of Research into the Education of Pupils of South Asian Origin*. Slough: NFER-Nelson.

TAYLOR, M. 1987. *Chinese Pupils in Britain*. Slough: NFER-Nelson.

TAYLOR, M. (with Hegarty, S.) (1988). *Worlds apart – A Review of Research on Other Minority Pupils*. Slough: NFER-Nelson.

TIZARD, B., BLATCHFORD, P. & PLEWIS, I. (1988). *Young Children at School in the Inner City*, London: Lawrence Erlbaum.

TOMLINSON, S. (1981). *Educational Subnormality - a study in decision-making*. Lon-don: Routledge & Kegan Paul.

TOMLINSON, S. (1982). *A Sociology of Special Education*. London: Routledge & Kegan Paul.

TOMLINSON, S. (1984). *Home and School in Multicultural Britain*. London: Batsford.

TOMLINSON, S. (1987). Curriculum Option Choice in Multi-ethnic Schools. In B. Troyna (Ed.), *Racial Inequality in Education*. London: Tavistock.

WRIGHT, C. (1987). Black Students. White Teachers. In B. Troyna (Ed.), *Racial In-equality in Education*. London: Tavistock.

3

Ursula Boos-Nünning and Manfred Hohmann
University of Essen

The Educational Situation of Migrant Workers'[1] Children in the Federal Republic of Germany

1. THE BASIC SITUATION

Between 1965 and 1982 the number of migrant pupils in the German school system[2] increased absolutely as well as proportionally. At first, this was mainly seen in *Grundschulen* and *Hauptschulen.* The number of migrant pupils escalated from 35 100 (0.5 per cent of the total number of pupils) in the year 1965 to 159 000 (1.8 per cent) in 1970 and 386 000 (3.5 per cent) in 1975 to 637 180 (7 per cent) in 1980 and the absolute peak with 720 700 (8.6 per cent) was reached in 1982. Since then the number of migrant pupils has been declining, though the relative proportion in the secondary schools' classes is still slightly increasing. From 1975 to 1982 the number of migrant pupils at vocational schools also increased: since 1983 they have been declining here, too.

Changes have also occurred in the composition of the migrant pupils. In the first period of workers' migration to the FRG Italians were the majority. In 1980 about 87 per cent of the total numer of migrant pupils originated from one of the six main countries of emigration (Turkey, Yugoslavia, Greece, Italy, Spain and Portugal) and this percentage remained constant since than. Turkish pupils, accounting for about 52 per cent, are the largest group; since 1980 this proportion increased only slightly (by three per cent).

For many years, much attention was paid to the 'problem' of children and young persons entering the host country at an age when school attendance is compulsory and these children had to be taken into classes regardless of their school attendance in the country of origin. This had repercussions on school organization and arrangement of lessons. For many years this was the main issue in discussions about the education of migrants and even led to speculations about far-reaching limitations of the rights of the migrant population (there was talk of not allowing children older than six years to migrate.) However, this issue has lost its importance because today by far the largest share of migrant pupils have been born in the Federal Republic of Germany. These data say little about the concrete situation in schools. The distribution of the migrant population over the states[3], within the states and even within the cities is very unequal, and the proportions of the various nationalities vary considerably from place to place. In some schools, the majority of pupils are of non-German nationality; in others a group of migrant pupils of different nationalities forms a small minority, and in some schools there are no migrant pupils. Not only is there an unequal distribution of the migrant population: there are also regional differences in the range of educational options available and differences in the policies of education in the states and cities (for example the availability of comprehensive schools and special schools). The selective effect of the secondary school system composed of three or four streams, and the system of vocational schools result in widely differing proportions of migrant pupils in different kinds of schools and individual schools. The observable trend for migrant schools to develop in conurbations is receiving additional impetus from the behaviour of German parents: they are moving away from areas with high migrant population and are increasingly avoiding *Hauptschule* (largely for reasons that have nothing to do with migrants; nevertheless this helps to increase the proportion of migrant pupils in such schools).

2. EDUCATION POLICIES FOR MIGRANT PUPILS

The policies for migrant education in the Federal Republic of Germany are primarily characterized by a lack of anticipatory planning or of at least medium-range concepts. They are reactions to economic-orientated development and are relatively consistently oriented towards the interests of all or part of the domestic majority, but not to the interests of the minority. There are exclusively administrative targets for the teaching of migrant pupils: guidelines and instructions from the *Ministries of Education and Culture* of the various states, allowing much leeway to the school administration, the schools and teachers. These state targets are usually based on agreements of the *Continuing Conference of the Ministers of Education and Culture of the eleven states of the Federal Republic of Germany* (KMK), which are only advisory in character. However, because KMK decisions must be reached unanimously, these decisions are important for administrative practice in the states (see the surveys in Siewert, 1980; Kischkewitz & Reuter, 1980; Rist, 1978; Boos-Nünning, 1979).

The basis of the first effort to organize the "teaching of migrant children" (KMK decision 1964) nationally, was the assumption that the migrants would only stay in the Federal Republic of Germany for a limited period of time (see Siewert, 1980). Thus, even then a kind of double strategy was formulated: appropriate measures were to be taken to facilitate the admission of migrants to German schools (it was agreed that in principle, school attendance is compulsory for migrant children). These measures were additional courses to teach German, possibly even in the preparatory classes. At the same time, 'special importance' was attached to giving migrants pupils support in their native language. On the whole, mainly from a perspective of implementation, this decision remained very vague, and in practice the action taken by individual states varied greatly: the relatively low number of pupils made it possible to remain indifferent to the new experienced situation.

The increasing number of migrant pupils, the deplorable situation in the preparatory classes, which have turned into miniature ethnic schools (i.e. non-German) in many states, and the start of a scientific and political debate about the migrants led to the KMK issuing a new agreement in 1971, now with a more appropriate title: "The teaching of migrant workers' children."

If they could follow the teaching without considerable language difficulties or, as a rule, after having attended a preparation class for one year, migrant children could start school in regular classes, according to their age or to their knowledge. The KMK advice included a detailed catalogue of measures that would guarantee "that the migrant workers' children could take more advantage of the educational chances provided by the German school system." However, native language teaching was not given much attention: it was stated that pupils "should have the opportunity" of receiving such teaching; but is was still up to the individual state to decide whether such teaching was "within the responsibility of the administration of education or not". It was not discussed which language should be declared as the native language; the task of native language teaching was described vaguely: "... to endeavour to preserve the pupils' connection with their native language and their home countries' traditions". In the 1971 KMK advice the point of 'integration' was clearly stressed. Thus, the KMK agreement of 1971 clearly contradicted official government policies towards migrants at that time, which were based on the idea that the migrants would return to their home countries after a few years, and the problem of integration would not arise.

Although the instructions issued by the individual states at that time or a short time later did, in principle, agree with the KMK advice, the necessary efforts to reach the aims of integration did not follow in practice. The increasing number of migrant pupils in conurbations led to segregation measures, because of the inflexibility of the system of school organization and under the premise of a 'limited capacity' of the German class (the KMK advice said that "the proportion of migrant children in a class ...... should not exceed one-fifth"). In 1971 Berlin was already permitting model types of secondary school that segregated migrants. It was contended that these were more appropriate to the migrant pupils' social situation and their needs and abilities in terms of their native language and certain other subjects than the regular German classes. Bavaria justified its 'open model' which is actually equivalent to a totally segregated school system for the whole duration of the compulsory school attendance period, even if a transfer to regular classes is formally possible, by pointing to the fact that measures have to be set to enable integration into the German school system as well as to link up with the educational system in the countries or origin, and that the importance of the native language for the children's mental and spiritual development had been underestimated until then. This concept has been severely criticized by Boos-Nünning (1981).

In 1976 the KMK issued a new advice that legalized all measures that deviated from the 1971 advice, especially the system of segregation (which contradicted the measures for integration, cf. Berlin and Bavaria). At the same time, the leeway for the states was widened: "It is up to the states to decide whether to try out other forms of educational support for migrant pupils."

In the preamble to the new advice the double task of the schools (i.e. to integrate foreign pupils and simultaneously prepare them for their return to the home country) was explicitly formulated. The importance of the states' efforts "to enable migrant children and young persons to attend German schools successfully and to maintain the possibility of reintegration into the schools in their countries of origin" was stressed. The concern in the future was identified as being to "enable the migrant pupils to learn the German language and to receive the German school-leaving certificates as well as to maintain and to widen their knowledge in their native language. At the same time, the education measures should help to socially integrate the migrant pupils for the duration of their stay in the FRG. Also, they serve to maintain these pupils linguistic and cultural identity". This advice, slightly modified in 1979, is still valid today.

Several amendments were made to the KMK advice of 1971, because meanwhile migrant pupils were not only attending *Grundschule* and *Hauptschule* but, even if disproportionally, had spread over the whole range of schools. The amendments included sections about "support of integration into secondary schools", "entry into special schools", "vocational schools"). However, the decisive change was the actual retraction of the concept of integration. Even though the preamble (and also the policy makers) declare that now the aims of "integration" and of "maintaining the possibility of reintegration (in the pupils' home country) were equal, and were as such also seriously intended, the proposed measures did not meet either of these aims.

- In direct contradiction to the aim of integration (as declared in the 1971 KMK advice) the KMK advice of 1976 offers three segregative models (alternative schools for specific nationalities, special classes and bilingual classes).
- Because the function of maintaining the national-cultural identity has been assigned to the teaching in native language – which is assumed to be necessary to ensure that migrants are prepared and able to return to their home country – a clear effort to give lessons in the native language should result from these directives. But this was (and is) not the case (see BAGIV, 1985). The organization of this teaching is still subject to the decision of individual states (and is regulated very differently between states); in secondary schools the "teaching in native language instead of a compulsory foreign language may be offered", but the native language may also be put "in place of a compulsory foreign language, if its

teaching is not possible"; in this case the language proficiency has to be proved in an examination. (KMK advice 1976 as amended on 26 October 1979).

Even given the fact that a body like the KMK is hamstrung by the obligation to reach decisions unanimously, the agreement of 1976/79 can only be interpreted as an abandonment of the aims of a uniform federal educational policy. As a consequence, this led to very differing models with very differing justifications in the states, but with similar results for the migrant pupils: these models did not change the disadvantage of this group.

3. PARTICIPATION IN EDUCATION, SCHOOLSUCCESS, TRANSFER TO PROFESSION

3.1 *Participation in education and success at school*

The abovementioned criticism of the results of the solutions proposed by the KMK to solve these problems raises questions about the chances the German school system can offer migrant pupils, as shown in the statistics on their participation in education, the school certificates they obtain and their transfers to vocational training. For migrant pupils the school situation has improved in several areas:

– comparing the numbers of migrant pupils with the corresponding age group of the population reveals that the fulltime compulsory school attendance for migrant pupils is practically 100 per cent. This does not apply to vocational schools: the attendance rate here is very low, but has improved slightly compared with earlier years (Budde et al., 1985).

– the proportion of migrants in the *Realschule* and Gymnasium is rising, though not to the same degree in all nationality groups. Turkish children are still considerably underrepresented in these higher streams.

– there has been an especially large increase in the number of migrant pupils obtaining the *Hauptschule* certificate. In the state of Nordrhein-Westfalen, 80 per cent of all migrant schoolleavers obtain the certificate. This is a clear improvement compared with earlier years.

However, the number of migrant pupils with the *Hauptschule* certificate is rising at a time, when possession of this certificate does not offer much perspective on future employment. Many such schoolleavers do not find training vacancies or jobs.

In contrast to the improvements mentioned above, there is also abundant evidence of a deterioration of the educational situation for migrant pupils. The most important is the increasing number of transfers to special schools – 80 per cent are transfers to special schools for children with learning problems. The proportion of pupils from the six main countries of origin of migrants attending special schools throughout the country rose from 2.5 per cent in 1970 to 4.6 per cent in 1980 and to 5.8 per cent in 1983 (the average attendance rate among native German children for special schools is 4 per cent: statistics from KMK 1984).

There are no sound explanations for this development. It cannot be excluded that the difficult conditions at school – for example the insufficient support of bilingualism – lead to problems that will be labelled as 'intellectual backwardness'. It is also conceivable that the failure of migrant children to meet the educational standards are currently in many subjects wrongly diagnosed as the result of backwardness, as many teachers overrate the pupils' knowledge of German because of their rather fluent colloquial speech. Perhaps pupils who would previously have remained in the preparation classes that were more common pre-1983, are nowadays increasingly transferred to special schools.

There are no certain reasons for the migrant pupils' poor performance at school: various explanations have been put forward and some empirical studies have been done (see, for example Boos-Nünning et al., 1976; Langenohl-Weyer, 1979; Damanakis, 1978; Schmidtke, 1979; Lukesch, 1981; Holfort, 1982; Glumpler, 1985; Hopf, 1981). However, these studies deal with particular aspects of the problem only. The researchers highlight various factors that hinder or prevent the migrant children's success at school, but so far no comprehensive theory, backed up by research, has been developed.

Scientists, policy makers and educationalists attribute the failure of many migrant children at school to the pre-school and school environment, the family, the migrant child's personality and circumstances (e.g. legal, social).

As regards the influence of the pre-school and school environment, the following reasons for poor performance of migrant pupils are pointed out: poor attendance of kindergarten; the way the migrant children's teaching is organized; allowing special classes for one nationality, the discrepancy between state government orders and school practice; inadequate organization and teaching in the preparatory classes and in the regular classes; the lack of curricula, support measures and special training for the teachers, especially for the teachers of German and foreign teachers, and the attitudes in teaching migrant pupils; the lack of integration of pupils into German classes. Even today a considerable number of migrant children does not attend a kindergarten (kindergarten attendance is not compulsory).

The family circumstances said to affect migrant children's school performance are: the children joining their family in the Federal Republic of Germany at a later age; their travelling back and forth between the country of origin and Germany (Damanakis, 1982), the parents' lack of ability to help with the homework; the excessive demands made on the children; and their non-involvement in school. The conflict between children's and parents' ideas, which results from the differing level of conformity to German norms and attitudes, is also cited as a reason for problems in the children's orientation in society and at school. Another factor is the way the migrant child develops his or her personality, in the face of the difficulties resulting from growing up in two cultures. The split between private (family) and social experience can lead to severe orientation problems, resulting in an inability to act and continuing psychological overburdening. These difficulties are described by expressions such as "seeking one's identity" and "protection of identity" or "disturbance in the development of the ego-identity".

The social factors comprise: the legal and political uncertainty, which precludes long-term planning for the future: the fact that migrant workers are almost exclusively employed in jobs that are looked down on (and eschewed) by Germans; and the discrimination by the German population as well as by German classmates (Holfort, 1982). Also cited are the poor living conditions which do not offer enough room to do homework undisturbed. The lack of future prospects and the poor prospects on the job market as well as in the area of training for an occupation lead to resignation and prevent success at school.

In addition to the negative connotations ascribed to migrants by virtue of their affiliation to the lower class, such as a low general and professional education, unrespected jobs without prospects of improvement and without autonomy at work, and poor general living conditions, young migrants have an insecure legal and social status and dubious standing in industrial law.

An essential reason for the migrant pupils' failure at school lies in the discrepancy between the ideas of German school and society on one side, and the migrant parents' orientation and social situation on the other, plus the mutual interdependence of all factors, and the inability of the persons concerned to deal with the situation resulting from the migration (cf. Boos-Nünning, 1984).

The German school system does not offer any means to remove the migrant parents' uncertainty, but intensifies their fears by demanding across-the-board conformity from the migrant pupils, and by singling out the children who do not adjust as 'problem cases'. This is in accordance with German society's willingness to accept adjusted foreigners only an attitude reflected in the aims of the teaching of migrant pupils (see section 5).

3.2 Transfer to profession

The disadvantage of young migrants is plainly visible when they attempt to enter a profession. In spite of the higher formal qualification of migrant pupils, there is no improvement in the transfer to professions. Absolute numbers of migrant apprentices are rising: from about 36 400 in 1979/80 tot 57 319 in 1986/87, but the proportion of apprentices in the age-group of 15 to 18 years is now stagnating after declining for some time. The proportion of migrants in the total number of apprentices is still only 3.2 per cent (1986/1987), compared to a training rate for German apprentices of 72 per cent. In recent years the number of young migrants who passed a complete training for an occupation or attended a secondary school that provides general education, remained relatively constant: it was about a third of the corresponding age-group.

The percentage of young migrants not in professional training or paid work – unemployed plus others – also rose from 14.1 per cent in 1972 to 25.7 per cent (the current rate for German youngsters is 9.8 per cent). The proportion is rising and mainly affects young persons between fifteen and eighteen years of age. Stoltenberg (1987) estimated that in 1984 75 000 migrants (37 per cent of the total) aged fifteen to under eighteen did not attend a school. For several groups the reality is even worse than the general statistics for unemployment can express, because:

- The statistics do not give a breakdown for the different nationalities. Turkish youngsters are probably one of the worse ethnic groups in terms of unemployment and non-attendance at school.
- Migrant young persons tend to concentrate on only a few occupations that require training. In 1982, 28.4 per cent of the migrant girls were trained as hairdressers and 12.7 per cent of the migrant boys as motor vehicle mechanics.

Henscheid (1986) shows more features of the young migrants' qualitative disadvantaging:
- About two-thirds are trained in small or medium businesses and
  more than a half is trained in the skilled trade.
- Some of the youngsters complete shortened, more practically
  oriented and less demanding training courses.
- An increasing number can be found in subsidized training courses
  (for example of the *Benachteiligtenprogramm, Berufsamt* [Profession-
  al Advisory Board] Berlin).

The young migrants' risk of being unemployed after the training is
estimated to be twice as high as that of young Germans. The facts
prove that the transfer to professions (from school into training or
work and from training to employment) for migrants especially
young Turks is plainly more difficult than for young Germans.

A survey of the facts makes it clear that for young migrants the process of choosing a profession and their integration into and education or a professional activity are subject to special difficulties.
Career advisers have come up with various reasons to explain this:
- Lack of sufficient school qualifications (no *Hauptschule* certificate,
  or only a *Hauptschule* certificate); in addition, especially for Turkish young people, the leaving certificate from a special Turkish
  class, which employers often regard as even less satisfactory.
- The preference for a few, often difficult to achieve professions and
  the narrow spectrum of professions for migrants, especially Turks.
- The lack of possibilities to influence Turkish parents.
- The qualifications demanded by the employers (formal qualifications or tests), which the migrant young people are unable to fulfil.
- The employers' rejection of migrant trainees, mainly in small busi-
  ness.

Therefore, the current professional situation of young migrants
shows characteristic contradictions: on the one hand their personal
qualifications and school qualifications have considerably improved;
on the other hand it is clear that migrants, especially young Turks,
have far less chances than young Germans and young people of
several other nationalities of finding a training vacancy. After their
training they are less often taken on and, even if they have the formal qualifications required, they have more difficulties in finding
long-term employment.

4. ORIENTATION TO EDUCATION OF MIGRANT FAMILIES

The opinion once held by many teachers that migrant parents, especially Turks, were not interested in their children's education at school was soon proved wrong. All empirical studies that asked parents about their plans for school and profession for their children found that

– migrant parents desire a school education that gives good qualifications, if possible, the attendance at a Gymnasium, and attach importance to school attendance as such
– they desire a good profession for their children, preferably a university education
– their expectations for education and profession are not different for boys or girls.

All current research indicates that migrant parents (including Turkish parents) are definitely oriented to the career and education of their children and strongly desire socially higher, even academic professions for them (Renner, 1975; Wilpert, 1980; Neumann, 1982; Mehrländer, 1983; Hecker, 1980, 1984).

When, often early in their child's school career, these wishes for professions prove to be unrealistic, they desire that the son, and also often the daughter, establish their own enterprise. Only seldom is immediate employment the aim after leaving school. Nevertheless, the young migrants do not ask for training vacancies or sometimes reject vacancies offered. Yakut (1986) ascertained the professional aspirations and job prospects of young Turks: this may show the possible reasons why this group fails to take up vacancies.

Current research reveals correspondence between Turkish parents and their children about the choice of occupation. This occurs mainly and most clearly in three areas:

1. Many Turkish parents correspond in their desire for an academic profession for their son or daughter. They want their boys to be doctors or engineers, the girls doctors, pharmacists or teachers, and so do the children themselves (though to a lesser degree). The demands of young Turks regarding education and their desire for an academic profession do not diminish as they grow older in the way it should regarding the actual conditions and chances. They become realistic only at the end of the compulsory time of school attendance, when they are confronted with the realities of the job market.
2. Another point of correspondence is, that if – after many setbacks

and disappointments – the educational career is continued in the 'dual system' (i.e. the day-release system, whereby young people in work are released to attend vocational school several times a week) an extremely narrow spectrum of professions, even narrower than that preferable to German pupils from *Hauptschule*, is strived for.

3. A third point of correspondence is that both parents and children prefer education at school rather than education in the dual system. Parents (and in some cases the young people) do not understand this system.

In these three areas one can assume a correspondence within some Turkish families either in tendency (such as the limited scope of job wishes) or basically (such as the preference for academic professions and the difficulties of understanding the dual system) even if the younger people have gained more insight into the German school system and education system and, more increasingly than their parents, recognize the futility of desires for higher professions. The families wish their child to be educated and become a person of some standing. The parents connect the idea of learning with education (*Bildung*) more than the children. They understand 'education' to mean training in a profession, not in the form of day release but wholly school. Turkish workers have found and are continuing to find that, in Germany they only do the unpopular jobs (i.e. the relatively badly paid jobs that are looked down on and offer little security). Their children, who have attended school for a longer period than they did themselves, should achieve 'better' professions. They should not be 'guest workers'. Ideas that are brought over from the country of origin and are rooted in the social structure there, mix with ideas based on the social situation of the Turkish workers here.

The preference for a school education rather than an education in the dual system may finally also result from the ideas about the education system in Turkey at the time of the migration.

It must be mentioned that teachers and social workers have reported that especially in the last years a growing number of young Turks and Turkish parents are admitting to a different motivation. These Turks see their activity in the Federal Republic of Germany only as a pragmatic solution to concrete and actual problems. They wish to earn enough money to be able to return to Turkey, or the young people want to support their parents' purchase of property or a house in Turkey and do not mind what kind of work they have to do for this.

Often they also need the money to afford the lump payments to avoid military service in Turkey. This group accepts a training vacancy mainly or exclusively because there is no job available for them. These young Turks, who at first look for a job at all costs, also accept vacancies in professions that require training, or in activities (also illicit work) without any prospects for the future and which are not accepted by German young people. This attitude, which can be described as 'educational pragmatism', is also a result of the difficult living conditions for migrants in Germany, and is accompanied by resignation, increased sensitivity and a greater risk of breaking up. This group wants to work to earn money and resists additional investment in education. The most recent studies which, however, were all carried out a few years ago, do not refer to this type of attitude; however a relatively high portion of the young migrants do not even try to get a training from the outset, or prefer an education in the dual system to a school-leaving certificate, because the latter does not offer financial compensation.

The unrealistically high orientation of young migrants and their parents to education and profession can therefore not be transmitted to the planning of a career at school or in a profession. Instead, Turkish, and also other migrant parents, transfer ideas brought over from the country of origin and altered during the process of migration, to the German school and education system.

5. DEVELOPMENT OF EDUCATIONAL AIMS

The pedagogical practice and theory of educating migrant children (*Ausländerpädagogik*) and youngsters has changed many times like education policy and the formulation of its aims and tasks. The *Ausländerpädagogik* arose as a consequence of political awareness of a need and, in a few cases, because of the initiatives of educationalists: the rapidly increasing number of migrant pupils in the educational system meant that issuing directives for school organization was not sufficient to solve the problem. Furthermore certain regulations could not be legalized, as for example, a long-term separation of migrant pupils into classes of one nationality. Therefore, accompanying pedagogical measures, mainly in the area of further training of the teaching staff, but also in the area outside school (e.g. help with homework) were assumed to be necessary and were implemented in the form of several projects and model experiments. From about

1970 to 1976 the discussion in the literature on migrant education and the standpoints of teachers brought up in discussions were – simply expressed – oriented on the following three premises and conditions:

1. The basic assumption was that migrant pupils, many of whom had already passed the larger part of their compulsory time of school attendance in the country of origin at that time, had to be prepared for entry into German schools by special teaching measures. At first, the school problems of migrant pupils were attributed mainly, if not exclusively, to difficulties of learning the German language; this led educationalists to believe that the pupils would have no more problems and could pass without further support, once they had sufficiently mastered the German language. Pedagogic endeavours concentrated on the modification of existing textbooks and the development of new ones, on thinking up teaching aids (often copied in large numbers as 'grey teaching aids') and on instructions teachers on the use of the textbooks and teaching aids. Soon, not only the migrant pupils' 'language deficits' were observed, but a great range of 'shortcomings' was identified: pedagogues pointed to the migrant pupils' lack of knowledge and social deficits and attempted to integrate these pupils into school and into German society. These actions, supported by activities outside school, were intended to improve the migrant pupils' chances in the school system by rectifying or lessening their linguistic or social shortcomings.

2. The regulations for school organization in the 1970s were based on the aim of achieving migrant pupils adjustment to the German school system. This aim was not achieved in pedagogical practice (nor was it sufficiently analysed in the pedagogical literature on migrants) except at the cost of separating the migrant pupils, and thereby reducing their possibilities of switching to the German system (and hence curtailing their professional and social chances in the Federal Republic of Germany). Even in the 1970s schools integrated pupils who were willing and able to be integrated – as later the federal government's migrant policy was to express more clearly – thus increasingly preparing them in the course of time for *Realschule* and Gymnasium but hardly offering them professional education, nor access to privileged professional positions. At the same time, however, migrant pupils were separated: in separate classes; in support groups, which rarely supported the migrant pupils, but merely served to relieve the problems of regu-

lar classes; in special schools; in measures established to prepare migrants for professions. The schools, too, equated integration with adjustment. The *Ausländerpädagogik* offered help, for the process of adjustment, in the form of special support for learning the German language, for certain other subjects and in the training of behaviour – up to training for interviews with potential employers and the training for tests to achieve a training vacancy.
3. It was assumed that migrant pupils were influenced by their parents and by the norms and values of their country of origin. Thus, German pedagogues working with migrant pupils should understand the social structure, the school system, the family and other particulars of the country of origin, and be able to integrate, to interpret and to influence in a reasonable way the 'strange' behaviour and the different orientations of the migrants.

Based on the foregoing assumptions that the migrant pupils' observed deficits had to be rectified, and backed by the social-political consideration that only a sufficient education at school provides the 'second generation' of migrant children and young people with chances for a profession and hence for their existence and further for their social integration – the latter also with the idea of preventing possible potential trouble for German society – a large number of projects and model experiments were initiated and financed in West Germany in the mid-1970s (Fuchs & Wollmann, 1987; Deutsches Jugendinstitut, 1987).

Since then, some pedagogues have considerably elaborated and redefined the abovementioned three basic tenets of teaching migrants in the Federal Republic of Germany. Thus, the assumptions about the reasons for the migrant children's difficulties at school are now more differentiated: besides language difficulties, the analysis now also includes cultural differences, the effects of the migration process and the social situation in the Federal Republic of Germany plus other particulars. Even today, opinions still vary as to how far the influence of these complexes of factors could be responsible for the failure of the education system.

On one hand the basic attitude to the problems of migrant pupils has not changed: this holds for the essential part of concrete practice at schools, and for educational administration and policy. The migrant children's personal abilities and their progress at school are still described as "insufficient", with no mention of the positive side of what they bring or could bring into school: their imperfect knowledge of the German language is noticed (and often equated with linguistic incompetence), the children's bilingualism is overlooked. The lack of knowledge of the German school system, of German families and of German society are deplored but the migrants' knowledge of the country of origin and their life in the migrant community is ignored. The disturbed socialization process is pointed out, but the children's individual ability to cope with two ethnic groups is ignored. Another dimension of this standpoint is, that – in theory and practice – the school is regarded as an area that is independent from and not influenced by social factors, so that the conditions the migrant pupils have to cope with, (such as the xenophobia, the migrant families' poor living conditions, insecurity in future planning because of restrictive political measures or intentions) are seen as accompanying factors that have little effect on the 'essential pedagogical work'.

The foremost idea is that within the school walls migrant and German pupils understand each other, and can work together, even if the atmosphere outside is aggravating, the political and personal pressure on the migrants is becoming heavier and the struggle for work is intensifying.

Together with the criticism of these ideas and their associated values and the doubt about their legitimacy, the concept of intercultural education developed. This term is used ambiguously and is frequently misused; often the old standpoints criticized above are hiding behind it. Sometimes the pedagogical idea of not demanding the children's one-sided adjustment to existing conditions, but of being willing to trace habitual values and forms and to challenge them is attached to it. Intercultural education also includes integrating the living culture of origin (the migrant's culture) into the process of education of the migrant children; thus it turns against the stigmatization of the culture of origin and the migrant culture, but also against the migrants' inflexible fixation to the culture of the country of origin. Intercultural education demands that the cultural origin of the children should no longer be ignored and seen as a stigma, but should be handled with equal rights in the daily routine. The consequence is, that the development of living conditions in the host country in which several cultures can live together, places demands not only on the migrants, but also on the local people, so that not only do the migrant pupils have to adjust but that also the German pupils and the German school have to change (Hohmann, 1983; also Boos-Nünning et al., 1983). The formulation of the aims of an intercultural education and, even more, their realization, requires fundamental changes at school and in society: the readiness to notice the other cultures and to put into perspective the own standpoint, to accept other forms and expressions even when they seem strange, to expect progress in adjustment not only from migrants, but also from German pupils, from the teachers and the school. This point of view includes not seeing the situation or the social structure in the country of origin as the reason for the migrant pupils' difficulties at school, but starting out from the migrant groups' culture in Germany, which is severely influenced by the legal and social circumstances under which the migrants live. The principle of intercultural education requires further modifications. Schools will have to open themselves in two respects: they must cease to distinguish between school concerns and the problems outside school; they must integrate the migrant children's living situation into the teaching and the daily routine at school, be more willing to cooperate with other groups, organizations and institutions, and initiate meetings between Germans and migrants.

6. CLOSING REMARKS

In recent years the interest in topics dealing with the school situation and the teaching of migrant pupils has diminished considerably in the Federal Republic of Germany and model programmes and measures are not financed willingly. This would be welcomed if it indicated a 'normalization' and if it meant that the migrant children's and young people's questions would be considered in other spheres of life. However, no such development is apparent to date: migrant pupils are handled as special problems or in special programmes, or they are not taken into consideration at all. Many of the model experiments that dealt particularly with the school problems of this group have aggravated this development unintentionally and without foreseeing the consequences, by reinforcing the idea that the migrants in the school system and in further education have to be dealt with as a special group, even as a problem group.

Many of the experiments and studies to date have been oriented on outdated conditions and circumstances, often because of the relatively long time needed for preparation and starting up. The development of teaching concepts, pedagogical measures, and also the development of teaching aids for pupils and teachers, referred to migrant children who entered Germany during their school career and had to be integrated into the German school and education system. Hardly any pedagogical measure or study, either in model experiments or in the pedagogical literature, considers the migrant pupils who have been born in the Federal Republic of Germany and who have a relatively good knowledge of the German language. The change that has been noticeable since 1980, i.e. the decline in the numbers of children entering Germany during their school career in favour of those children who grew up in Germany and in many cases attended kindergarten, but still have difficulties in coping with the demands of the German school system because of discrepancies in socialization within and outside the family, is usually not considered. Also, only a few pedagogical measures and experiments are directed to the migrant pupils' situation in *Realschulen* and Gymnasiums, and also in special schools. The problem of the referrals to special schools, which for some years was especially important in the discussion about the teaching of migrants, is now hardly considered. For these groups, which have not yet been scientifically investigated and analysed, projects oriented on studying, implementing and testing innovations are necessary. They are also useful for those groups of migrant children and young people, for which we have evidence (for example, Turkish girls) that they are still especially disadvantaged in the area of training for a professions.

NOTES

1 It is government policy in the Federal Republic of Germany to refer to 'migrants' or *Gastarbeiter* – terms that suggest the transience of these people.

2 Education in the FRG is compulsory for children aged 6-18. After primary school (*Grundschule*) children enter one of three streams: Gymnasium (pre-university schooling), *Realschule* (intermediate secondary) or *Hauptschule* (basic secondary). The latter two prepare pupils for entry into vocational schools at age 16.

3 The Federal Republic of Germany consists of eleven states. The states are independent in their formulation of educational policies.

REFERENCES

BAGIV – Bundesarbeitsgemeinschaft der Immigrantenverbände in der Bundesrepublik Deutschland und Berlin (West) (Eds.) (1985). *Muttersprachlicher Unterricht in der Bundesrepublik Deutschland. Sprach- und bildungspolitische Argumente für die zweisprachige Erziehung von Kindern sprachlicher Minderheiten.* Hamburg: Rissen.

BOOS-NÜNNING, U., HOHMANN, M. & REICH, H.H. (1976). *Schulbildung ausländischer Kinder.* Bonn: Eichholz.

BOOS-NÜNNING, U. (1979). Language and language tuition for ethnic minorities in the Federal Republic of Germany. OECD-paper Paris.(In German (1981), *Schulmodelle für ethnische Minderheiten. Drei Bundesländer im Vergleich.* Essen/Landau: Publikation Alfa.

BOOS-NÜNNING, U. (1981). Muttersprachliche Klassen für ausländische Kinder: Eine kritische Diskussion des bayerischen 'offenen Modells'. *Deutsch Lernen, 2,* 40-70.

BOOS-NÜNNING, U., HOHMANN, M., REICH, H.H. & WITTEK, F. (1983). *Aufnahmeunterricht. Muttersprachlicher Unterricht. Interkultureller Unterricht. Ergebnisse einer vergleichenden Untersuchung zum Unterricht für ausländische Kinder in Belgien, England, Frankreich und den Niederlanden.* München: Oldenbourg. (In English 1986). *Towards intercultural education. A comparative study of the education of migrant children in Belgium, England, France and the Netherlands.* London: JLT.)

BOOS-NÜNNING, U. (1984). Schulprobleme ausländischer Kinder und Jugendlicher: Soziale und familiäre Ursachen. In H.J. Brandt & Haase, Cl.-Pl. (Eds.), *Begegnung mit Türken – Begegnung mit dem Islam. Ein Arbeitsbuch,* Bd. IV. , 39-55. Hamburg: Rissen.

BOOS-NÜNNING, U. & HENSCHEID, R. (1986). Ausländische Kinder an deutschen Schulen. *Politische Bildung: "Ausländer" in der Bundesrepublik Deutschland – "Gastarbeiter" oder Einwanderer?* H. 1, 64-82.

BUDDE, H., HENSCHEID, R., KAUFMANN-SAUERLAND, L., KLEMM, K. & SCHULZ, G. (1985). *Gutachten zu Massnahmen zur Verbesserung der beruflichen Integration ausländischer Jugendlicher.* Unveröffentlichtes Manuskript. Essen.

DAMANAKIS, M. (1978). *Sozialisationsprobleme der griechischen Gastarbeiterkinder in den Grund- und Hauptschulen des Bundeslandes Nordrhein-Westfalen.* Kastellaun: Henn.

DAMANAKIS, M. (1982). Aus ausländische Pendelkindern Neu-Deutsche machen. *Lernen in Deutschland, 8,* 6-16.

DEUTSCHES JUGENDINSTITUT (Eds.) (1987). *Ausländerarbeit und Integrationsforschung. Bilanz und Perspektiven.* München: DJI.

FUCHS, H.E. & WOLLMANN, H. (Eds.) (1987). *Hilfen für ausländische Kinder und Jugendliche. Wege aus dem gesellschaftlichen Abseits?* Basel: Birkhäuser.

GLUMPLER, E. (1985). *Schullaufbahn und Schulerfolg türkischer Migrantenkinder.* Hamburg.

HECKER, U. (1980). Repräsentativ-Untersuchung über die Bildungs- und Beschäftigungssituation ausländischer Jugendlicher in der Bundesrepublik Deutschland. Erste Ergebnisse. In U. Hecker &. D. Schmidt-Hackenberg (Eds.), *Bildungs- und Beschäftigungssituation ausländischer Jugendlicher in der Bundesrepublik Deutschland. Teil 1: Grunddaten der Befragung.* Berlin/Bonn: Bundesinstitut für Berufsbildung.

HECKER, U. (1984). *Ausländische Jugendliche in Ausbildung und Beruf. Eine Untersuchung zur Situation der zweiten Generation in der Bundesrepublik Deutschland.* Berlin/Bonn: Bundesinstitut für Berufsbildung.

HENSCHEID, R. (1986). Berufliche Chancen und Berufsbildung ausländischer Jugendlicher. In *Einführung in die Ausländerpädagogik.* Unveröffentlichtes Manuskript. Essen: Institut für Migrationsforschung, Ausländerpädagogik und Zweitsprachendidaktik.

HOHMANN, M. (1983). Gibt es eine Didaktik für den Unterricht mit ausländischen Kinder? In A. Regenbrecht & U. Franke (Eds.): *Ausländerpädagogik an Universitäten.* pp 10-18. Hamm: Verband Bildung und Erziehung.

HOHMANN, M. (1983). Interkulturelle Erziehung – Versuch einer Bestandsaufnahme. *Ausländerkinder in Schule und Kindergarten,* 4, 4-8.

HOHMANN, M. (1987). Interkulturelle Erziehung als Herausforderung für allgemeine Bildung? In D. Glowka, M. Krüger-Potratz & B. Krüger (Eds.), *Vergleichende Erziehungswissenschaft: Informationen, Berichte, Studien Nr. 17: Erziehung in der multikulturellen Gesellschaft.* pp 98-115. Münster: Westfälische Wilhelmsuniversität.

HOLFORT, F. (1982). *Benachteilung ohne Ende? Zur sozialen Integration ausländischer Kinder.* Düsseldorf: .Swann.

HOPF, D. (1981). Schulprobleme der Ausländerkinder. *Zeitschrift für Pädagogik,* 6, 839-861.

KISCHKEWITZ, P. & REUTER, L.-R. (1980). *Bildungspolitik zweiter Klasse? Ausländerkinder im Schulsystem der Bundesrepublik Deutschland.* Frankfurt/M.: R.G. Fischer.

LANGENOHL-WEYER, A., WENNEKES, R, BENDIT, R. LOPEZ-BLASCO, A., AKPINAR, Ü. & VINK, J. (1979). *Zur Integration der Ausländer im Bildungsbereich, Probleme und Lösungsversuche.* München: Inventa.

LUKESCH, H. (1981). Zur Situation von Ausländerkinder an deutschen Schulen, Ergebnisse einer empirischen Untersuchung in Nordrhein-Westfalen und Hessen. *Zeitschrift für Pädagogik,* 27, 779-892.

MEHRLÄNDER, U. (1983). *Türkische Jugendliche – keine beruflichen Chancen in Deutschland?* Bonn: Neue Gesellschaft.

NEUMANN, U. (1982). *Erziehung ausländischer Kinder. Erziehungsziele und Bildungsvorstellungen in türkischen Arbeiterfamilien.* München: Oldenbourg.

RENNER, E. (1975). *Erziehungs- und Sozialisationsbedingungen türkischer Kinder. Ein Vergleich zwischen Deutschland und der Türkei.* Rheinstetten: Schindele.

RIST, R. C. (1978) *Guestworkers in Germany. The prospects for pluralism.* New York: Praeger. (In German, 1980, *Die ungewisse Zukunft der Gastarbeiter, Eingewanderte Bevölkerungsgruppen verändern Wirtschaft und Gesellschaft.* Stuttgart: Klett-Cotta.)

SCHMIDTKE, H.-P. (1979). Ausländische Kinder im Elementar-, Primar- und Sonderschulbereich. In G. Hansen & K. Klemm (Eds.), *Kinder ausländischer Arbeitnehmer.* pp 61-72. Essen: Neue Deutsche Schule.

SIEWERT, P. (1980). Zur Entwicklung der Gastarbeiterkinder und der schulpolitischen Abstimmung der Kultusministerkonferenz. In Max-Planck-Institut for Bildungsforschung - Projektgruppe Bildungsbericht (Eds.), *Bildung in der Bundesrepublik Deutschland. Daten und Analysen.* 2 Bände. pp 1053-1112. Reinbek: Rowohlt.

STOLTENBERG, G. (1987). Zur Situation der beruflichen Ausbildung ausländischer Jugendlicher – Massnahmen des Bundesministers für Bildung und Wissenschaft, Ergebnisse und Umsetzung. In Deutsches Jugendinstitut (Eds.), *Ausländerarbeit und Integrationsforschung – Billanz und Perspektiven* pp 315-351. München: DJI.

WILPERT, C. (1980). *Die Zukunft der Zweiten Generation. Erwartungen und Verhaltensmöglichkeiten ausländischer Kinder.* Königstein/Ts.: A. Hain.

YAKUT, A., REICH, H.H., NEUMANN, U. & BOOS-NÜNNING, U. (1986). *Zwischen Elternhaus und Arbeitsamt: Türkische Jugendliche suchen einen Beruf.* Berlin: Express.

4

Jacqueline Costa-Lascoux

National Centre for Scientific Research (CNRS)

Immigrant Children in French Schools: Equality or Discrimination

French schools, which had permitted illiteracy to be eliminated in the population as a whole, and provided access to France's literary and artistic heritage and encouraged the social and occupational furtherment of large numbers of people, today find that their dual function of education and democratization of knowledge is being questioned.

Schools are currently the subject of a discussion on both social and cultural aims. Certain people stress the exceptional success of a public service which, within a single century (1881-1988), has contributed towards forging a more open society and which, in the last twenty years, has been able to absorb and train a large school population. Others hold very critical views. Guy Bayet, President of the Société des agrégés[1] (the Society of Grammar School Teachers), has denounced the institutional, financial and scientific bankruptcy of the school system (Bayet, 1987). As for Hervé Hamon and Patrick Rotman, they conclude their investigation into secondary education with the following statement: "If we quite dispassionately list the solutions offered and the obstacles that obscure the horizon, the resulting forecast is pessimistic. Realistically, the opposition wins. The disorder which pervades the system is equalled only by its rigidity. The reforming procedures are equalled only by the inertia or hostility or the personnel" (Hamon & Rotman, 1984).

In his report entitled *Education et Société. Les défis de l'An 2000*, submitted to the Ministry of Education, Jacques Lesourne summarizes the main questions as follows:

"A question about the aims: Does the objective of the educational system consist in developing talents, creating responsible citizens, conveying specific knowledge, teaching people how to learn? Should it or should it not seek to educate man in all his dimensions?

A question about the effects of democratization: despite the efforts in this direction, success at school continues to be closely tied to social origins.

A question about the social, individual and collective effectiveness of education: Does the race for certificates retain its 'profitability' for the individual and does it improve the growth prospects for the national economy?

A question about selection methods: the current system does not generate positively experienced, differentiated successes, but rather the development of feelings of failure and frustration in the majority of pupils.

A question about the ability to steer the educational system in view of its complexity, inertia and its tendency to produce adverse effects which are not identified until later.

It is of little importance whether these questions are well or poorly formulated. The essential fact is that, despite the success of the educational system, they convey the existence in contemporary society of a malaise emanating from this very system." (Lesourne, 1988.)

The repeated discussions on the 'lowering of standards'[2] among pupils, on failures at school, and the failure of training to adjust to a changing labour market, relate primarily to immigrant pupils or pupils of 'foreign origin'. Jacques Berque's report (1985) emphasized the role of immigration as a revealer of dysfunction in a school system.

1. DYSFUNCTION REVEALED BY THE DEPRIVED

After World War II, and particularly after the years of growth (the 'Glorious Thirty'[3]), employment structures and qualifications changed more rapidly than teaching programmes and educational methods. But these socio-cultural difficulties did not appear to shake the basic principle of schools open to all, which would promote equal opportunity. Radical criticism of schools after the events of May 1968, seized on the situation of the children of immigrants in the educational system to denounce the faults of the system. However, the presence of foreign children in French schools is an old phenomenon, directly related to the large waves of migration in the inter-war years.

In a survey carried out in 1927, Georges Mauco recorded 257 665 foreign children between the ages of 6 and 13, representing 8.4 per cent of the total school population: 201 532 attended state schools, 33 964 attended private schools[4], but 22 159 escaped compulsory schooling. Non-attendance of school by such children was one of the weaknesses of the system at that time (Mauco, 1932).

It was not until the Act of 9 August 1936 on the prolongation of schooling that it was clearly stated that: "Primary education is compulsory for children of both sexes, whether of French or of foreign nationality, aged between 6 and 14."

The numbers of children of foreigners in schools clearly followed the flows of migrants: very low numbers in the 1950s (1 per cent at grammar schools and colleges), against 10 per cent of current numbers. In 1952-1953, private schools had 8 500 foreign pupils, representing a minute proportion of the total numbers (Boulot & Boyzon-Fradet, 1988b).

Before 1974, with the exception of a few surveys, no systematic statistical data were kept on the numbers of children of foreign nationalities. For the period after 1974 the numbers of foreign pupils show a perceptible progression: 6.8 per cent of the rolls in 1974-75; 8.9 per cent or 1 085 342 pupils in 1986/1987, the latter being made up of 10.3 per cent of the pupils in state schools and 2.1 per cent of the pupils in private schools.

Another development is equally significant: the proportion of foreign children in nursery schools (aged from 2 to 5) is now identical to that of French children. In other words, all children spend a minimum of 13 to 14 years of their lives at school: before 1970 only half the children spent so long at school. School is consequently the first place where French and foreign children live together, and also the place where the preparation for adult life, in particular, for working life, is at stake.

2. STAKES IN SCHOOLING

The prolongation of schooling, whether in the form of an institutional obligation (compulsory schooling extended to age 16) or a socio-economic fact (backwardness at school and repeating of years result in pupils leaving school at age 18 or 19), has transformed national education into a vast enterprise involving 14.5 million people out of a working population of 35 million, i.e. 41 per cent. The educational system is sagging under the demographic weight but also under the hierarchical and bureaucratic structures.

The complexity of the educational system stems particularly from the diversity of its goals and its public, and the size of the task it has to accomplish:

- The object of the educational system is to transform people by means of successive stages of learning.
- Its public is from a wide variety of social and cultural origins, economic levels and linguistic communities. The sedentarization of immigration, and particularly of communities originating from distant countries, has accentuated this phenomenon.
- The will to educate the whole of an age group, and to carry its training as far as possible, makes the system so huge.
- The imprecision of the objectives is inherent to an educational system which during the 14 to 20 years of schooling of an age group, has to respond to the wide range of socio-economic and political possibilities and upheavals occurring during such a period.
- The educational system is often a place for conflicts: "Conflicts between families wishing to ensure that their children will have a relatively better position in the society of the future. Conflicts between pupils in search of certificates and the institutions which issue such certificates. Conflicts between the organized groups of teachers and central government. Conflicts between all the actors with regard to the allocation of resources. Conflicts at the heart of society as a whole with regard to priority objectives in the area of education and training. This dimension is in the nature of things, but realism dictates that it should not be concealed." (Lesourne, 1988.)

Is it surprising that, as a result of its contradictions, the educational system produces effects that are difficult to measure? Should one take account of the final exam results, the level of the last class attended or the job obtained at the end of the course?

To position the children of immigrants in the French educational system, it is advisable to have in mind a composite collection of data. The taxonomic review made by Serge Boulot and Danielle Boyzon-Fradet (1988a) on the basis of national education statistics is particularly revealing in this area.

The general statistical records of foreign pupils in the French educational system show the perspectives of the measures implemented. But once the statistics indicate a relatively negative conclusion, its interpretation has to be moderated by the results of surveys and research carried out amongst 16-25 year-olds of immigrant origin.

2.1 Compulsory schooling and equality of opportunity

French schools are dominated by the philosophy of equality. However, abstract institutional equality, guaranteed by the fact that education is free and secular, has proved inadequate. It has subsequently given way to the notion of equality of opportunity, which, by means that included specific measures, was intended to re-establish the balance between pupils, across the boundaries of differing socio-cultural origins.

In the name of equality of opportunity, pupils must have access to identical knowledge, within identical structures and according to identical methods of teaching. Four reservations have to be made with regard to this fundamental premise, which has long been the only one applied in French schools:

1. Education in a private institution is possible: this applies to nearly 20 per cent of the total school population, but to only two per cent of foreign pupils;
2. At an early stage, sometimes even before compulsory schooling, schools eliminate pupils who do not conform to the model, by directing them towards special classes;
3. The equipment varies noticeably from one school to another, a disparity which often reflects differences in the quality of the neighbourhoods, and which also corresponds with inequality of teacher training (the youngest and least experienced teachers often finding themselves assigned to schools regarded as 'difficult to teach in').
4. The departure from 'sectorization'[5], introduced experimentally in 1982 and extended again by the Socialist government at the start of the 1988/1989 school year to more than 40 per cent of schools, in itself aggravated the genuine danger of the 'ghetto'. The percentages of foreign children in primary education and the chart of schools (see below) taking pupils of foreign nationalities, provide a good indication of the phenomenon of strong geographical concentration of immigrant communities. What is observed at the provincial level is emphasized at the district level in the large cities: some schools have more than 80 per cent foreigners, representing more than fifty nationalities.

Table 1: Percentage of foreign children in primary education 1983-1984

National average: 11.10 %

Paris	30.81 %	Alpes-Maritimes	13.33 %
Seine Saint-Denis	29.05 %	Bas-Rhin	13.14 %
Hauts de Seine	23.32 %	Bouches-du-Rhône	13.10 %
Rhône	23.27 %	Eure-et-Loire	12.91 %
Val-de-Marne	21.85 %	Jura	12.80 %
Doubs	18.84 %	Saône-et-Loire	12.63 %
Yvelines	18.58 %	Corse-Sud	12.58 %
Territoire de Belfort	18.13 %	Drôme	12.39 %
Haut-Rhin	18.11 %	Savoie	11.92 %
Loire	18.09 %	Yonne	11.86 %
Ain	17.58 %	Aude	11.69 %
Isère	17.44 %	Ardennes	11.50 %
Val d'Oise	17.33 %	Haute Corse	11.15 %
Guyane	17.06 %	Côte d'Or	11.00 %
Haut-Loire	15.10 %	Meurthe-et-Moselle	10.69 %
Moselle	13.92 %	Cher	10.61 %
Essonne	13.89 %	Nord	10.37 %
Loiret	13.73 %	Gard	10.26 %
Puy-de-Dôme	13.67 %	Oise	10.25 %
Vaucluse	13.61 %	Vosges	10.11 %
Seine-et-Marne	13.34 %		

Source: Ministry of Education.

The 4 027 289 pupils in education in the regular classes of primary schools fall into generations of approximately 800 000 pupils, corresponding roughly with the age groups of the INSEE (National Statistical Institute). There is a slight variance from this average in the classes at either end of the primary education[6]:

– for the CP (preparatory course, intended for pupils aged 6), the excess numbers of foreigners may have two causes: on the one hand the demographic bulge of 1980 and 1981; and on the other hand the higher level of repeating of classes at this level (10.8 per cent in 1984/1985);

– for the CM2 (second year intermediate course, intended for pupils aged 10), it is essentially connected with the level of repeating of classes (8.6 per cent in 1984/1985).

The study of cohorts of pupils starting the sixth grade at school in 1982/1983/1984 and starting the CP in 1973 provide elements of comparison between the courses of the French pupils and those of the foreign pupils.

- On average, the foreign pupils start the preparatory course later than the French pupils, 9.2 per cent of them being admitted to the course at the age of seven, whereas this percentage is only 1.4 per cent for French pupils. However, this phenomenon is related to the time of arrival in France: among pupils born in France, the level of admission to the CP at age seven falls to four per cent, which, for comparable socio-economic categories, approaches the level for French pupils.
- French pupils starting the CP at age seven are rather less successful than the others, whereas the level of normal schooling of foreign pupils starting the CP at age seven is equivalent to that of pupils starting the CP at age six.
- In view of the assumed linguistic handicap of foreign students, a significant difference in the amount of repeating of classes could be expected between foreign and French pupils. This difference does exist but is not substantial: 19.2 per cent of French children in the 'unskilled worker' category repeated the CP, compared with 25 per cent of foreigners born in France. The levels for children of skilled workers are 13.3 per cent and 17.3 per cent respectively.
- Repeating the CP results in little chance of reaching the top grade: only 5.4 per cent of pupils who repeated the CP reached the top grade.

In other words, the school course is at risk right from the start, at primary school; successive repeating of classes will only serve to aggravate the disadvantage acquired during the early years of schooling. Hence the importance, particularly for foreign pupils, of schooling starting with the nursery school, to prepare them for learning written expression and for mastering the language. All the surveys testify to the decisive role of early schooling in avoiding the need to repeat the preparatory class.

But here a contradiction in the French educational system becomes apparent. The will of the authorities to avoid steering certain pupils toward the 'short routes' (*filières courtes*), has been translated into measures intended to take the majority of pupils as far as the *baccalauréat* (the final exam of secondary school). This has resulted successively in the disappearance of autonomous educational structures, the elimination of streams starting in the sixth grade and, very re-

cently, attempts to integrate 'maladjusted' pupils into ordinary classes. The creation of vocational *baccalauréats* completes the 'unification'. Henceforth all the courses should result in the same degree of
equality, at least in theory!

In fact, "the need to lead an increased proportion of young people to
the *baccalauréat*, combined with the closure of the labour market, has
resulted in a considerable increase in the number of pupils repeating
upper school classes. It is a race in which certain participants have to
make several attempts at surmounting hurdles, rather than a continuous course, modulated according to each person's own rhythm.
This situation has become socially difficult to accept in a context in
which repeating a class is considered as a failure and in which its
intrinsic value is not fully demonstrated. This is why educational
plans envisage courses differentiated in time: learning to read in
three years, preparation for the *baccalauréat* in four years and vocational training in the form of sandwich courses." (Boulot & Boyzon-
Fradet, 1988a.)

In order to produce equality the strategy of unification has temporarily patched up certain differences, but has given rise to others.
Therefore, in a system in which age acts as a factor for educational
selection (particularly in the paths of excellence), what will happen
to 'mentally handicapped' children? In a society in which 74 per cent
of an age group will reach the level of *baccalauréat*, what new selection criteria will be used in the labour market?

The heterogeneity of the public cannot be totally 'mastered' by the
unitary nature of the educational system: the introduction of uniformity does not constitute equality of treatment. Conscious of the un-
favourable effects of an attitude, laudable in its intentions but too
abstract to make good the real handicaps of the most deprived pupils, the authorities introduced specific measures. Three of them are
particularly worthy of attention: the reception classes for non-French
speaking foreign children, the courses in languages and cultures of
origin, and the zones of priority education. Two of these relate exclusively to foreign children or children of foreign origin; the third
includes a large proportion of them.

2.2 *Specific measures or positive discrimination?*

Since the Revolution of 1789 the French language has been one of the
most powerful instruments of national unification. The circular implementing the famous Falloux Act of 1851 proclaimed: "French will
be the only language used in schools." It was not until the Deixonne

Act of 1951 that plans were introduced, in response to decades of regional demands, for the "best means of encouraging the study of local languages and dialects in the regions in which they are used". The Deixonne Act has been implemented since 1969. More recently, in 1981, Henri Giordan was commissioned to produce a report on "the implementation of a policy of dynamization of the regional cultural fabric", in order to "permit the blossoming of the linguistic and cultural differences in which France is rich..." and "to make an early start with a policy of promoting regional and minority cultures" (Giordan, 1982).

In the cultural and linguistic context peculiar to France, the measures of specific support for foreign pupils and the promotion of languages and cultures of origin have acquired the significance of *measures deviating from common law.*

Interest focused in the first place on language difficulties, since they were assumed to be the principal cause of failure at school. Subsequently, the cultural dimension was evoked, not without a naive, folkloric perception of distant civilizations. Finally, explanations and remedies were sought in the socio-economic sphere. "To say that, where the socio-economic situation of the parents is identical, immigrant children are not distinguished by a higher level of failure, is largely true, but it does not solve the problems: on the one hand, institutions and public opinion experience the effects of a situation first of all; on the other hand, the purely economic explanation is not very effective in tackling the cultural and religious question. The conflict lies in the differences of lifestyles and racism. To take such a statement for granted, without searching for other means of correcting the unfortunately, all too real difficulties, would be to wait for a general advancement of the inhabitants of France, including foreigners, to reform our education." (Boulot & Boyzon-Fradet, 1988a.)

The compromise of the French educational system reflects these varying perceptions of the position of young immigrants. Three essential measures have been taken:

1. The creation of special reception classes for non-French speaking foreign children.
2. The introduction in schools of the teaching of languages and cultures of origin (LCO).
3. The establishment of structures for information and for training the personnel concerned, in particular the Training and Information Centres for the Education of the Children of Migrants (CEFI-SEM[8]) and the 'zones of priority education' (ZEP[9]).

3. SPECIAL RECEPTION CLASSES FOR NON-FRENCH SPEAKING FOREIGN
   CHILDREN

Created in 1970 on an experimental basis in primary schools, under
the name of 'initiation classes' (for children aged between 7 and 12),
and in 1973 in secondary education, under the name of 'adaptation
classes' (for children aged between 13 and 16), special reception classes for non-French speaking foreign children were conceived as temporary structures for encouraging rapid integration. Within one year
the pupils were to acquire a linguistic capability which would permit their integration into normal education. In a sense, the transitory
nature of the special reception classes meant that they did not form
an exception to common law. At the beginning of the 1970s the needs
appeared to be limited and destined to resolve themselves progressively. This explains the relatively low numbers of school pupils in
such reception classes, compared with the arrival of foreign children
in the context of family reunion (see table 2).
The overall figures do not reveal the needs by age group. Moreover,
the interpretation of national statistics should take account of the
geographical distribution of the pupils. It is very difficult to establish
precise correlations between the arrival of foreign children and the
specific structures assuming responsibility for them. Where there
were insufficient numbers of children, they were placed in ordinary
classes. Therefore, the rate of diffusion of non-French speaking foreign pupils into the common system cannot easily be determined.
On the other hand, major trends are clearly obvious from the national statistics: observation of the development of the data reveals a
latency period in the implementation of the measures, which leads to
a significant number of special reception classes, providing education for a reduced number of pupils (16.8 pupils per class in primary
education in 1972/73 and only 9.8 in 1985/86!) Today the rigidity of
the procedures for opening new classes, still does not permit a
prompt response to the arrival of pupils.
More fundamentally, the question posed is that of the status of the
majority language of the country of residence. From the educational
point of view, the reception class experiment relied on 'French as a
foreign language' methods, which is inappropriate to the situation of
foreign children learning the language in a French-speaking context.
This unsuitable teaching has veered towards certain practices which
are astonishing with regard to the objective persued, but which do
fall within the logic of equality of treatment: the initiation and

Table 2: Family reunion and education in special reception classes.
Development from 1970 to 1987 (state education*)

Years	Family reunion		Children in reception classes		
	Total	Children**	Total	Prim. ed.	Sec. ed.
1970	80 952	46 027	(100 classes)		
1971	81 496	44 802	(288 classes)		
1972	74 955	40 412	6 513	6 513	
1973	72 647	38 881		7 683	(40 cl.)
1974	68 038	36 947		8 381	(60 cl.)
1975	51 824	27 097***	13 506	8 671	4 835
1976	57 377	30 628	15 678	11 196	4 482
1977	52 318	26 997	13 135	12 080	1 055
1978	40 123	20 525	11 955	11 356	599
1979	39 300	20 730	14 340	11 707	1 633****
1980	42 020	23 223	13 063	11 155	1 908
1981	41 560	23 129	12 366	10 546	1 820
1982	47 366	26 117	13 228	10 665	2 563
1983	45 731	23 994	11 620	8 953	2 667
1984	39 586	19 335	10 016	7 034	2 982
1985	32 512	14 859	8 252	5 308	2 944
1986	27 140	12 689	7 933	4 621	3 312
1987	26 769	13 242		4 182	(414 classes)

*   Private schools provide education for a negligible number of foreign
        pupils in special reception classes (in 1986/87: 74).
**   These figures include all 'children' aged from 0 to 20 and above.
***   From 1975 onwards, the members of families from the EEC are not includ-
        ed in these figures.
****   Data for periods prior to 1978/79 include pupils educated in other struc-
        tures (final studies classes in particular).

adaptation classes have assumed increasing responsibility for children with educational difficulties, whatever their national origins.
The reception classes ended up mixing non-French speaking pupils
with French pupils of low intellectual ability, as if the type of
teaching suited to one group was suited to the others. The assumption of equivalence between linguistic difficulties and intellectual
difficulties is highly questionable.

However, linguistic research has considerably advanced the knowledge of phenomena such as 'second language acquisition' and
'diglossia', which vary according to the language context, situations

which are not confined to a more or less exact knowledge of a particular vocabulary or a particular syntax. The reception class experiment appears to have been unaware of this research. In these circumstances, should one be surprised at the low level of training and preparation of teachers assigned to the special reception classes? Moreover, since no provision of information to the personnel as a whole had been seriously arranged, these classes, when they existed at all, found themselves isolated within the schools. "In total, being too inward-looking, the initiation class 'ghetto' or even 'cocoon' is, in any case, too often marginalized with respect to the rest of the school. They 'demobilize' other teachers, such as those giving integrated remedial courses, insofar as they operate without liaison with the other educational activities: since 'specialists' deal with these problems, non-specialists feel themselves relieved of this task and tend not to integrate the presence and the specific characteristics of these children into their activities." (Berque, 1985.)

Serge Boulot and Danielle Boyzon-Fradet rightly point out that: "Nearly twenty years after their creation, these structures have still not been evaluated. It is impossible to say whether they contribute to the sound educational integration of the pupils. This lack of information ought to result in the utmost caution with regard to authoritarian administrative decisions: systematic decompartmentalization of these remedial classes might have a negative effect on genuine consideration for the specific needs of certain pupils. Similarly, straight suppression of these classes for reasons of the decline in family reunion or of the risks of 'ghettoization' would only be meaningful after the definition of a general policy and the scientific evaluation of the various existing measures... In any case, it is not necessary to make an amalgam when one considers educational provisions for foreign children: they are virtually all subjected to the common regime: in 1986/87 only 6 429 pupils out of a total of 1 085 342 were in reception classes." (Boulot & Boyzon-Fradet, 1988a.)

Planned as an experiment, and introduced into certain city districts with a strong concentration of immigrants, the special reception classes are a typical example of institutional responses that fail to produce the anticipated effects. They are imprisoned in a rigid system: they anticipate the structures and the numbers, as well as additional logistics, but they do not display the range of competence and teaching methods suited to the expressed needs. The reasons put forward to justify the inevitable rigidity of the structures always relate to material resources. In fact, no serious evaluation (not even of this particular point) has been made. The training of teachers and a reduction in the numbers in certain 'normal' classes with foreign pupils, along with extra-curricular support, might have been more successful in attaining the objective of 'non-ghettoization', and at a lower cost.

Two ideas have commonly been put forward for 'finding solutions' to the educational integration of children of foreign origin: special reception classes for learning French and, later on, teaching of the languages and cultures of origin – the latter being intended to provide a smooth transition into the culture of the host society as well as to prepare the pupils for a possible return to their country of origin. The discussions and reflections on identity and differences are characteristic of the 1980s: their expression in the educational system is one of the most significant aspects of this discussion on 'identity'.

4. THE TEACHING OF LANGUAGES AND CULTURES OF ORIGIN

The circular of 21 December 1925, authorizing the teaching of "modern languages by foreign instructors" in schools after normal courses, represented the first introduction (via a concealed door) of modern languages for foreign pupils. It was a concession made by France to recently settled immigrant communities. This was evidently a compromise between the French government, seeking manpower (via the intermediary of the representatives of the Coal Mines and of the Agricultural Federation for the Devastated Areas), and the Polish government. In reality, the 1925 circular did not offend against the general functioning of schools; it was a very limited addition.

It was not until 1983 that the measures relating to the teaching of foreign languages by foreign teachers became the subject of a more positively stated policy. The first attempt at integrating language courses into 'third-period education' (i.e. the three hours a week reserved for 'awakening' activities in primary schools), related to the teaching of Portuguese.

In the late 1960s the Minister of Education, in conjunction with the Portuguese government, decided to introduce three hours teaching of Portuguese for Portuguese pupils on an experimental basis with the assistance of teachers recruited and remunerated by Portugal.

Other experiments of the same type were introduced very rapidly for Italian, Tunisian and Spanish pupils. On 9 April 1975 a general circular established rules for the "teaching of national languages to immigrant pupils in the context of 'third period' education in primary schools". This teaching formed part of the bilateral agreements signed in 1975 with Morocco, in 1977 with Yugoslavia, in 1978 with Turkey and in 1982 with Algeria. In 1987 a total of eight countries assigned approximately 2 000 teachers to provide these courses. These teachers are trained, remunerated and supervised by the countries concerned (the supervision is carried out jointly with the French authorities and the Training and Information Centres for the Education of the Children of Migrants (CEFISEM).

The teaching of languages and cultures of origin viewed the integration of foreign pupils in terms of four principal objectives:
- to preserve the ties with the family and social environment, both in France and in the country of origin;
- to acquire a more objective and more precise knowledge of the culture of origin, as opposed to stereotyped and often disparaging views;
- to encourage a better actual and psychological balance, which is essential for a general education and for success at school;
- to achieve greater mastery of the language of origin, in order to acquire French language easier.

In truth, these courses, which deviated from the French educational system, encountered numerous difficulties, both at the practial level and in the elaboration of didactic methods:
- the lack of educational material and premises, the late arrival of foreign teachers, who, moreover, worked in several educational establishments, raised numerous material and organizational obstacles;
- the courses in languages and cultures of origin often generated substantial operational complexity, since the schools concerned were those where there were large numbers of foreign pupils of a very wide variety of nationalities. Where there are courses in Arabic, Portuguese and Turkish in the same school, the pupils of a single class who are nationals of those countries leave the class at different times, thereby making it difficult, if not impossible, to apply the principle that basic teaching should not be given during the language and culture of origin courses;
- pedagogical integration has not proved to be very satisfactory: course content and teaching methods have not only been poorly coordinated with the teaching of other subjects, but have also often emerged as retrograde and therefore discredited in the eyes

of the pupils – lacking in individualization and in openness to the contemporary world.
The recorded results clearly convey the limits of this 'integrated' teaching, which reached less than 20 per cent of the pupils potentially involved. There are considerable variances from this average, depending on the languages concerned: fewer than two per cent Yugoslavs and four per cent Spaniards, more than 25 per cent Turks and more than 20 per cent Portuguese. On the other hand, all Italians take these courses. In fact, some children of French nationality and Italian origin, and some French pupils taking early courses in Italian, are included in the statistics. Italian has moved into the category of a modern foreign language which far more pupils than those with Italian 'antecedents', take an interest in.

Table 3: Integrated courses in language and culture of origin in primary schools (state establishments)
*Development from 1981/1982 to 1986/1987 ** *

Languages	81/82	82/83	83/84	84/84	85/86	86/87
Arabic						
Algerian	6 232	9 549	25 668	30 559	27 289	23 340
Maroccan	3 775	4 195	6 723	4 740	3 813	5 339
Tunisian	3 131	3 501	3 506	4 011	3 639	3 212
Spanish	996	905	1 452	813	494	411
Italian	8 149	8 216	8 503	12 519	10 335	10 142
Potuguese	16 644	17 409	18 166	19 585	16 881	14 735
Turkish	4 382	3 880	5 209	7 029	7 802	8 047
Serbo-Croat	143	44	71	104	107	108
Total	43 452	48 165	70 497	79 360	70 360	65 334
% **	***		12.36%	17.74%	20.24%	19.32%	17.52%

*   Data relating to these courses available only from the 1981/1982 school year onwards.
**   % of pupils pursuing integrated courses in relation to pupils potentially involved.
***   Data not available.

In secondary schools, the teaching of languages and cultures of origin acquires a different significance. Indeed, all pupils, whether foreigners or French, may in theory choose between fourteen modern languages, including Arabic, Spanish, Italian and Portuguese, which are also languages of the countries of emigration. This teaching is provided by French teachers. However, there is no equal provision of, or demand for, teaching of all the languages accounted for by immigration. Eight countries of origin have signed an agreement with France, to organize language courses on the same conditions as in primary school, i.e. in the context of optional teaching. It is therefore possible for two types of language teaching to exist side by side in the same school: that provided by French staff and that provided by foreign staff, supervised by the authorities of the country of origin. Moreover, there are 'foreign assistants' in numerous French grammar schools and colleges, while the French teachers of foreign languages may themselves obviously be 'second generation' or French by acquisition of nationality (particularly by marriage), the language they teach being their mother tongue.

In reality, three languages dominate: English, German and Spanish, which accounted for 96.44 per cent of the choices in 1985/1986. English is well ahead: 63.81 per cent of the choices and 75 per cent as first foreign language in 1983; a development which has become steadily more pronounced since the 1960s. Italian, which is in fourth place, with 2.49 per cent is only in fifth place as a first foreign language (0.27 per cent) after Portuguese (0.28 per cent). Arabic represents only 0.19 per cent of the choices and 0.14 per cent as first foreign language. On the other hand, a trend seems to be developing towards the choice of optional languages – Arabic, Vietnamese, Chinese, Hebrew – by pupils in the *grands lycées* (grammar schools with preparatory classes for the *grandes écoles* – university-level colleges, specializing in professional training), in anticipation of an occupation oriented towards scientific co-operation or international commerce. This is a long way from the integration of languages and cultures of origin for the benefit of the children of immigrants, but this 'upward valuation' of 'rare' languages – and no longer of 'mother' tongues – may perhaps have a positive influence on the conception of foreign languages.

Indeed, it cannot be denied that there is a 'hierarchy of languages', which reflects the unequal development and the cultural influence of the individual countries. The international use of a language, and its capacity for communication and representation, exceed the usefulness of a mother tongue, which has emotional value, but which does not always open up the possibility of social mobility or of advanced technological learning.

Numerous misunderstandings exist with regard to languages referred to as 'mother tongues' or 'languages of origin', because insufficient account has been taken of socio-linguistic analysis and research[10]. Bilingualism acquired in a *'lycée international '*(international grammar school[11]) is not the same as that of an immigrant child. Composite, often impoverished and deformed, the languages spoken within families with little education, who emigrated several years previously, do not satisfy academic criteria. A considerable effort is therefore required on the part of pupils following mother tongue courses, and this is added to the courses taken jointly with the other pupils. Far from valuing their origins and reuniting families, this teaching underlines the 'failure' of their parents, their 'lack of culture', and the gap between them and the society of origin. Parents do not take lightly to being 'taught a lesson' in a foreign country. Moreover, which language should be given preference when the country of origin is itself characterized by multilingualism?[12]

In addition to these socio-cultural difficulties, a double reproach is directed at the teachers of languages and cultures of origin: namely that they exercise a right of inspection with regard to the community on behalf of their government and act as political or religious propagandists; and that they do not seek to work together with their French colleagues in order to coordinate the teaching[13]. It is true that the educational methods used for languages and cultures of origin are often anachronistic and authoritarian when compared with the methods used by French schools. In addition, certain people see in this an incitement to return to their country of origin. If mastery of the language or *a* language of the country of origin is beneficial to successful reintegration, it will be difficult for the optional courses given under current conditions to reverse the relationship between emigrant societies and the developed countries (Poinard, 1988).

The speeches in favour of languages and cultures of origin, which marked the decade 1975-85 are nowadays more critical. The results of the first experiments were those forecast by certain people who were not listened to at the time (see Boulot & Boyzon-Fradet, 1988a, 1988b). Increasing disliking on the part of pupils towards courses 'for immigrants' has been observed. The demands of the parents themselves tend now towards a return 'to common law', and not for a derogatory system. "Let French schools do what they know how to do!" The application of 'common core' teaching, even if it has to be further divided to include courses in foreign languages and 'distant' cultures, would appear to provide a better guarantee of the equality of pupils, whatever their origin. The specific approach, on the other hand, is successful in the extra-curricular area. The most positive reforms have been those that have permitted better adaptation of the institution itself by means of teacher training and an adequate response to the educational needs. The creation of the Training and Information Centres for the Education of the Children of Migrants (CEFISEM), the zones of priority education (ZEP) and the extra-curricular activities, have perhaps done more to guide the children of immigrants along the path of equality of opportunities, than the reinforcement of cultural particularism, which undervalues those who are already deprived.

5. ADAPTATION OF THE INSTITUTION: CEFISEMs AND ZEPs

The twenty CEFISEMs created between 1975 and 1984 comprise teams of varying numbers around a basic cell consisting of two primary school teachers and a general college education teacher (PEGC[14]) – at least in theory. Certain CEFISEMs have established ties with universities and research via external intermediaries. Others have been able to develop joint action with regional or local authorities, or both. Schools have opened up to the outside world, to specialists, to social partners. Communication has been established, from the nursery school to the university.

Hailed as an innovative experiment, the CEFISEMs have, unfortunately, not benefited from sufficient logistical support, particularly since 1985. The announcement in the press of their possible disappearance has demonstrated their fragility. Will the programme of the new Minister of Education, appointed by the Rocard government, move towards the maintenance or even reinforcement of the structure? The very idea of this information and training, with the improvements that could be proposed on the basis of the experience acquired, is worth developing, in parallel with a renewal of experiments such as the ZEPs and the reform of colleges.

The *zones of priority education* respond to a different logic than that of specific teaching based on the origin of the pupils. It is a matter of determining what are the educational needs and the internal or external factors in schools that may explain underachievement or failure at school. In this way, on the basis of analysis of the causes of failure, notably the socio-economic handicaps common to pupils of differing origins, geographical areas have been defined in order to make use of material and personnel resources corresponding with the needs. If there is specificity in educational policies, it is in response to difficulties and needs encountered and not on the basis of preconstituted population categories.

The objective is to "contribute to correcting social inequality by selective reinforcement of educational activity in the zones and social environments in which the level of failure at school is highest". It tends toward "the subordination of the increase in resources to their discounted return in terms of democratization of school education". (Circular of 1 July 1981.)

The idea is not new: born in Great Britain at the end of the 1960s, and developed in France by the SGEN-CFDT[15] teaching federation at roughly the same time, it was prescribed in the socialist programme of 1980. But the originality of the principles of the ZEPs created in 1981 is undeniable:

- "Henceforth it is no longer blasphemous to talk of malformation of the educational system" (Berque, 1985). It is admitted that a fundamental role is played by non-school factors: socio-economic background, cultural environment and integration. Therefore, repeating of classes, orientation towards the short route or special education, and whether or not certificates are obtained, are just as much indicators of individual courses as of the integrating capacity of schools and of the quality of the socio-economic environment. This conception of the school as the stake of society as a whole, is the basis for the 'priority zones'.
- "It is no longer believed or proclaimed that school is capable on its own of resolving social problems. Quite the contrary..." (Boulot & Boyzon-Fradet, 1988a). The mobilization of the partners is broader, the expectations better evaluated and failure less irreversible.
- The variety of methods used does not question the principle of egalitarian treatment of the pupils: the disciplines taught, the curricula, the examinations and the certificates remain the same. What is involved is not the making of a 'school for the poor', but the modification of the relationship to the school by involving partners capable of coordinating their efforts towards the reduction of inequality. The educational action "adapts the teaching to the diversity of the pupils' references" and is completed by out-of-school educational activities. These diversified practices are conceived as an application of the egalitarian principle, not as a deviation, from it.

– The resources in terms of posts, fincancing, and training periods
are allocated on the basis of needs and of an 'area plan' which
allows everyone to participate on a local basis, even those who
used to be least associated with educational tasks: from administrative managers to politicians, with representatives of associations or of employers too.

The method of determination and functioning of the ZEPs was particularly original. Indeed, the creation of priority zones was accompanied by an 'inventory' of the educational system in schools, colleges
and grammar schools. Reports were requested and consultation was
undertaken. Parallel to these measures, two educational innovations
were implemented:

1. The reform of the colleges, introducing differentiated educational
   practices, flexible and adjustable 'level groups', with individual-
   ized school support – but the tutorial system remained at the
   planning stage, principally because of reservation on the part of
   the teachers;
2. The educational action plans (PAE) which arrange interdisciplinary and inter-class work on a particular topic, in order better to
   adapt practices to the "diversity of the pupils references". This
   formula is particularly appreciated by the pupils.

As a result of their global view of the problem of failure at school,
the priority zones meant that foreign children were not to be treated
'separately'. However, rather clumsily, the first circular of July 1981
fixed a 'quota' of 30 per cent of foreign pupils as one of the indicators determining such a zone. As early as December of the same
year, the technical appendix to the second circular had to specify that
the proportion of foreigners was one "social and demographic criterion" among others (CSP[16], unemployment, large families, residen-
tial density, placement of children and educational support intervention in an open environment"). How regrettable it is, however, that
the term 'zone', with its pejorative connotations in current French
was maintained!

The will not to particularize the children of immigrants and not to
marginalize them with culturalistic presuppositions, marked a turning point in the approach to difficulties of schooling. It has to be
noted, however, that three out of the five environmental indicators,
were devoted to the presence of foreign pupils (percentage of non-
French speaking pupils and of foreigners in primary education, by
school and by sector; percentage in middle-school classes, by college). Though the quota of 30 per cent had disappeared, the presence

of foreign pupils was still numbered among the factors aggravating the school situation, since the equation, non-French speaking pupils = foreign pupils, was very quickly assumed.

Rules of institutional management, mental rigidity, administrative routine and corporatistic defences, combined to produce an example of adverse effect. Despite the objective clearly expressed in the second circular, the directors of establishments based their requests for ZEPs (which represented additional advantages and resources) on the 'determining' criterion of the number of foreign pupils enrolled. Whereas the Ministry of Education had wanted to prevent the 'ghetto' effect, the situation came close again to the logic of quotas (28.9 per cent of foreign children in the schools located in ZEPs, against 10.8 per cent at the national level). Consider again the statement made by Boulot and Boyzon-Fradet (1988a): "It was thought that this veritable revolution in the conception of the school could turn up its nose at the difficulties and resistance, relying on voluntarism to act as the motor of the change of mentality. But the initial enthusiasm was very soon confronted with reality: corporatism on the part of the teachers' unions, persistent hierarchical structures, an administrative logic incompatible with the notion of an interdisciplinary, multipartite, decompartmentalized project, insufficiency of information of the social body as a whole, the absence of training, particularly for teachers, in the preparation of coherent projects, confusion of the respective roles of the various parties, and dialogue difficulties...

Moreover the resources deployed did not live up to the hopes: little creation of posts (in fact it was rather a redistribution, made possible by the population decrease), no institutionalized periods of consultation between the teachers, no real coordination of the zones, no long-term plan for readjusting the projects and relaunching the campaign each year."

As a whole, the scope of the ZEPs was limited by the weight of the educational system and the inadequacy of the resources deployed: in 1984/1985, a year in which the priority zones were at their peak, there were 383 zones involving 4 600 schools, representing:

– 8.5 per cent of pupils in primary education;
– 10.5 per cent of those in colleges, 8.2 per cent of those in vocational secondary schools;
– 0.7 per cent of the pupils in grammar schools.

As early as 1985, the ZEP experiment was virtually dormant. All the supporters of school reform were to return to the established principle, and this regardless of their political or ideological affiliations.

Thus, the Lesourne report, commissioned by René Monory, under-
lined the contribution of the ZEPs "towards initiating the break with
the teachers' educational monopoly, and the coordination of schools
with other institutions that take part in local development, specula-
ting on the power of this synergy to prevent or remedy the failure."
Several of the programmes of the candidates in the presidential elec-
tion of 1988 made explicit reference to this, and the new Minister of
Education, Lionel Jospin, has taken up the project again to develop
the experience gained from it. One should again remember the
deviations experienced successively by all reforms, accumulating
ideological bias, epistemological errors, the dearth of resources and
the interactions of power or interest that curb the most generous
proposals.

There is limited scope for succeeding in modifying the French educational system, which has been elevated to the rank of an institution
for more than a century. The imperatives of a high-level scientific
training, and consideration for the most deprived, are not without
contradiction. How can we succeed in providing an education in
solidarity and in the respect for equality while at the same time preparing young people for a society based on competitiveness? One of
the preconditions for the efficacy of measures is their clarity. In the
French system a number of constant factors appear, which cannot be
ignored:

- the dangers of a 'right to differ' becoming a 'right to ethno-devel-
  opment' compel us to think in terms of the right to equality;
- the equality of treatment prescribed in the texts is exposed to the
  risk of the adverse effects of a formal equality with no actual
  resources to restore balance to the detriment of the prevailing
  social domination or inequality;
- failure at school is the most serious future event that can be hypo-
  thesized for an individual, but more so in environments in which
  'socio-cultural handicaps' and marginalization become cumulative.

However that may be, the desires of the youth of the second generation should be heard. Their demand is first of all for equality with
their classmates and peers. The 'marches for equality' in the early
1980s and the demonstrations by secondary school pupils and students in the autumn of 1986 related essentially to this subject. A
return to fixed, stereotyped identities would in fact jeopardize the
entry of this second generation into working life.

NOTES

1 'Agrégé': holder of 'agrégation', highest competitive examination for teachers in France.

2 Evergreen argument put forward by supporters of elitistic academic education opposed to the alleged lack of strictness of school reformers.

3 'Glorious Thirty': stylistic device which has its root in French history. Years between 1945 and 1975 corresponding a constant economic growth rate and, consequently, to an increase in purchasing power and to a change in the French way of life.

4 Most of to-day's French private schools are in fact denominational schools, grant-aided and controlled by the state ('établissements privés sous contrat avec l'état').

5 'La sectorization': division in areas. Parents from a particular area must send their children to the schools of that area and are not permitted as a rule to choose a school further away.

6 French primary education is divided into five grades:
   - preparatory course ('cours préparatoire')
   - elementary course 1st year ('cours élémentaire 1ère année')
   - elementary course 2nd year ('cours élémentaire 2e année')
   - intermediate course 1st year ('cours moyen 1ère année')
   - intermediate course 2nd year ('cours moyen 2e année')

7 French secondary education is divided into seven grades from age 11 to 17:
   - 6th form ('sixième')
   - 5th form ('cinquième') ⎫
   - 4th form ('quatrième') ⎬ education given in a 'collège' = middle school
   - 3rd form ('troisième') ⎭
   - 2nd form ('seconde') ⎫ education given in a 'lycée' = upper school
   - 1st form ('première') ⎬ which leads to the 'baccalauréat', giving
   - final year ('classe terminale') ⎭ university entrance qualification

8 CEFISEM: Centres de Formation et d'Information pour la Scolarisation des Enfants de Migrants.

9 ZEP: Zones d'Education Prioritaire.

10 One only has to consult the REMISIS documentation network and the abundant CNDP-Migrants documentation to discover the authoritative socio-linguistic works.

11 Grammar school in which there are not only language courses, but also courses *given in* foreign languages.

12 Is it necessary to recall that the majority of North Africans in France are Berber-speaking and that the North African States recognize a plurality of languages? The phenomenon of 'chain migration' from a village or a region reinforces the minority aspect or at least localizes the linguistic expression of numerous immigrants.

13 It should be noted, however, that the staggered course timetables do not encourage meetings between foreign and French teachers and that the latter have themselves scarcely made any efforts in this direction.

14 PEGC: Professeur d'enseignement Général des Collèges.

15 SGEN: Syndicat Général de l'Education Nationale.
    CFDT: Confédération Française et Démocratique du Travail.

16 CSP: Categories Socio-Professionelles.

REFERENCES

BAYET, G. (1987). Les trois faillites de l'école. *Revue des Deux-Mondes*. Paris.
BERQUE, J. (1985). *L'immigration à l'école de la république*. Rapport remis au Ministre de l'Education Nationale. Publié à la Documentation Française. Centre National de Documentation Pédagogigue.
BOULOT, G. & BOYZON-FRADET, D. (1988a). L'école française: égalité des chances et logique d'une institution. *Revue Européenne des Migrations Internationales (REMI), 4 nos. 1-2.*
BOULOT, G. & BOYZON-FRADET, D. (1988b). *Les immigrés et l'école: une course d'obstacles.* Paris: Harmattan/CIEMI.
GIORDAN, H. (1982). *Démocratie culturelle et droit à la différence.* Paris: La Documentation Française.
HAMON, H. & ROTMAN, P. (1984). *Tant qu'il y aura des profs.* Paris: le Seuil.
LESOURNE, J. (1988). *Education et société. Les défis de l'an 2000.* Paris: La Découverte/Le Monde.
MAUCO, G. (1932). *Les étrangers en France.* Paris: A. Colin.

5

Eugeen Roosens
Catholic University of Leuven

Cultural Ecology and Achievement Motivation[1]

Ethnic minority youngsters in the Belgian system

1. Major Immigrant Groups

When compared with France, the UK and the Netherlands, it is striking that Belgium has only an insignificant number (official figures 1985: 9 607) of immigrants stemming from its former colony, Zaire, or its two overseas protectorates, Rwanda and Burundi (Dumon & Michiels, 1987).

However, Belgian companies and Belgian authorities actively stimulated immigration from Southern Europe after the World War II, in order to attract cheap labour. At present, hundreds of thousands of migrant workers, their wives and children reside in Belgium (official figures 1985: 269 316 Italians, 55 141 Spaniards, 72 495 Turks and 123 188 Moroccans). Skilled and highly trained migrants from the Netherlands (official figures 1985: 66 317) and France (103 215) and other industrialized countries have also settled in Belgium. Roughly speaking, one out of every eleven inhabitants in Belgium is an immigrant (Dumon & Michiels, 1987). In Brussels, one resident in five is not Belgian, and in some of Brussels's nineteen townships more than 40 per cent of the population is non-Belgian. At present, approximately one out of every two new-borns in the Brussels area has immigrant parents. Compared with most other European countries, Belgium has become an immigration country par excellence, although it forcefully repudiates this epithet.

The migrants arrived quietly and gradually. As early as the 1930s, some employers – specifically in the coal mining industry – began to recruit foreign labourers to make up for local shortages in the labour market, and they continued to do so after World War II because attempts to attract Belgians who were then unemployed (an estimated 100 000) to coal mines were unsuccessful. Going down into the mines was too dangerous and too ill-paid for them (Roosens, 1981).

In 1945, with government approval, campaigns to recruit labourers for the mines of Wallonia and Limburg were initiated in foreign countries, and in a short time 60 000 workers (mostly Italians) were signed up. It seems useful to note here that these workers did not come to Belgium on their own initiative, but were encouraged to come by recruiting organizations. They came at the invitation of Belgian employers to do jobs Belgians would not do. In the labour-intensive coal mining industry, they contributed to provision of cheap energy which, among other things, benefited Belgium's competitive position in the international market. In view of the economic advantages, neither the government nor the unions objected to the importation of foreign labour force. In addition, the foreigners posed no threat to Belgian workers because for a number of years they were restricted to the mining sector. When it appeared that the strategy of importing cheap labour was working excellently, other sectors of production – e.g. the steel industry, the construction industry, and the domestic service sector – asked the government for permission to follow suit, particularly in the 1960s. In effect, the jobs that Belgians refused to do were taken over by foreigners from countries to the south.

Furthermore, the migrant labourers have been serving other purposes besides filling gaps in the production system. For example, in Wallonia the immigration of foreign families was considered to be a partial solution for the underpopulation in the region – particularly after the publication of the Sauvy Report in the beginning of the 1960s. In certain areas of Wallonia, the authorities have repeatedly advocated immigration as a technique of repopulation (Roosens, 1981).

The labour relationship between local employers and immigrant workers, which clearly developed in a context of fundamental inequality between Belgians and non-Belgians, is the primary source of the social distance which exists between the autochthones and allochthones of the immigrant labourer type. Immigrant labourers constitute an 'underclass', to use the term of Rex and Tomlinson

(1979). Those who had recruited immigrants clearly profited from the vulnerable position of these immigrants in their own countries. That is, the guest workers were recruited precisely *because* they had belonged to the lower, poorer socio-economic levels of their countries; in addition, these countries were and are developing areas. It is obvious that employers sought workers who would be satisfied with very little. The guest workers' status in Belgium is thus low in two senses: the immigrants come from the lower socio-economic levels of countries that have a low level of socio-economic development as a whole.

Moreover, when the immigrants have phenotypical traits that distinguish them from the Belgians – as is the case with many North Africans and Turks – their 'classification' is a simple matter. In a certain sense, therefore, before they arrived in Belgium these immigrants were already 'classified' into population categories by the international division of labour and international relations on the one hand, and by the socio- economic levels of their countries of origin, on the other.

Nevertheless, they have not become caste-like minorities. A certain number of factors, counteracting the formation of quasi-castes, can be detected (Roosens, 1988).

First of all, the policy adopted by most European countries to bring about some form of European unity by 1992 makes the presence of EEC immigrants unavoidable. The autochthonous populations seem to be accepting this as a fact of life. It may also become increasingly difficult to devise policies to exclude the Turkish and the Moroccan minorities without invoking negative reactions from their respective countries of origin, particularly since the European Commission is asking that the measures taken to integrate EEC immigrants also be applied to non-EEC immigrants and their families.

A second factor counteracting caste formation is the official recognition of the Islamic religion by the Belgian authorities in 1974. Islamic parents now have the right to demand that courses in Islam be given in Belgian state schools. And, moreover, if Islam organizes itself formally, Islamic leaders will have the right to establish their own school system, which would be funded almost totally by the Belgian government. The position of Islam as an officially recognized religion could become a powerful political weapon. Parents would be able to remove their children from Catholic and other Belgian schools and thus deprive these schools of a significant proportion of their enrolment, which they can ill afford to lose. The dramatic demographic decline of the native population makes children of immigrants welcome guests in many institutions.

Furthermore, the status of Islam as a world force, or at least a world phenomenon, may encourage a growing number of Turks and Moroccans to identify themselves publicly as Muslims. This form of 'religious' identification may help to counter caste formation in Belgium, where, at least officially, all religions and world views are considered equal. Paradoxically, perhaps, Islamic identification may reinforce feelings of ethnic belonging among both Turkish and Moroccan immigrants (Kepel, 1987).

Finally, first generation immigrants tend to compare their present situation with their former position and prospects in their country of origin. In very many cases, they feel more like winners than losers. They certainly do not feel like members of a lower caste.

These factors may well prevent caste or quasi-caste formation and enhance the status of non-EEC immigrants, even if their presence is not accepted by a vast proportion of the majority.

Caste formation might start, however, with the so-called second and third generations. As far as is known up to the present, all researchers working in Europe, whatever their philosophy, report that the children of the above-mentioned immigrants have a strikingly high proportional failure rate in the school system. If this process continues for generations, the formation of a quasi-caste system cannot be excluded.

2. CHILDREN AND GRANDCHILDREN OF IMMIGRANTS

It is commonplace to say that the second generation sits between two cultures. In fact, this expression conceals as much as it reveals. There is evidence that the immigrant family never perfectly maintains the culture it acquired in the home country. Instead, an immigrant version of the home culture is created, in which the social context that gives many elements of a culture meaning and significance has been lost. For example, both parents very soon appear to be incompetent in the eyes of their children when it comes to orienting themselves in the new social environment; many children have to help their parents in their contact with local authorities, such as health centres, social services, and administrators. An immigrant father can do very little or nothing at all for his family or for the employment of his children. This is in great contrast with what he could have done in his home country. The immigrants' native language attenuates: many old expressions disappear, and new words – generally bastard words and pidgin structures – appear (Leman, 1982). Furniture and household apparatus are acquired on the Belgian market and alter the form and social context of the women's domestic tasks (Cammaert, 1983). In addition, many immigrant couples were married in a social structure that differs from the Belgian structure; in the home country, men and women may spend the greater part of the day in single-sex groups of relatives and friends. Many couples from Southern Europe find that living in an apartment is an isolated situation that requires them to adapt (Cammaert, 1983; Roosens et al., 1979).

With these realities in mind, one can state that the children who grow up in an immigrant family perceive or acquire norms, values, expectation patterns, dress codes, and the like that are impossible for them to link to a broader meaningful context, because they have never experienced the world of the home country as an everyday, direct reality. A Berber living in Brussels can demand that his daughter dresses as in the country of origin, that she strictly shuns the company of unrelated men and boys, that she never visits a disco bar, and that she helps her mother with household chores after school. But the entire Belgian context demonstrates that he is 'wrong'. Immigrant parents thus fight with unequal weapons for the preservation of behavioural patterns that they consider essential because of their own internalizations and because of pressures from both the surrounding immigrant environment and the home region.

In summary, one may argue, as Leman (1979) does, that the children of an immigrant family are confronted not by a coherent culture but with cultural fragments, and that they psychologically internalize this fragmentation. A relatively coherent synthesis that grew from generalizations of experience and has been found to be viable – which is precisely what is called a culture – is not offered to the second generation. Although no cultural pattern ever offers a perfect synthesis, there is still a great difference between what many Belgian children receive from their homes in the way of coherent reference frames and what immigrant children get.

The school situation of the second generation is comparable with the family situation: there too, the immigrant children have to do their schoolwork in an emotional and semantic context alien to their parents. The home environment offers only a limited number of contact points with the cultural elements that are transmitted to the children in the school context, whereas the home experiences are virtually ignored by the school programmes. Conflicts between norms, belief content, attitudes, and role patterns are not explained, and in most cases, no assistance in working through them is offered. The vast majority of teachers have never received the necessary training to do so. The immigrant children are thus raised with diverging fragments of a world image and with diverging experiences, and they themselves must create a viable synthesis that is usable for everyday life. In many cases, the school, the peer group, and the world of mass media will win out over the parents. Gradually, the parents come to be seen and judged by their children according to the reference frames of the dominant majority. Although definitive ruptures between the children and parents are not strikingly frequent, it still remains a manifest reality that the children distance themselves culturally from their parents, objectively and subjectively. They have learned to speak the language of the autochthones, strive to obtain fashionable clothing and entertainment 'of their time', and they ask for 'modern' food, if not Belgian 'national dishes'. In general, the life-style of the parents is perceived as that of out-of-date people who know no better (Cammaert, 1983; Roosens et al., 1979). This does not mean that the parents lose the respect of their children completely, or that all affective bonds are broken. On the contrary, in many cases the mother, at least, plays a more affective role than is the case in the country of origin (Leman, 1982; Cammaert, 1983). Nor does it mean that the second generation definitively breaks with or discounts all of the cultural characteristics of the home country.

The question of relative status is clearly different for the second generation than for the first, because the members of the second generation cannot refer to a promotion in status with respect to the country of origin that most of them barely know. Their point of departure is the point of arrival of their parents, but measured with Belgian norms. Because of the aspirations of their parents and also through their own aspirations and the schooling they receive, a certain percentage of the second generation inevitably enters into competition with a number of autochthons. In this competition, the latter frequently resort to the argument that autochthons must be given priority.

For their part, the parents themselves, generally without consciously knowing or wishing it, launch their children into another cultural world by encouraging them in their striving for socio-economic improvement. There is only one way to achieve this improvement, and this route inevitably runs through extended schooling or an intensive training period in an industry. Even if Belgian schools were to incorporate special immigrant language and cultural courses into their curricula, the logic of competitive technological Western society and its attendant service sectors would impose a certain degree of uniformity on the life pattern of immigrant pupils, and this could not be reconciled with large portions of the culture from their home countries. Such pupils would only be able to maintain some traits of the symbolic-expressive sector of their culture.

However, this does not prevent people who assimilate large portions of the surrounding culture from firmly maintaining their own *ethnic identity*.

This self-affirmation by means of origin, culture traits and historical background seems to me to be a way of having oneself recognized as being socially equal by 'the others'. At the same time, this self-manifestation confers a feeling of psychological continuity and uniqueness to the group and the individual. That one is recognized in terms of one's ethnic belonging by outsiders seems to be more important than clinging to objectively verifiable cultural traditions (Barth, 1969; de Vos, 1975; Levine & Campbell, 1972; Glazer & Moynihan, 1975; Bentley & Carter, 1983; Jacobson-Widding, 1983; Roosens, 1986). In other words, it could well be that someone who wants to be recognized as a Berber or as a Muslim is very similar to me culturally, but that he would also take great offence if I were to misjudge his specific ethnic identity on the grounds of this cultural similarity. More generally, one may state that we are evolving toward a world that is becoming ever more uniform on the instrumental level, but that, at the same time, is becoming more keenly aware of symbolic expression in areas of life not dominated by the operational sector.

So far, I have been trying to outline what I consider to be relevant dimensions of a global situation that might affect the ways immigrant children learn and achieve at school. How and to what extent these factors interfere with school achievement remains an open question. I am firmly convinced that the only way to discover how things really work is to plan and implement basic empirical research, covering a number of successive years. In section 5 of this chapter I propose a set of interrelated research hypotheses which draw upon the interpretation of the phenomena exposed in the preceding sections.

3. School Achievements and Educational Policy

The yearly figures published by the Ministry of Education report in general terms on wide geographical areas, so that individual patterns of schools do not show up, and high concentrations of disadvantaged minority children are difficult to locate. In many cases, EEC immigrants (e.g. children from Dutch parents in Flemish schools) are not distinguished from non-EEC immigrants, and children with Belgian nationality but with a different life style and home language are counted as Belgians. Critical review articles agree about the nature of the data collection under discussion here: it is beyond doubt that these statistics confirm the existence of problem areas, but the way the data have been collected and processed do not allow any falsifiable conclusions to be drawn (Mens en Ruimte, 1985; Heyerick, 1985).

Fortunately, certain studies published by private institutions have more to offer. For example, a detailed picture of the statistics relative to the various Flemish Catholic secondary schools can be found in a 1987 issue of *Welkom*, published by N.V.K.T.O. (1987) in Brussels. It is apparent from these data that the children of Mediterranean minorities achieve less well than native children, and that Moroccan and Turkish youngsters are clearly lagging: they are overrepresented in the academically feeble sections, and lag behind throughout the school curriculum. 3 021 immigrant children, or 1.80 per cent out of a total of 168 167, attend secondary schools with a general educational character, possibly leading to higher education, whereas 2 280, or 2.29 per cent of a total of 99 447, are enrolled in vocational schools, and 3 729, or 6.25 per cent of a total of 56 608, are pupils in programmes for 'special education'. Generally speaking, 13.90 per cent of the immigrant children are two years behind the average standard when they enter the secondary school system, compared with only 1.70 per cent of the Belgian children. These few figures illustrate in a representative manner what can be found throughout the wealth of data presented in *Welkom*, and confirm the official, overall figures published by the Ministry of Education.

Weekly seminars on school problems of immigrant children, sponsored by the Flemish Ministry of Education, are held at the Centre for Social and Cultural Anthropology of the Catholic University Leuven (CULeuven), where experts from all over Europe air their views on the problem of minority schooling. These seminars started on February 1, 1987 and are programmed until March 1990. When reviewing presentations by researchers from the most advanced centres in Europe, I came to the conclusion that in-depth or basic research about the insertion of immigrant children in the schools of the host countries and about the effects of the measures taken to facilitate their 'integration' is scarce. Ideological discussions and impressionistic conclusions predominate.

Over the months, the participants in this postgraduate seminar have discovered that, with one exception, no single political entity in Belgium has ever put forward any consistent view, let alone promulgated any adequate directive, in the field of minority schooling. However, a few arbitrary measures have been taken. A first Royal Decree, in 1975, allowed for the organization, under certain conditions, of special courses on the local language, for primary school children of foreign origin. In 1978, the Islamic religion was accepted as a subject in the school curriculum. And in 1980 a number of transition classes between primary and secondary school were given government grants. The implementation of the last-mentioned measure, which theoretically allows for some genuine experiments in intercultural education, was almost exclusively put in the hands of young, inexperienced teachers, functioning in the framework of a special employment programme (Verlot, 1988).

Although Belgium has backed the various EEC directives concerning multicultural education in the schools, the only realization of this programme boils down to a limited number of bicultural or intercultural 'experiments'. The best known are the EEC experiments in Limburg, started in the mid-1970s, which have led to the spread of intercultural education in more than 40 schools, starting in 1982, and an EEC experiment at the secondary school level, initiated in 1983. Another well-known experiment is the Foyer programme, in Brussels, which I will discuss briefly later.

The financial means to implement other sensible programmes are visibly lacking. We are far removed from a school system in which intercultural topics would be part of teacher training. And since no stimulus is offered to do so, only a small proportion of the hundreds of students at teachers' training colleges attend courses on multicultural education if these are set up at university.

However, the participants in the Leuven seminar have reached a certain consensus on a number of topics. Everybody agrees that all the children of the nation – both autochthons and allochthons – should be educated to live in a pluri-ethnic and multicultural society. Consequently, all future teachers must be given appropriate academic training in the field of interethnic and intercultural issues, and massive complementary training should be offered to those already in the profession. Opinions differ on the strategies to be followed: some participants stress the importance of changing people's attitudes, whereas others favour insight and knowledge. These differences of opinion among educationalists may well be a worldwide phenomenon. Nevertheless, all factions agree that professional research is lacking and that measures should be taken very urgently, in order to avoid adventuresome experiments as well as damaging 'innovations'.

There is bibliographical evidence that hundreds of initiatives have been taken in schools, all over Belgium, in order to remedy retardation, underachievement and other problems with minority pupils. Most of these interventions have never been backed by any school authority. Only a limited number of initiatives are subsidized by a government department or departments. With a few exceptions, the effect of these operations has rarely been evaluated.

These few exceptions, where scientific standards and critical theory are used in evaluating the experiments, clearly show that studies of this kind are illuminating and useful, both from a scientific *and* a practical level. Repeated evaluations by professional people, for example, have demonstrated that in the Foyer experiment in Brussels (where three languages are combined, following a certain pattern) immigrant school children are successful in all three languages, and, furthermore, social interaction between autochthonous and allochthonous children seems to be very satisfactory; allochthons do not lag behind in mathematics (Danesi, 1987). Besides, a comparison between this Brussels case and what has been practised in bilingual Canada in the last fifteen years not only confirms scientific findings about human learning in general, but also provides a practical model, which could be used all over Europe (Danesi, 1987).

Generally speaking, however, it is striking that, until now, almost all research efforts have been 'practice-oriented' in the naive sense of the term. It follows that most results are poor and disappointing: implicit and explicit values and norms of all possible types get mixed up with basic research questions. Moreover, the small amount of research money is scattered over a number of tiny projects which are extremely limited in time and personnel, thus precluding sound and fruitful research.

One of the most significant initiatives taken by a Belgian cabinet minister in recent years, is, as far as I can see, the launching of a research programme about 'success and failure' related to school experience in the lives of young minority people. This research programme was started on March 1, 1988 at the Centre for Social and Cultural Anthropology of the KULeuven. In the near future, another project will probably be started, on the conditioning of young preschool children in their home environment. Since I feel that the set-up and orientation of these projects might contribute to the elaboration of a European programme, I will sketch these research designs very briefly in section 5 below.

4. SUGGESTIONS FOR THE RESEARCH POLICY

It seems to me appropriate that two kinds of research be promoted: survey research and basic research. Both are essential.

4.1 Survey research

Survey research should be able to provide a clear picture of the situation in several areas:

1. Precise data on the distribution of the children and young people in all branches of education in function of ethnic origin.
2. In this kind of research, information can be gathered simultaneously about all kinds of facts that are considered of importance for the school situation of the child. Data on the family of the children and young people can be mapped. At the same time, a series of concrete questions can be asked about the linguistic aspects of the children and their environment: What language is spoken at home between the parents, between the parents and the children, among the children, among the children and their friends, etc.?

For this kind of research, which is done under the auspices and with the moral support of the authorities, the researchers must go to the respondents. Their visits to the various educational institutions would also permit them to compile data on the schools themselves.

Such data, which can be made available to the public by a documentation centre like WEDEM (KULeuven) and its collaborating institutions, would provide a solid foundation for all other kinds of research, and also for policy making.

It seems obvious that such research would best be set up as an integrated project. In this way, considerable savings could be made on operating costs. Several research centres could work together.

4.2 Basic research

The survey research can be combined with research that examines the course of the entire schooling process in depth.

We know, for example, virtually nothing about the phase that precedes the schooling of the child. An in-depth comparative study on socialization and raising in the family context would be valuable for many professional fields. One would discern how the parents, and particularly the mother, orient their young children; what value orientations function with the parents themselves; how they experience their own position and that of their children in the Belgian context; how they try to improve this position or why they resign themselves to it. Such a study would offer an insight into cultural transference from generation to generation and the influence of the preschool environment on the school behaviour of young children. At the same time, the process of becoming bilingual or multilingual could be observed in its initial phase. It is also important to learn if parents have dreams or expectations about the future of their children and if they adopt specific concrete strategies in order to guide their children to better socio-economic positions in society. I will outline a research project on that topic in section 5 below.

Another field that urgently needs research is the choice made in school regarding the study specialization and course package. Here, too, one could best consider an in-depth comparative study whereby the entire choice process is mapped, with all the possible factors that play a role in it. This research would illuminate a critical phase that lies in the middle of the secondary-school career. As noted in the following section, the research conducted by CIMO (*Centrum voor Interculturalisme- en Migratie-Onderzoek*, KULeuven) covers the final phase of the school process and the transition from school to the job market.

In addition to illuminating important steps in the course of the schooling process, it would be very useful to undertake comparative research on the efficiency of the various experimental programmes. For example, the *Elkaar Ontmoetend Onderwijs* (literally: "meeting-each-other education") could be compared with bicultural education as it is being promoted in Brussels by Foyer, and both forms could be compared with the local, Belgian system.

It would also be useful to compare various types of school in terms of their efficiency. An extensive study conducted in England (see the chapter by Sammons in this volume) shows that the quality of the school can make all the difference and that the quality of the school benefits all categories of the school population, irrespective of their ethnic origin. Such a study would naturally involve a thorough examination of the attitudes, the motivation, and the commitment of the teachers and their ability to work together. It would also show what explicit and implicit picture the teachers form of their allochthonous pupils.

5. THE OUTLINE OF TWO RESEARCH PROJECTS

5.1 Success and failure in the school experience of minority pupils [2]
Reviews of the literature (Camilleri, 1985; Cottaar & Willems, 1985) indicate that there is a lack of reliable analyses of the processes that take place among children in primary and secondary school and during the post-school period or the period of further education. The literature on the United States also has an obvious lacuna on this point (van den Berg-Eldering et al., 1983; Camilleri, 1985; Ogbu & Matute-Bianchi, 1986; Ogbu, 1988). Logical conclusions and inferences are drawn without their being supported by a sound, empirical substructure.

To begin with, the existing literature has little to say on the concrete motivation of the children and adolescents. Neither is much known about the motivation and self-perception of school-leavers (Verkuyten, 1988). Almost all studies assume implicitly – and some do so explicitly – that success and failure must be seen in terms of the majority group. This position, of course, can be held if research is conducted for governmental agencies that specify this success or failure self-evidently in terms of their own culture, and for policy makers this is perhaps the only solution. But that does not keep this approach from neglecting a very important part of the mechanism. For it is precisely in this motivation, in the value orientation, in the interpretation of cultures and the world that surrounds them, that these adolescents can differ greatly from the autochthonous adolescents without their being able to manifest it directly or to formulate it verbally. Research on Japanese and Korean groups (Wagatsuma & de Vos, 1984; Lee & de Vos, 1981) shows that it is indeed possible to obtain more profound insights by means of participant observation and by culturo-anthropological use of projective techniques (de Vos & Rommanucci-Ross, 1975).

After a thorough study of what values the subjects themselves apply in their categories of 'success' and 'failure', it will be possible to look for the socio-cultural elements and then, in collaboration with psychologists, for the psychological elements that specify in terms of the socio-cultural context this success and failure as seen by the subjects themselves, and also as seen by the surrounding majority. This socio-cultural context implies the family of the subjects, their peer group, the school, and the more diffuse general environment with which these adolescents are concerned.

When studying the successes and failures, one can work with five, already existing hypotheses. However, I believe that these hypotheses contain a considerable number of stereotypes, since fundamental research in this area is very exceptional.

The first hypothesis: The language and cultural differences between the home environment of certain categories of immigrant children and what is taught at school are so great that one may speak of a true educational subordination for the majority of the children, a subordination that they will never overcome in their lives. Cultural discontinuity is the most important factor (Roosens, 1979; van den Berg-Eldering et al., 1983).

The second hypothesis: What is observed with children of 'guest workers' is not at all specific for children from immigrant environments but is primarily related to the socio-economic position these children and their parents occupy in the wider social system, precisely as in the case of children of the autochthonous disadvantaged (Boulot & Boyson-Fradel, 1984).

The third hypothesis: The failure of immigrant children of some groups is a function of the quasi-caste status of their groups. Their situation is different from that of the autochthonous disadvantaged, in the sense that it involves decisive factors that the latter are not affected by. This position is supported by exceptional success of some immigrant groups, like the Sikhs, the Japanese, the South Koreans, and the Chinese in the United States, and the spectacular failure of others, like the Mexicans and the Black Americans in California (Ogbu & Matute-Bianchi,1986). Migration, therefore, need not per se lead to failure. Many children of certain immigrant groups succeed better than the Anglos in the United States. This raises the question of what makes them do so well. These groups also have more cultural differences to overcome than some other populations that fail, such as adolescents of Mexican origin. Those who succeed also have minority status, numerical and social, but seem to be able to handle it well and also to fit into the dual context of school and family without difficulty. They are aware that discrimination is practised, but this does not seem to affect either their performance or their self-image in a tangible way. And this takes place while other groups seem to be unable to accomplish anything positive under the dead weight of their quasi-caste position. The decisive factor would thus be that one has 'surrendered' and has internalized the failure because a quasi-caste position has socially and psychologically sealed off all exits.

The fourth hypothesis: In success and failure according to the norms of the majority, the parents' disposition is decisive. Parents who firmly decided to succeed in the host country and plan and provide for their children a definitive residence and career in that country, will act in such a way that their children succeed much better than those of families that see the migration as a temporary phase and that continue to cling to the relations that stayed behind and to their region of origin. A family group of the former type will more easily overcome all the hindrances of the migration, including the linguistic and cultural difficulties (Zeroulou, 1985).

The fifth hypothesis: It is very improbable that inborn characteristics play such a great role that they explain the spectacular successes or failures of certain minorities, since comparable populations from the same ethnic group, the same region, and the same socio-economic status succeed in one situation and fail in another. As far as I can see, it is not feasible to test this hypothesis directly, but it may be interesting to follow the theme in the literature and note relevant phenomena that emerge in the research process (Ogbu & Matute-Bianchi, 1986).

I am inclined to suggest that the first, third, and fourth hypotheses be combined as the point of departure without, however, deprecating the second. I would develop this combination as follows.

First, one could say, as noted above, that success and failure must be considered not only according to the criteria and manner of judgment of the surrounding Northwest European majority, but also according to the norms of the immigrants themselves. This distinction is generally made, at least implicitly, for the first generation: it is stressed that many immigrants make comparisons with their former situation in the country of origin and are thereby motivated and feel themselves rewarded. Such a distinction between success in terms of the majority and the minority is generally also made for the second generation, whose members no longer make comparisons with the home region of their parents but with their peer group. References are seldom made to the way in which the parents define success and failure for their children. In particular, the way in which they operationalize this success and failure and draw conclusions from it in relation to the education and the preparation of their children could well have a decisive influence. Personally, I am inclined to assign this factor particular importance, not only as regards the migration events worldwide but also in the area of the economic survival and the economic development of the Third World.

In the initial hypothesis that I sketch here, two main components are involved in the determination of what parents do to motivate and to prepare for the success of their children: a cultural factor that transcends the parents and is related to the system from which the parents themselves came, and an individual factor, the way in which the parents react as individuals to this cultural factor (Roosens, 1988).

In order to have a meaningfully differentiated study that faithfully reflects the internal diversity of the migration, three ethnic or national categories are being studied: young people (boys and girls) of Spanish, Turkish and Moroccan origin. This allows for the elaboration of the following contrasts: Islamic versus non-Islamic, migration from an EEC country versus migration from a non-EEC country, school versus post-school situations and transition between them, failure versus success, boys versus girls.

5.2 Early socialization and education in a multicultural setting [3]

Another theme that I believe is prominent in the investigation of education as a cultural event in an interethnic context and that is very appropriate for anthropological research is the transfer of the general orientation, motivation, and value orientation of the allochthonous parents to their young children when they begin their school careers. In other words, the answer is sought for the question of what is the socio-cultural input of the parents in the school system before the school period and in the first years of schooling (Spindler, 1982, 1987; Trueba & Delgado-Gaitan, 1988; see also the chapter by Eldering in this volume). Such research can also shed light on the marginality or the emancipation process of the parents and determine whether and in what way marginality or emancipation is transmitted by the parents to their children. What is called a quasi-caste system is generated precisely by continuous marginality of several generations of specific ethnic groups (Wagatsuma & de Vos, 1984; Ogbu & Matute-Bianchi, 1986).

Insofar as estimations can be made in this regard, it seems that people of Moroccan origin run the most risk of marginality in the short and medium term. Hence, I have proposed studying the situation of Moroccan subjects. Moreover, previous research has provided much information on this population since 1974. The younger parents of Moroccan origin can be traced through the kindergartens. This can be done in Antwerp or in Brussels or in both zones, depending on what the preliminary research reveals. From this population, about twenty families will be selected, in which the father has by his own efforts, acquired a place in the local socio-economic environment that can be considered enviable in terms of his own environment. In addition, twenty men will be selected who very obviously can be considered failures and marginal.

A male researcher will follow these forty men for a period of three years (Agar, 1986). A female researcher will undertake parallel research with their wives.

Both researchers will pay special attention to the following themes:

1. How these categories of men and women conceive their own 'success' or 'failure' and/or that of their spouse, depending on their situations and as a function of the course of their careers.
2. How the whole of their situation interferes with the raising of the children in the household: general child raising patterns, proposed role patterns, the achievement motivation that is or is not stimulated in the child, values and behaviour models that one tries consciously to inculcate or that are transmitted unconsciously.
3. During the research period, at least one child per family will be observed in school. In the course of the research, it must be determined which children will be observed, and the heuristic value of the respective cases must be used as the criterion.

Whereas the project on 'success and failure' is studying the transition from the school or the part-time training programme to the adult world, the research proposed here will examine the transition from the family to the school.

The transmission of values and other cultural dimensions from one generation to the other is one of the basic problems in social and cultural anthropology; what happens with these processes and contents in acculturation situations is another basic problem. The transmission of the self-image from one generation to another is another basic dimension.

For studying all of these themes, use can be made of an adapted form of the observation technique that is explained in the *Six Culture Project* of Harvard (Whiting & Whiting, 1977). A large number of observations and parts of conversations, covering a maximum of 30 minutes of observation, are collected in three years. Tape recordings can be made, so that the researcher has the exact words and, with this as the basis, can reconstruct the visual and the spatial aspects of the situation. The data thus obtained are not only valuable for quali-- tative analyses but can also be subjected to all kinds of quantitative processing. This research technique has been successfully applied in this form by Cuvelier in the context of the *Geel Project* (see Roosens, 1979).

With this, the anthropological use of the *Thematic Apperception Test* (method developed by G. de Vos, see de Vos & Rommanucci-Ross, 1975) and the Q-sort of Block (1978) can be combined.

Another important factor that deserves urgent attention in this context is the discrimination inflicted by the surrounding environment and particularly by the relevant figures of the majority, including the imposition of negative stereotypes, and the accompanying stigmatization (de Jong, 1987). Generally, immigrants cannot acquire a socioeconomic position in Belgian society autonomously from, and independently of, the influences of majority groups. Majority groups assign them their place. Not rarely, this assignation is downward: the attempt is made, directly or indirectly, to keep immigrants in lower positions. In all of this, indirect discrimination, stereotyping, and stigmatization play important roles (Penninx, 1988). This downward pressure and the associated social climate can have their effect in many circles that are relevant for the immigrants and can even, over the years, create negative self-images in many members of the minorities (Wagatsuma & de Vos, 1984, Verkuyten, 1988). An autochthonous teacher, for example, whose pupils are predominantly immigrant children whom he knows are branded by the surrounding society as backward and uncivilized, can become thoroughly discouraged when he sees, after years of effort, that the allochthonous children do, indeed, get 'bad results' or even manifest a revulsion for the school. And then if the autochthonous children are pulled out of the school *en masse* because 'too many foreigners' have 'lowered' the level of the school, that teacher may well adopt a defeatist attitude that will influence the pupils negatively.

For this reason, it is recommended that a third researcher be employed who would be assigned the complex task of studying the attitudes, negative and positive images, stereotypes, actions, and reactions among the surrounding, relevant members of the majority groups with respect to the children being studied and their families. A study of attitudes and practices of the teaching staff and of the overall school climate is of essential importance. Such a combination of perspectives, whereby the problem is studied from the point of view of both the minority and the majority, is rare. This is not surprising, for such a combination is not easy to achieve.

The results of such research can be combined with those of the project on school success and failure (see the former subsection) and interpreted within one and the same explanatory framework.

The project sketched here is intended for application to a group of young Islamic families: this has the added advantage of providing the opportunity to follow the evolution of a category of people who, researchers have the impression, are moving toward a strong Islamic identification. This presenting of oneself as a Muslim by members of the second generation seems to be a recent phenomenon (Bastenier & Dassetto, 1985; Kepel, 1987). With these developments, one can profitably relate existing and evolving theory to the 'new religions' or 'sects' that have mushroomed by the thousand in Black Africa and elsewhere (Barrett, 1967, 1982). Many of these religions fulfil a number of orientation and self-confirming functions in social categories that have sunk into marginality or threaten to do so. In the case of Islam in Northwestern Europe and more particularly in Belgium, strong identification with this religion can conceal but also reinforce the less prestigious ethnic identity. In other words, it could be that a person prefers membership in a world religion to membership in an ethnic minority as a social manifestation. However, ethnic belonging can also be interwoven with religious belonging and in this way be absolutized.

Of course, such developments can have major repercussions on the attitudes of the parents toward the Belgian school to which they entrust their child. It is also not to be ruled out that voices will be raised among Islamic parents for the construction of an Islamic school system, which is theoretically possible, particularly since Belgium recognized Islam as a religion in 1974. The repercussions of the Islamic standpoint of the parents on the children seems to be relevant in terms of the formation of the social self-image of the child and of the criteria with which the child evaluates his or her own achievements and situation.

In addition to yielding scientific insight and correcting current generalizations, the research presented here will allow the findings to be processed into programmes for the training and additional schooling of teachers at all levels of education. Using the material in this way

could have a considerable impact on the insights and attitudes of
those responsible for formally educating children and young people.
It is obvious that insight into the fundamental areas discussed here is
essential for policy. To date, there has been virtually no policy.

Without hoping for a spectacular reversal of current attitudes, one
may argue that the compilation and dissemination of reliable information and insights can contribute to the elimination of marginality
and promote the emancipation of the less advantaged.

NOTES

1 Some passages of this contribution were previously published in E. Roosens
(1981) and E. Roosens (1986b).

2 This research project was started on April 1, 1988, by CIMO, Catholic University of Leuven.

3 This research project will be started in the foreseeable future by CIMO, Catholic University of Leuven.

REFERENCES

AGAR, M. (1986). *Speaking of ethnography*. Beverly Hills: Sage Publications.
BARRETT, D. (1967). *Schism and renewal in Africa*. London: Oxford University Press.
BARRETT, D. (Ed.) (1982). *World Christian encyclopedia*. London: Oxford University Press.
BARTH, F. (1969). *Ethnic groups and boundaries: the social organisation of culture difference*. Boston: Little, Brown.
BASTENIER, A. & DASSETTO, F. (1985). Organisations musulmanes de Belgique et in-
sertion sociale des populations immigrées. *Revue Européenne des Migrations In-
ternationales*, 1(1), 9-21.
BERG-ELDERING, L. VAN DEN, F. DE RIJCKE & L. ZUCK (Eds.) (1983). *Multicultural
education: A challenge for teachers*. Dordrecht: Foris Publications.
BLOCK, J. (1978). *The Q-sort method in personality assessment and psychiatric research*.
Palo Alto: Consulting Psychologists Press.
BOULOT, S. & BOYSON-FRADEL, S.(1984). L'échec scolaire des enfants de travailleurs
immigrés: un problème mal posé. *Les Temps modernes*, 40 (542-544), 1092-1914.
CAMILLERI, C. (1985). *Anthropologie culturelle et éducation*. Paris: Unesco, 73-99.
CAMMAERT, M.-F. (1983). *Grens en transgressie in de wereld van de Berbervrouw.
Nador (N.-O. Marokko)-Brussel*. Ph.D. dissertation. Leuven: Centre for Social
and Cultural Anthropology, KULeuven.
CAMMAERT, M.-F. (1985). *Migranten en thuisblijvers: een confrontatie*. Assen/Leuven:
Van Gorcum.
CARTER BENTLEY, G. (Ed.) (1983). Theoretical perspectives on ethnicity and natio-
nality, Part I. *Sage Race Relations Abstracts*, 8(2),1-53.

COTTAAR, A. & WILLEMS W. (1985). *Overzicht onderzoek minderheden*. The Hague: Adviescommissie Onderzoek Minderheden.

DANESI, M. (1987). Enkele twee- en drietalige onderwijsprogramma's bij immigrantenkinderen in Canada en België met het oog op de gewenste plaats van de 'moedertaal' in het onderwijs. In J. Leman (Ed.), *Taal- en cultuurgevoelig onderwijs voor migrantenkinderen*. Brussels: Cultuur en Migratie, 27-50.

DUMON W. & MICHIELS, L. (1987). *OCDE, Système d'observation permanente des migrations, Belgique, Sopemi 1987/2*. Leuven: Sociologisch Onderzoeksinstituut, Departement Sociologie.

ELDERING, L. (1988). *Ethnic minority children in Dutch schools: Underachievement and its explanations*. Paper presented at the International Workshop on 'Education and the cultural development of ethnic minority children'. Kerkrade, Netherlands, 12-14 September.

GLAZER, N. & MOYNIHAN, D. (Eds.) (1975). *Ethnicity: Theory and experience*. Cambridge: Harvard University Press.

HEYERICK, L. (1985). Problemen van migrantenkinderen en hun leerkrachten in het Vlaams basisonderwijs. In A. Martens & F. Moulaert (Eds.), *Buitenlandse minderheden in Vlaanderen-België*. Kapellen: Uitgeverij De Nederlandsche Boekhandel, 103-113.

JACOBSON-WIDDING, A. (Ed.) (1983). *Identity: personal and socio-cultural*. Stockholm: Almqvist and Wiksell International.

JONG, W. DE (1986). *Inter-etnische verhoudingen in een oude stadswijk. Factoren van invloed op etnische tolerantie*. Delft: Eburon.

KEPEL, G. (1987). *Les banlieues de l'Islam: naissance d'une religion en France*. Paris: Editions du Seuil.

LEE, CH. & VOS, G. DE (1981). *Koreans in Japan. Ethnic conflict and accommodation*. Berkeley: University of California Press.

LEMAN, J. (1979). La deuxième génération des travailleurs migrants. Fragmentés en non déstructurés. *Recherches Sociologiques*, 10(2), 247-270.

LEMAN, J. (1982). *Van Caltanissetta naar Brussel en Genk. Een antropologische studie in de streek van herkomst en in het gastland bij Siciliaanse migranten*. Leuven: Acco.

LEMAN, J. (1984). *Integratie anders bekeken*. Brussel: Cultuur en Migratie.

LEVINE, R. & CAMPBELL, D. (1972). *Ethnocentrism: theories of conflict, ethnic attitude and group behavior*. New York: John Wiley and Sons.

'MENS EN RUIMTE' (1985). *Uitbouw van een permanent informatiesysteem van sociale indicatoren voor het meten van de integratie van gastarbeiders in de Vlaamse Gemeenschap*. Brussels: Mens en Ruimte v.z.w.

OGBU, J. & MATUTE-BIANCHI, M.E. (1986). Understanding sociocultural factors: Knowledge, identity and school adjustment. In *Beyond language: Social and cultural factors in schooling language minority students*. Los Angeles: Evaluation, Dissemination and Assessment Center, 73-142.

OGBU, J. (1988). Unpublished research proposal.

PENNINX, R. (1988). *Minderheidsvorming en emancipatie*. Alphen aan den Rijn: Samsom.

REX, J. & TOMLINSON, S. (1979). *Colonial immigrants in a British city: a class analysis*. London: Routledge and Kegan Paul.

ROOSENS, E. (1979). *Mental patients in town life: Geel – Europe's first therapeutic community*. Beverly Hills/London: Sage Publications.

ROOSENS, E. (1981). The multicultural nature of contemporary Belgian society: the immigrant community. In A. Lijphart (Ed.), *Conflict and coexistence in Belgium*. Berkeley: University of California, Institute of International Studies, 61-92.

ROOSENS, E. (1986a). *Micronationalisme*. Leuven/Amersfoort: Acco.

ROOSENS, E. (1986b). Immigrants in Belgium: The sociocultural structure. *Kroeber Anthropological Society Papers (University of California, Berkeley), 65-66*, 15-25.

ROOSENS, E. (1988). Migration and caste formation in Europe: the Belgian case. *Ethnic and Racial Studies, 11*(2), 207-217.

SAMMONS, P. (1988). *School effectiveness and school organisation: Some findings from a recent study of junior education in the United Kingdom*. Paper presented at the International Workshop on 'Education and the cultural development of ethnic minority children.' Kerkrade, Netherlands, 12-14 September.

SCHWARTZ, T. (1976). The Cargo cult: A Melanesian type-response to change. In G. De Vos (Ed.), *Responses to change: Society, culture and personality*. New York: Van Nostrand, 157-206.

SPINDLER, G. (Ed.) (1982). *Doing the ethnography of schooling: educational anthropology in action*. New York: Holt, Rinehart and Winston.

SPINDLER, G. (1987). *Education and cultural process: towards an anthropology of education, 2nd edn*. Prospect Heights: Waveland Press.

TRUEBA, H. & DELGADO-GAITAN, C. (Eds.) (1988). *School and society: learning content through culture*. New York: Praeger.

VERKUYTEN, M. (1988). *Zelfbeleving en identiteit van jongeren uit etnische minderheden*. Arnhem: Gouda Quint BV.

VERLOT, M. (1988). *Research note*. KULeuven.

VOS, G. DE & ROMMANUCCI-ROSS L. (Eds.) (1975). *Ethnic identity: Cultural continuities and change*. Palo Alto: Mayfield.

WAGATSUMA, H. & VOS, G. DE (1984). *Heritage of endurance. Family pattern and delinquency formation in urban Japan*. Berkeley: University of California Press.

'WELKOM', 1986-1987, 4(14). Brussels: N.V.K.T.O.

Whiting, B. & Whiting, J. (1977). *Children of six cultures*. Cambridge, Mass.: Harvard University Press.

ZEROULOU, Z. (1985). Mobilisation familiale et réussite scolaire. *Revue Européenne des Migrations Internationales, 1*(2), 107-117.

6

Lotty Eldering
Leiden University

Ethnic Minority Children in Dutch Schools

Underachievement and its Explanations

1. INTRODUCTION

The present social position of ethnic minorities in the Netherlands and the educational opportunities of their children are strongly influenced by the history and character of the immigration as well as by the way the immigrants have been received in the Netherlands. In the first part of this chapter I will therefore outline the history of immigration (section 2), the numbers of immigrants and their distribution over the country (section 3), and the general and educational policy regarding immigrants (sections 4 and 5). In the second part the situation of ethnic/cultural minority children in the educational system will be depicted (section 6), and the reasons for educational underachievement will be explored (section 7). The chapter will be concluded with a few words about research in the Netherlands and with a number of recommendations for further research (section 8).

2. THE HISTORY OF MIGRATION TO THE NETHERLANDS

The immigrants who have entered the Netherlands since World War II can be divided into two broad categories:
– immigrants from the colonies: the Dutch East-Indies (including the

Moluccan Islands), Surinam and the Dutch Antilles;
– foreign workers and their families from Mediterranean countries
  (Greece, Italy, Yugoslavia, Portugal, Spain, Turkey, Morocco, Tunisia) and the Cape Verde Islands.

They came in different periods and for various reasons. Those from
colonies emigrated mainly for political reasons, those from Mediterranean countries did so mainly for economic reasons. Most immigrants of the first category were Dutch citizens who were already
oriented towards Dutch society, whereas the second category consis-
ted predominantly of migrant workers, who came here as foreigners
in the broadest sense of the word.

2.1 Immigration from colonies

Dutch East-Indies
In the years before and after the Independence of Indonesia in 1949,
about 150 000 persons of Dutch-Indonesian origin emigrated to the
Netherlands. Most of them were absorbed into Dutch society within
two decades. The explanation for this quick assimilation lies partly
in the attitude and orientation of the immigrants, and must partly be
attributed to the economic growth and expanding tertiary sector in
the Netherlands. The descendants of these immigrants are not considered to be a minority group and they are not a target group in the
current Dutch policy for ethnic minorities (see table 1).

Moluccan Islands
In contrast, the Moluccans who arrived in the same period as the immigrants from the Dutch East-Indies are very much an underprivileged minority group. They came to the Netherlands involuntarily,
as a consequence of a court decision. At the time they numbered
about 12 000 (ex-servicemen and their families). Since their stay here
was meant to be only temporary, they were housed together in former camps and were not granted access to the labour market for the
first few years. Governmental policy with regard to the Moluccans
has led to a long-lasting segregation and isolation, and to the Moluccan community having a deep distrust of the Dutch government.
Not until the 1970s did the Moluccans start to participate in Dutch
society more on an individual basis. Even today more than half of
them continue to live poorly housed in segregated neighbourhoods
in about 60 communities. From the outset their children have attended schools with a Dutch curriculum and Dutch as the language of

instruction. Not until 1985 were special provisions made for Moluccan children to attend lessons in the Moluccan-Malayan language
(see scheme p. 117)

Surinam and the Dutch Antilles
The history of migration from Surinam to the Netherlands is closely
related to the tradition of the Surinamese elite during the colonial
period. Until the beginning of the 1970s, the Surinamese migrated to
the Netherlands in pursuit of higher education. In ethnic terms they
were predominantly Creole-Surinamese (descendants of African
slaves). From the mid-1960s onwards the economic circumstances
and prospects in Surinam worsened. In addition to push-factors in
Surinam, there were also a number of pull-factors in Dutch society,
which stimulated the emigration: in addition to the already mentioned educational opportunities for higher education these were a
flourishing labour market and a well developed system of social
security. One factor that facilitated the emigration was the absence of
formal obstacles. Under the Charter for the Kingdom of the Netherlands of 1954 Surinamese and Antilleans received *de jure* Dutch citi-
zenship. In the years before and after the independence of Surinam
in 1975 the number of emigrants grew enormously, while at the same
time their average educational level fell considerably. A large part of
those who emigrated in those years belonged to the Hindustani,
Javanese and other ethnic groups of Surinam. They had decided to
move to the Netherlands for fear of Creole domination after independence. By 1975 more than 30 per cent of the whole population of
Surinam was residing in the Netherlands.
The process of chain-migration – the Surinamese already in the
Netherlands providing accommodation and employment for new-
comers – has resulted in concentrations of Creole-Surinamese in Amsterdam and in Rotterdam and of Hindustani-Surinamese in The
Hague.
The emigration from the Dutch Antilles has been markedly different
from that of Surinam. There are far fewer Antilleans than there are
Surinamese immigrants, and secondly the Antilleans migrated mainly for economic reasons.
Within the Surinamese and Antillean population in the Netherlands
there are substantial differences with regard to ethnicity, cultural and
religious backgrounds, proficiency in the Dutch language and educational levels. At the end of the 1970s the numbers of men and
women were more or less equal.

2.2 *Immigration from Mediterranean countries*

The growth of the economy and tertiary sector in the 1950s caused serious sectoral labour shortages in the Netherlands. The first workers of foreign nationality, who were recruited for the mining industry in the south of the Netherlands came from Italy. The demand for manpower grew enormously over the following fifteen years and could not be met by Dutch supply. The Dutch government therefore provided an official framework for the recruitment of foreign workers in the 1960s: during that decade labour-recruitment agreements were concluded with Mediterranean countries. In 1960 the Italians were the only significant group, numbering about 3 000. From 1961 to 1968 Spanish workers were mainly recruited, followed by Turks and Moroccans from 1964 onwards.

The composition of the Mediterranean population in the Netherlands has altered drastically over the past fifteen years. In 1975 about half of the migrants of Mediterranean origin were Turks and Moroccans; by 1990 their percentage will have increased to about 90 per cent.

The emigration from the Mediterranean countries differs from the migrations from Surinam and the Antilles in several respects. The Mediterranean foreign workers came here primarily for economic reasons and they were foreigners in the broadest sense of the word: they had another nationality, a low degree of proficiency in Dutch and Dutch culture was strange to them. The migration from Mediterranean countries took place in several phases. First, the workers (predominantly male) arrived, leaving their families behind in their country of origin. After a couple of years, however, wives and children followed (in the case of the Turks, after five years on average; the Moroccans after as many as nine years). On January 1st 1983 only 70 married foreign females were resident in the Netherlands for every 100 married foreign males. For the Turks these figures were 79:100 and for the Moroccans 61:100 on that date (CBS statistics). Even now this family reunion process, which began in the 1970s is not yet completed.

A relatively large number of Turks and Moroccans living in the Netherlands with their families have one or more children residing in the country of origin. These children were left behind (in the case of the Moroccans) or returned to their country of origin (in the case of the Turks). These families remain partly oriented towards their country of origin.

The migration from the respective Mediterranean countries develop-

ed according to its own dynamics. A recent analysis of the emigration from Morocco to the Netherlands shows that before 1975 the
migrating families were mainly young and small (with three children at the most), chiefly from urban areas on the Atlantic Coast and
in Central Morocco, whereas after that year, the families that decided
to emigrate were mainly older and larger and were from rural areas
in the North and the East of Morocco. More than 50 per cent of the
Moroccan families now residing in the Netherlands originate from
Northern and Eastern Morocco. Most of them have rural backgrounds and speak a Riffian-Berber language (Haffmans & de Mas,
1985). This explains why from 1975 to 1983 Dutch schools were confronted with large numbers of illiterate Moroccan youngsters who
were over 10 years old. Unfortunately, we do not have such detailed
information about the emigration from Turkey, or from other Mediterranean countries.

3. NUMBERS AND DISTRIBUTION OF IMMIGRANTS

3.1 In general
In table I the relevant immigrant categories and target groups of the
Dutch minority policy are presented according to the criteria mostly
used: country of nationality and country of origin. Since most residents of Surinamese and Antillean origin have Dutch nationality,
other criteria for identification have to be used, such as country of
birth or country of birth of parents (usually the mother). Table 1
shows that numerically speaking, Turks, Moroccans, Surinamese,
Antilleans and Moluccans are the most important immigrant groups
with an officially recognized minority status. On January 1st 1987
they numbered about 570 000 or five per cent of the population in
the Netherlands.
Equally important are the figures about their distribution and concentration. According to recently held *Quality of Life Surveys* among
Moroccans and Turks, Surinamese and Antilleans and among Dutch,
more than 50 per cent of the ethnic groups live in cities of more than
100 000 inhabitants, compared with only 26 per cent of the native
Dutch (table 2). In the big cities, including Amsterdam, Rotterdam
and The Hague 10-20 per cent of the population are immigrants and
in the year 2000, half of the school pupils will be children of immigrants (Memorandum, 1988).

Table 1: Immigrants and ethnic minorities in the Netherlands (Jan. 1st 1987)

criterion mostly used for identification	categories	numbers in thousands	percentage of the total of aliens	target group minority policy
country of	Netherlands	14047.1		ref.group
nationality	Greece	3.8	0.7	yes
	Italy	17.0	3.0	yes
	Yugoslavia	11.6	2.0	yes
	Portugal	7.5	1.3	yes
	Spain	18.2	3.2	yes
	Turkey	160.6	28.3	yes
	other Europe	126.0	22.2	no
	China	8.3	1.5	no
	Cape Verde Is	2.0	0.4	yes
	Morocco	122.7	21.6	yes
	Tunisia	2.6	0.4	yes
	Vietnam	6.5	1.1	no
	other non-Europe	76.3	13.4	no
	without nat.	4.9	0.9	
	TOTAL	14615.1		poss.ref. group
	among whom			
	EC (excl.Neth.)	159.7		no
	Mediterr. c.	344.1		yes
	North Mediterranean c.[1]	58.1		yes
country of birth (also of mother)	Dutch Antilles	55.2		yes
	Surinam	195.0		yes
other criteria	Moluccans	33.3		yes
	refugees	26.5		yes
	caravan-dwellers	30.0		yes
	gypsies	3.7		yes

1. Greece, Italy, Yugoslavia, Portugal, Spain.

Source: Ankersmit, T., et al. Statistisch Vademecum 1988, CBS.

*Table 2: Degree of urbanization of Turks, Moroccans, Surinamese, Antil-
  leans and Dutch (in percentages)*

	villages in rural areas population 2 000-10 000	small towns population < 100 000	cities population > 100 000	Amsterdam Rotterdam The Hague	Total
Turks (1984)	13	34	22	31	100
Moroccans (1984)	13	30	19	38	100
Surinamese (1984)	26	13	11	50	100
Antilleans (1985)	31	25	17	27	100
Dutch (1983)	47	27	13	13	100

Source: Leefsituatie-onderzoeken. 1984, 1985, 1986, CBS.

3.2 Immigrant children in Dutch schools

There is a close connection between the way funds are allocated to
the schools by the central government or the municipalities and the
way school children are registered.

In the Netherlands, the allocation of funds is related not only to the
number of pupils, but also to the socio-economic condition of their
parents and their ethnic backgrounds. As regards immigrant children, before 1980 schools received extra funds for non-Dutch speaking children only (i.e. children of Mediterranean workers). But slowly the awareness grew that children from Surinam and the Antilles
often had a low proficiency in Dutch too. Hence, new arrangements
were made, under which schools could also receive extra funds for
Surinamese and Antillean children who had been in the Netherlands
for less than four years. Since the Educational Priority Policy became
effective in 1985, all children from ethnic-cultural minority groups
have been rated in the same way, regardless of their length of stay
and proficiency in Dutch (for an explanation of the educational policy and its target groups see section 5 and scheme 1).

As a consequence of the successive changes in educational policy, the
official statistics give different numbers and percentages of immigrant children before and after 1980 and also before and after 1985.

The numbers of pupils (majority and minority) in Dutch kindergarten and primary schools are presented in table 3.

Table 3:   Pupils in Dutch kindergarten and primary schools
(absolute numbers and percentages)

	1980[1]	1984[1]	1985/86[2]
Categories			
Total no. of pupils	1 837 383	1 574 817	1 468 720
Total no. of Cu-Mi pupils[3] (percentage)	90 437 5%	97 721 6%	122 871 8%
of whom Mediterranean countries	64 396	76 675	69 817
(Turkey)			30 794
(Morocco)			27 954
(other Mediterr. c.)[4]			11 069
Surin./Antil.	22 737	17 378	48 978[5]
Moluccans	3 304	3 668	4 076

1. *Source: Ministerie van Onderwijs en Wetenschappen, 1984.*
2. *Source: Ministerie van Onderwijs en Wetenschappen, 1987.*
3. In educational policy documents, ethnic minority pupils are called cultural minority pupils.
4. Other Mediterranean countries: Greece, Italy, Yugoslavia, Portugal, Spain, Tunisia and Cape Verde Islands.
5. This number includes a residual category of Cu-Mi pupils.

Close examination of table 3 leads to the conclusion, that whereas the absolute number of pupils in Dutch schools has been decreasing steadily since 1980, the number of pupils from ethnic minority backgrounds has increased over the same period. In a provisional estimation the following distribution is assumed: 25 per cent Turkish, 25 per cent Moroccans, 25 per cent Surinamese and Antilleans and 25 per cent other minority pupils (Ministerie van Onderwijs en Wetenschappen, 1987).
As mentioned above, about half of the Turks, Moroccans, Surinamese and Antilleans live in cities (table 2). Within these cities a further

concentration in certain districts and neighbourhoods has occurred. Minority pupils living in these neighbourhoods, however, are not distributed over the schools at the same rate. From 1980 to 1984 the number of schools with more than 50 per cent minority pupils increased by 70 per cent from 227 to 368. At the same time the number of schools without minority pupils also increased (Ministerie van Onderwijs en Wetenschappen, 1984). This process has been continuing for more than ten years; yet until recently the problems of schools with a high percentage of ethnic minority pupils – so-called *black schools* – have been largely ignored and only now have they become an important issue for public debate.

4. OFFICIAL POLICY ON IMMIGRATION AND MINORITY GROUPS

In the preceding sections the terms 'immigrants' and 'ethnic cultural minorities' have been used interchangeably. Although there is a strong connection between immigration and minority formation, not all immigrants have a minority status, and, similarly not all persons in a minority condition are immigrants or children of immigrants.

A minority group is characterized by having a *low social position* over a long period, mostly several generations. The concept of social position can be defined as the average of the positions members of a group occupy in the central institutions of a society: labour market, housing market, educational system and political-juridical system. These institutions control the distribution of scarce and highly valued resources in society. In nearly all the relevant fields of public life, immigrants initially have a low or even marginal position. Central questions are how long these groups will continue to have a low social status and whether or not a particular society considers stratification along ethnic lines undesirable.

In the Northwestern European countries the awareness has grown that most immigrants will settle permanently and that, if no effective policy measures are taken, they remain in a minority situation for many generations.

Since 1980 the Dutch government has been developing a policy for immigrants. Its main objectives are:

– improving the social position of residing immigrants (as well as restricting further immigration),
– preventing and combating prejudice and discrimination,

– furthering the emancipation of the immigrant groups by respect-
ing their cultural, religious and linguistic backgrounds (Minderhedennota, 1983: 10).

Not all immigrant groups and not only immigrants are considered as
target groups of the Dutch policy for minorities (see table 1). To date,
most attention has been given to the first aim, the improvement of
the social position. To this end, *Quality of Life Surveys* have recently
been held among Dutch (1983), Moroccans and Turks (1984) and
Surinamese and Antilleans (1985) aged 18 years and older. The interviews of the surveys concerned housing conditions, work and unemployment, educational levels, health, language spoken at home,
household composition, religion and degree of urbanization.

For the assessment of changes in the social condition of minorities a
monitoring system has been developed by the Central Bureau of Statistics. Each year a *Statistical Vademecum*, containing relevant data
and figures about the *participation in* and *accessibility* of provisions
and institutions that regulate the distribution of societal resources
will be published. In this chapter I will not go into details about the
general indicators used to monitor this participation and accessibility; instead I shall limit my treatise to participation in the educational
system. But first an overview of the Dutch educational policy for immigrant children will be given.

5. EDUCATIONAL POLICY AND PRACTICE

Three periods can broadly be distinguished in Dutch educational
policy concerning children of immigrants, each with its own underlying premises: before 1980, between 1980 and 1985, and post 1985
(see scheme 1).

5.1 *Policy before 1980*
Prior to 1980, educational policy was based on the assumption that
children of migrant workers would only stay in the Netherlands
temporarily and that they would return to their home country after a
couple of years. The educational policy regarding these children can
be characterized as a 'two-track' policy intended to integrate them in
the Dutch school system as well as to prepare them for return. They
received extra lessons not only in the Dutch language, but were also
taught in the language of their home country. These mother-tongue
lessons were given at the request of the parents for a maximum of six

Scheme 1: Dutch educational policy for ethnic/cultural minority pupils in Primary Education

Educational policy	before 1980	1980-1985	from 1985
Title	Educational policy for non-Dutch speaking children	Educational policy for cultural minorities	Educational priority policy
Target groups	Children of migrant workers from Mediterranean countries	Children of immigrants (Mediterranean, Surinamese, Antillean and Moluccan backgrounds)	Minority and majority children from working class families (living in same neigbourhoods)
Basic assumptions	- temporary stay of migrant workers and families	- permanent settlement of immigrants - special policy needed to prevent immigrants from becoming minorities - equivalence of cultures	- similarity of disadvantages between minority and majority children from working-class families (same socio-economic position) - to remove disadvantages, provisions in and out of school must be long-lasting - Dutch society is a 'multicultural society'
Educational aims	- integration in Dutch educational system - preparation for return to home country ('two-track policy')	- equality of educational opportunities in Dutch schools - acculturation (knowledge, acceptance of each other's culture)	- preventing educational arrears at an early stage - preparing children for living in a multicultural society
Special provisions Dutch-language teaching	- dependent on degree of Dutch proficiency	dependent on: - ethnic group - years of stay (<2 yrs,>2<4 yrs)	- schools are free to decide how to use staff and resources
Mother-tongue teaching	- in principle possible for at most 6 hours/ week (preparation for return)		- maximum 2.5 hours/ week during school-time (supporting the integration in Dutch educational system) - extension to kindergarten grades - extension to Moluccan children
Intercultural education	non-existent	non-compulsory	Compulsory according to the 1985 Elementary Education Act

hours a week. Their main purpose was to facilitate re-integration in the school system of the country of origin.

In the second half of the 1970s it was gradually realized that most migrant workers would not return to their home country as quickly as had been assumed and that their children would stay in the school system for much longer (cf. van den Berg-Eldering, 1978). In addition it became clear that children of Surinamese and Antillean backgrounds needed special attention too.

5.2 Policy between 1980 and 1985

The assumptions underlying educational policy altered radically after 1980. No longer was the policy based on the assumption that children of migrants would only stay in the Netherlands temporarily. On the contrary, it was assumed that the majority of migrant workers and their families from Mediterranean countries as well as the immigrants from Surinam and the Antilles would settle in the Netherlands for good. This had been one of the main conclusions of the Report *Ethnic Minorities* issued by the WRR Advisory Committee in 1979 (Ethnic Minorities, 1979). A second conclusion of this Report was that a special policy should be developed, in order to prevent the immigrants from drifting into the lowest layers of society (minority condition). A long-term policy was recommended for these groups.

In 1980 the Ministry of Education and Science launched a plan for an educational policy for children of ethnic/cultural minorities. This plan stipulated that educational practice should concentrate on two fields: *equality of educational opportunities* and *the equivalence of cultures*.

In conformity with the general policy, not only Mediterranean workers and their families, but also immigrants from Surinam, the Dutch Antilles and the Moluccan Islands were to be considered ethnic/cultural minorities (see table 1).

The first educational goal – equal opportunities – had to be achieved by putting more emphasis on Dutch language teaching and by intensifying contacts between minority parents and the school.

In order to achieve the second goal – equivalence of cultures – two types of provision were proposed:
– teaching the immigrant children their mother tongue (Moroccan, Turkish, Spanish, Italian, Yugoslav, and Greek languages and cultures),
– intercultural education.

Dutch language teaching

It goes without saying that in the Netherlands command of the Dutch language is a prerequisite for a successful school career. In the Netherlands, however, there is no tradition of teaching Dutch as a second language (note the distinction between the teaching of a language as a second language and as a foreign language). The absence of such a tradition proved to be a serious obstacle during the first ten years of the presence of the non-Dutch speaking children in the Netherlands. The number of hours for Dutch language teaching awarded to a school depended on the number of children of ethnic/cultural minorities in that school, on how long they had been in the Netherlands and on their country of origin. The underlying assumption was that children from Mediterranean countries needed more lessons in the Dutch language, particularly during the first two years of their stay, than, for instance, children from Surinam or the Dutch Antilles (for a more detailed picture, see Extra and Vallen in this volume).

Mother-tongue teaching

In the 1970s the Netherlands made arrangements with several Mediterranean recruitment countries about the teachers, teaching materials, curricula and responsibilities involved in teaching the children of immigrant workers their mother tongue and culture. The language to be taught was the official language of the country of origin, in the case of Moroccan children the standard Arabic language. Surinamese and Antillean children did not receive lessons in their mother tongue, since Dutch was the official language in their countries of origin.

Originally, mother-tongue teaching was set up to facilitate the reintegration of the children of migrant workers should they return to their home country. As a result, the contents, methods and curriculum of mother-tongue teaching were modelled on those prevailing in the country of origin.

Although responsibility for these lessons in the mother tongue, formally rested with the principals of the Dutch schools, in fact most children of migrant workers were participating in two segregated educational systems: the regular Dutch system and the mother-tongue section controlled by foreign teachers (bicultural education).

In 1980, however, the teaching of the mother tongue was reviewed in the light of the new educational policy that had the permanent settlement of the immigrants in the Netherlands as its starting point.

It was thought desirable that these lessons concentrate more on the children's daily life in the Netherlands and integrate better into the regular curriculum of the Dutch school. In the policy plan of 1980 *the goals of the mother-tongue teaching* were formulated in *psychological rather than in linguistic terms*: fostering the well-being and the ethnic awareness of children and guarding them against alienation from their parents and their family, rather than teaching them the official language of their home country.

One question that arises is whether all these proposals could be put into practice, since they made great demands on both the Dutch and the foreign teachers. For instance, it was stipulated that foreign teachers should have a good command of the Dutch language and adapt their teaching to the Dutch pedagogical-didactic principles, that new curricula and teaching materials ought to be developed and that Dutch and foreign teachers should collaborate.

Another question that has frequently been raised is to what degree these lessons contribute to better achievements of immigrant children in Dutch schools (van den Berg-Eldering, 1986). In a recent report, the current situation of the mother-tongue lessons has been pictured (Ministerie van Onderwijs en Wetenschappen, 1988). In recent years the number of pupils following these lessons has grown enormously as a consequence of the extension of mother-tongue teaching to kindergarten grades (four- and five-year-old children), and to the Moluccan minority. In 1987 about 65 per cent of the children participated.

The Inspection Report concludes further that despite the growing participation of pupils, the mother-tongue lessons suffer from a-series of shortcomings, which may influence their effectivity in a negative way. These shortcomings concern the teachers and the schoolteam as well as the pupils. Thus, it appears that the reading proficiency of older pupils in their home language is often insufficient to enable them to read textbooks from their home country and that the vocabulary of young pupils is too poor to permit them to communicate with the teacher. Another handicap is that many teachers are insufficiently qualified to teach young children in kindergarten grades. About 70 per cent of the teachers are appointed to two or more schools. This leaves them few opportunities to cooperate with Dutch teachers, and to integrate their lessons in the whole curriculum. Dutch teachers and school management, too, make few attempts to involve the mother-tongue teachers in matters concerning the curriculum and pedagogic-didactic approach. To this day, mother-tongue teaching remains a controversial issue for policy makers, educationalists, linguists, teachers and parents alike, despite its being prescribed by the 1985 Elementary Education Act.

Intercultural education

Over the last fifteen years Dutch society has been changing into a multicultural society. The idea behind intercultural education was that it should prepare children of ethnic/cultural minorities and those of the indigenous Dutch majority to live harmoniously side by side in that multicultural society. According to the 1980 policy plan, the prerequisites for such a harmonious co-existence are knowledge and acceptance of the respective cultures and even readiness to adopt elements of each other's cultures (acculturation). Intercultural education is intended to contribute to this process of acculturation. The assumption that Dutch society is a multicultural society was also enshrined in the 1985 Elementary Education Act. However, many teachers do not know how to translate this abstract assumption into daily educational practice. According to recent research, less than half of the Dutch schools include intercultural activities in their curriculum (Fase & van den Berg, 1985). Whereas most teachers believe that intercultural education should concentrate on combating prejudice and discrimination, in reality most activities involve only folklore (customs regarding life-cycle rituals, eating, clothing, music, dancing, etc.) and history (of the countries of origin). In addition to these problems of implementation, the principles underlying intercultural education are being challenged by some of those involved in policy making and educational practice. For instance, can equivalence of cultures exist in a society in which the respective ethnic-cultural groups hold different socio-economic positions (minorities and majorities)?

5.3 Post 1985: Educational Priority Policy

The basic assumption of the Educational Priority Policy, which came into effect in 1985, is that children of immigrant workers and those of indigenous Dutch working-class families are to a high degree comparable. They live in similar houses in the same neighbourhoods of the big cities; they attend the same schools and their parents hold more or less the same socio-economic position in society (lower-class jobs, low educational levels). This assumed similarity was the main reason for developing one educational policy for all underprivileged children in the Netherlands. In this policy, priority (i.e. additional

funds) is given to schools and to geographical areas with a high percentage of children from both categories. Pupils are rated according
to the educational level and economic position of their parents and
their country of origin. Thus, pupils from ethnic minority groups are
given nearly twice as much (1.9) weight as 'average' Dutch children.
This weighting forms the basis for assessing the school score and the
school score determines the number and sort of staff or funds allot-
ted to a school by the Ministry of Education and Science. At present,
about 70 priority areas receive additional funds for the schooling of
disadvantaged children. To reduce the educational arrears of these
children at an early age, emphasis is placed on the first four years of
primary education (including kindergarten).

A remarkable feature of Dutch educational policy is the government's limited influence on the way these funds are used by the
schools. As a result of this, a great variety of activities are being
undertaken, all with the same aim: to improve the performance of
disadvantaged children.

Besides this, schools may organize lessons in the mother tongue of
ethnic minority children to a maximum of 2.5 hours a week, during
schooltime. Attendance at these lessons is, however, not compulsory.
So far, no results of this educational priority policy in terms of the
educational performance of the children are available; the policy has
only been operational since 1985/1986. But its main assumption –
that children of ethnic minority backgrounds are similar to those of
the native Dutch working class - is already being questioned.

Recently, people involved in policy making at the municipal level
and in teaching in the schools have become more aware of the poor
level of cognitive development of ethnic minority children at the
moment they enter kindergarten (at the age of four). This can be
attributed to a number of factors. First, the percentage of Moroccan
and Turkish fathers who are unemployed is growing (currently 40-
50 per cent). As a result, contacts between their families and Dutch
people are rare and the young children do not learn Dutch either at
home, or in the street. At the same time, the number of 'black
schools' – i.e. schools with hardly any indigenous Dutch pupils – is
increasing, particularly in the big cities. Recently, the municipal
councils of The Hague and Amsterdam launched a plan to use the
mother tongue to instruct non-Dutch speaking children in the basic
skills during the first years of primary education.

Clearly, the assumption that children of immigrants who were born
in the Netherlands would have the same educational level upon

their entrance into schools as children of Dutch workers is highly questionable.

6. THE UNDERPRIVILEGED CONDITION OF ETHNIC MINORITY PUPILS

How can arrears in the education of minority children be measured and which indicators might be used to this end? The above mentioned monitoring system for periodically assessing the condition of ethnic minorities in the Netherlands will use as main indicators for educational assessment: final level of educational achievement, and flow patterns (primary education → types of secondary education).

The evaluation of the educational priority programme will provide detailed data about the educational performance of ethnic minority pupils. This programme, which has been effective since 1985, will be evaluated extensively by a longitudinal study of successive cohorts. The first cohort study in primary education, involving 849 primary schools and about 50 000 pupils, was carried out in 1988. Pupils in grades 4, 6, and 8 were tested on Dutch language proficiency, mathematics, social competence, and intelligence. In 1990 and 1992 the cohort studies will be repeated (Kloprogge, 1989). The longitudinal nature of the research will provide, in the near future, a good overall as well as a detailed picture of the educational performance of disadvantaged ethnic minority and majority pupils, and their progress under the educational priority programme (cf. Tomlinson and Sammons in this volume for the situation in the UK).

The picture given in this chapter must, necessarily, be global, and will be based upon scarce and often non-representative research data and statistics. The following will be used as indicators of the educational situation of ethnic minority pupils: distribution of pupils over school types, educational performance, and participation.

6.1 Distribution of pupils over school types

Table 4 indicates how Dutch and Mediterranean pupils are distributed over all types of fulltime education. From this table it cannot simply be concluded that ethnic minority pupils are disproportionally distributed over the schools as a result of educational arrears, because the age structures of the various categories are an intermediate factor in these figures. The percentages of Mediterranean children in primary schools (since 1985 they include the kindergarten grades 1 and 2) are substantially higher than those of Dutch children.

However, it cannot be denied that the unequal distribution of Dutch and Mediterranean pupils over the various types of secondary, higher and university education is mainly caused by educational arrears. Differences in age structures play only a minor role here. As to differences between the categories of pupils from Mediterranean countries, the figures in table 4 indicate that children from North Mediterranean countries occupy an intermediate position between Dutch

Table 4: Pupils in all forms of full-time education. School year 1985/1986 (in percentages)

Forms of education	Dutch[1]	N.Medit. c.[2]	Medit. c.[3]
prim. education	43.4	54.0	65.2
prim. special educ.	3.0	4.2	4.0
Sub-total	46.4	58.2	69.2
general sec. education (mavo, havo, vwo)	24.6	22.5	11.9
junior sec. vocational education (lbo)	10.7	10.0	16.6
senior sec. vocational education (mbo)	8.6	5.8	1.9
Sub-total	43.9	38.3	30.4
higher voc. education (hbo)	4.6	1.4	0.5
university education	5.3	2.2	0.6
Sub-total	9.9	3.6	1.1
Total	100	100	100
absolute numbers	3 192 680	1 6076	98 742

1. Including pupils from Surinamese and Antillean origins with Dutch nationality.
2. Greece, Italy, Yugoslavia, Portugal, Spain.
3. Countries under 2) plus Turkey, Morocco, Tunesia.

Source: Ankersmit, T. et al., Statistisch Vademecum, CBS, 1988.

and Moroccan/Turkish children. But differences also exist between Turkish and Moroccan pupils. In the school year 1985/86, only one out of three Moroccan youngsters was enrolled in a school for general secondary education, compared with two out of five Turkish youngsters. In the same year, about 75 per cent of the Moroccan and 67 per cent of the Turkish twelve year olds were still in primary education, compared with only 35 per cent of the Dutch.

In table 4 no distinction is made between indigenous Dutch pupils and pupils of Surinamese or Antillean origin, since the Central Bureau of Statistics uses only nationality as criterion. Other sources provide a better insight into the educational situation of Surinamese and Antillean pupils. A survey in 1982 of 1271 pupils in grade 8 of 342 primary schools showed that in that year teachers advised more than 70 per cent of the Moroccan and Turkish pupils to enroll in junior secondary vocational education, as against only 35 per cent of the Dutch pupils. The percentages for the other ethnic minority groups were 52 per cent of the Surinamese/Antilleans, 47.5 per cent of the Moluccans, and 49 per cent of the pupils of North Mediterranean countries. Of the Moroccan and Turkish pupils in this survey, only 42.5 per cent and 50.3 per cent had participated in Dutch education for more than 4.5 years, as against 71 per cent of the Surinamese/Antillean pupils, and 98.7 per cent of the Moluccan pupils (van Esch, 1983). A study of Surinamese pupils of 24 schools in 1982 showed important differences between Creole and Hindustani Surinamese pupils (Koot et al., 1985). Of the Creole Surinamese group, 36 per cent were advised to enroll in junior secondary vocational education, and 57 per cent had been advised to enroll in general secondary education. The corresponding figures for the Hindustani Surinamese group were 57 per cent and 34 per cent, respectively.

Comparison with recent data of 1987 shows that, generally speaking, ethnic minority pupils (pupils weighted at the 1.9 rate) begin to approach disadvantaged Dutch pupils (pupils weighted at the 1.25 rate) with regard to the teacher's advice for enrolment in secondary education. But the differences between the various ethnic groups are still great (Kloprogge et al., 1989).

6.2 *Educational performance*
Ethnic minority children not only more often attend lower types of secondary education, but they also perform less well at school and they frequently leave school prematurely without having sat for an examination.

The above-mentioned survey of 1271 pupils in grade 8 of primary school showed great differences in test scores between the various ethnic minority groups. The average scores of minority pupils were 100 compared with 129 of their indigenous Dutch classmates. Pupils from North Mediterranean countries scored highest (108) among the minority groups, followed by Surinamese/Antillean (107), Moluccan (104), Turkish (101), and Moroccan pupils (90) (van Esch, 1983). Within the category of Surinamese pupils, Hindustani scored lower on report marks than Creole pupils, according to the research of Koot et al. (1985).

A study in Rotterdam, in which pupils were followed for three years until the end of the second grade of secondary education from 1982 until 1984, showed a similar pattern (de Jong, 1987). In the report on this research it was concluded that, on average, ethnic minority pupils lagged behind educationally by two years at the end of the second year of secondary education. This means that these pupils had then achieved the educational level Dutch pupils generally have at the end of primary school. However, there were striking differences between the various ethnic groups. Chinese children were only six months behind their Dutch classmates, but Moroccan and Turkish children had an educational lag of 2.5 to 3 years. Between these extremes were the Surinamese/Antillean children, and the pupils from North Mediterranean countries, with a lag of 1.5 to 2 years. We have to keep in mind that these differences in test scores and report marks between the various ethnic groups may be strongly influenced by differences in length of stay and proficiency in Dutch language. If this is the case, the data which will be produced in the national evaluation of the educational priority programme will give a more positive picture of the differences between the various ethnic groups, and between the ethnic minority pupils as a whole and the Dutch pupils.

6.3 Participation in education
A third indicator for educational inequality is the degree of participation in education. Generally speaking, nearly all pupils younger than twelve attend school. The *Quality of Life Surveys* indicate that in the age category of 18 to 24 years old, about 20 per cent of the Turks, 40 per cent of the Moroccans and 41 per cent of the Dutch receive full-time education. These figures may lead to the hypothesis that Moroccans try to catch up on their educational lag by staying longer in full-time education (cf. the research results of Mabey mentioned in

the chapter by Tomlinson in this volume). However, one has to bear in mind that these figures refer to Turkish and Moroccan males only and to Dutch males and females.

Several research findings show that Moroccan and Turkish girls in the ages between 13 and 16 participate much less in full-time education. Their drop-out rates vary from 25 per cent to 35 per cent (Penninx, 1988). The girls who stay in education, however, are enrolled in 'higher' school types more often than boys (Luykx, 1988).

6.4 Conclusion

The general conclusion from this short review of research into educational inequality must be that although the ethnic minority pupils show substantial educational arrears compared with Dutch pupils, there are equally striking differences both within this global category and within the various ethnic-minority groups. The Moroccan and Turkish pupils are worst off, whereas the Surinamese/Antillean pupils and those from North Mediterranean countries approach the level of the Dutch pupils. Another conclusion would be that Moroccan and Turkish girls may have higher drop-out rates than boys of the same nationality, but that they also attend 'higher' school types, when staying in education.

7. EXPLANATORY MODELS

In the foregoing sections, the question of how to explain the underachievement of ethnic minority children was occasionally touched upon. A relevant issue with regard to this question is whether the educational performance of these children can be explained by general theoretical models, or should be explained by specific factors related to immigration, minority position, and ethnic/cultural backgrounds.

The educational achievement of children depends on many factors inside and outside schools. Research done in recent decades has shown that there is a strong connection between parents' socioeconomic status in society, and the educational achievements of their children. How this connection is to be explained has also been an important issue for research. For instance, are all SES variables (educational achievement level of parents, and their occupation and income) of equal weight in this connection? What kind of factors within the family mediate between SES variables and school performance (educational goals and styles, expectations of parents, etc.)? More recently, attention is also being given to factors within schools that might influence the learning process of children (attitudes and skills of teachers, curricula, the way schools and classes are organized and managed) (see also Sammons's chapter on school effectiveness in this volume). With regard to indigenous Dutch underprivileged children, researchers in the Netherlands currently use theoretical models in which socio-economic and socio-cultural background variables as well as teacher and school variables are seen as input factors influencing the school performance and flow patterns of these children (cf. Slavenburg, 1986). Some scholars doing research on ethnic minority children use these models too, by adding a few specific variables which, in their view, might contribute to these children's poor performance, such as country of origin, nationality, length of stay, proficiency in the second language, religion (cf. de Jong, 1987). In the evaluation of the Dutch educational priority programme, a similar approach will be used. Those using this approach implicitly or explicitly assume that underachievement of immigrant children is temporary and that their performance will approach that of indigenous children of working-class families as time goes on. According to these theories ethnic minority children born in the new country are more or less comparable with indigenous children from the same socio-economic backgrounds.

It goes without saying that the *length of stay* in the new country and *the age at which children immigrate* strongly influence their school career and subsequent position in society. Several research findings show that 'half-way' generation children – children who immigrated half-way through their school career – perform poorly at school and have high drop-out rates. Most of them leave school without having passed an examination. These youngsters run the risk of becoming marginalized in society: truancy, school failure, unemployment, marginal position in the family, delinquency, drugs etc. (Fase & de Jong, 1983; Fase & Risseeuw, 1984; de Vries, 1981; Werdmölder, 1986).

The majority of ethnic minority children in Dutch schools now belong to the so-called second generation children. These children were born in the Netherlands[1], and they will follow the Dutch school system from the outset. The question arises whether these second generation children will attain higher educational levels and will gain a better position in society than their parents and older siblings. The Dutch Educational Priority Policy has as its main assumption that children of immigrants who were born in the Netherlands begin their school career at the same educational level as children of indigenous manual workers.

Other scholars assume that the underachievement of ethnic minority pupils will last longer, or will not even disappear with time. Adherents to these theories attribute the underachievement to characteristics of the receiving society and its institutions, to characteristics of the minority groups themselves, or to a mixture of both. According to Tierney (1982), discrimination and racism at several levels in society perpetuate the minority position of parents, and this causes the poor school performance of their children. In a review of research, Cummins (1984) explores the factors that might influence the academic achievement of ethnic minority pupils. He discusses bilingualism, quality of education, and home-school cultural mismatch, and concludes that none of these factors can provide a complete explanation of minority pupils' achievement patterns, and that the role of broader social factors has to be examined.

A fruitful theory in this respect is the theory developed by Ogbu, an American-Nigerian anthropologist. On account of its possible relevance for the explanation of school performance of ethnic minorities in the Netherlands, Ogbu's theory will be treated here in more detail (Ogbu, 1987). The challenge for educational anthropology is, in Ogbu's view, to explain the variability in school performance of ethnic minority pupils. Why do some minorities successfully cross language and cultural boundaries and perform well in school, whereas others do not?

The primary problem in the school performance of ethnic minority pupils does not lie in the mere fact that children possess a different language, dialect or communication style, but "the main factor differentiating the more successful from the less successful minorities appears to be the nature of the history, subordination and exploitation of the minorities and the nature of the minorities' own instrumental and expressive responses to their treatment, which enter into the process of their schooling" (Ogbu, 1987, p.317).

The three sources that contribute to school performance are society, community (including the family), and school. Ogbu identifies two relevant types of ethnic minorities: *immigrant minorities* and *caste-like* or *involuntary minorities*. Chinese and other Asian immigrant groups in the United States belong to the first type; American Indians, black Americans and Mexican Americans are examples of the latter. Both types initially have a low socio-economic position in society, and are characterized by cultural differences in relation to the dominant group in society. The quality of these cultural differences, however, is not the same for both types. The cultural differences of immigrant minorities are differences in content, which existed prior to emigration, whereas those of the caste-like minorities arose after emigration, and as a response to the contact with the dominant group in society. The contact situation, involving the domination of one group by another, resulted in the development of a new collective identity in opposition to that of the dominant group, and in the development of secondary cultural differences. The involuntary minorities have experienced the barriers in the opportunity structure for generations, and they know that these barriers are not temporary but institutional. As a response, they have developed alternative folk theories of getting ahead with alternative strategies.

Initially, the immigrant minorities are more optimistic about their future and that of their children. They accept the dominant group's folk theory of getting ahead, and they believe that their children can get ahead through hard work and school success. They view the opportunity structure in the new country in a more positive way, since they compare it with that of their country of origin. They see cultural and linguistic differences as barriers to overcome in order to achieve their long-range goals of future employment, rather than as markers of identity to be maintained, as involuntary minorities do.

As a consequence of these perceptions and expectations about the future, immigrant minorities (communities and families) develop strategies enhancing the school performance of their children. Parents and communities tend to insist that children follow school rules of behaviour and respect school authority.

As regards the involuntary minorities, complex community forces make it more difficult for their children to overcome their initial school problems. They tend to equate school learning with learning a white American cultural frame of reference, and to equate following the standard practices and activities of the school that enhance school success and social adjustment with 'acting white'. Communities and parents give the children ambivalent messages about society and school learning.

Erickson (1987) discusses the positive and negative aspects in Ogbu's theory. The positive points in this theory, which Erickson called "the perceived labor market explanation", are its empirical support and theoretical force. It is a comprehensive theory, linking phenomena across diverse levels of social organization. One of the main weaknesses of the theory is its implicit mechanistic view of society (economic determination), which leaves no room for human agency, and thus no hope that education might change the future lives of pupils.

Ogbu's theory has given a new impetus to the discussion on the school performance of ethnic minority children in the U.S. between educational anthropologists (cf. Jacob & Jordan, 1987; Spindler, 1982; Trueba, 1988).

In the Netherlands the field of educational anthropology has as yet not been developed. It might be fruitful to follow the theoretical developments in this field in the USA, and to study their applicability and validity with regard to ethnic minority pupils in the Netherlands.

8. RESEARCH IN THE NETHERLANDS

8.1 Present state of the art

Recently, a general inventory of research on ethnic minority children for the years 1979-1985 was made by our department of intercultural education at Leiden University[2].

The main conclusions of this inventory are:
- the number of research projects in this field has grown enormously since 1982. Whereas only eight research projects were carried out in the years 1979-1981; more than a hundred projects started during the period 1982-1985,
- about 75 per cent of the projects have been funded by the national government. Partly because of budgetary constraints, universities have only recently begun to invest in research in this field. One of the initiatives is the creation of a chair in intercultural education at Leiden University,
- so far, most attention has been given to ethnic minority children of school age and those over twelve; children of preschool age (less than six years old) have received least attention,
- more than 80 per cent of the research projects concerned Turkish and/or Moroccan children,
- more than half of the projects studied school education and language acquisition. Other relevant issues were health, social welfare and delinquency.

It is evident that the research conducted so far, reflects to a high degree the dynamics of the immigration process and the needs for understanding primarily felt by Dutch society and its institutions. This explains why so much attention has been given to the condition of the 'half-way' generation children and so little to children of pre-school age. The former category was seen as a high-risk category, whereas the latter was thought of as a category that would quickly assimilate and integrate in the school system. The awareness that the second generation children – i.e., children who are born in our country – begin their school career with serious developmental arrears is only growing slowly (van den Berg-Eldering, 1988a). In a trend study of educational research (Everts et al., 1985) it has also been concluded that ethnic minority children below school age (less than six years old) are underrepresented in research. The authors of that study analysed 150 Dutch research publications that appeared up to 1984 and in which ethnicity played a role. The most relevant conclusions of their analysis are:

– very little is known about the condition of ethnic minority children under school age. Apart from research into second language acquisition of these children, there is also a need for research into their cognitive and socio-emotional development,
– the relationship between school and family, and in particular those factors within the family that are closely connected with the development of children and their school success or school failure need more attention in research. The role of the mother in the socialization of her children and her position within the family needs to be clarified,
– although the interest of researchers in educational processes at school is growing, hardly any research has been done on the role of teachers and the way they function in multi-ethnic settings. The same applies to issues such as the organization and management of multi-ethnic classes containing children with different levels of Dutch proficiency,
– relatively little attention has been paid in research projects to specific issues such as mother-tongue teaching of ethnic minority children, second language acquisition and maintenance or loss of first language competency.

For some years now, researchers have been paying more attention to young children's proficiency in Dutch and to their socialization and development. In 1987 the department of intercultural education of Leiden University started a large research project concerning ethnic minority children of preschool age. In this project the socialization and cognitive development of these children are being studied, as well as the possibilities for home-intervention programmes (van den Berg-Eldering, 1988b).

8.2 Recommendations for further research

This chapter will be concluded with a few recommendations for further research. These areas are only globally indicated and need to be worked out in more detail in a follow-up study.

Areas for further research

1. The socialization and enculturation of second generation children. Generally speaking, school careers of children are strongly influenced by the socio-economic position and cultural orientation of their parents. The cultural orientations of parents from ethnic minority groups and their values, goals and expectations regarding the upbringing and education of children need to be studied.
2. The cognitive, socio-emotional and language development of ethnic minority children under school age. Relevant in this respect is the role of the mother in the family, and the way she interacts with her child and stimulates its development.
3. The interplay of socio-economic condition of ethnic minority parents in society and socialization patterns of the family and their relation with school performance (see Ogbu's theory in section 7).
4. The school careers of ethnic minority children. Within this field of research a distinction has to be made between the various ethnic minority groups, as well as between boys and girls. School careers and factors causing drop-out have to be studied over a long period (longitudinal design).
5. Educational processes at school: curricula and organization of multi-ethnic classes and schools, and the role of teachers.
6. The language development of ethnic minority children at pre-school as well as at school age; first as well as second language acquisition.

Finally, a few remarks have to be made with regard to the nature of past and future research. So far most research projects have been of the survey type (interviews or questionnaires), and their span has been a couple of years at the most. In order to gain a better insight into the dynamics and complex processes of the socialization and development of children and of the effects of intervention and schooling, research projects of a more qualitative kind are called for (participant observation, repeated in-depth interviews). Educational anthropology, as developed in the USA by Spindler (1974, 1982) and his followers, may serve as a model in this respect. Secondly, it is recommended to start up longitudinal research projects: for instance, on school careers and on the long-term effects of intervention programmes (cf. Berrueta-Clement et al., 1984; Lombard, 1981).

NOTES

1 Under Dutch law, children born in the Netherlands do not have Dutch nationality, but take the nationality of their father.
2 This inventory has been made by Ms. Lucy Waarts-Grinwis, one of our research assistants.

REFERENCES

ANKERSMIT, T., ROELANDT, TH., & VEENMAN, J. (1988). *Minderheden in Nederland. Statistisch Vademecum* (*Minorities in the Netherlands, Statistical Vademecum*). Voorburg: C.B.S.
BERG-ELDERING, L. VAN DEN (1978). *Marokkaanse gezinnen in Nederland* (*Moroccan families in The Netherlands*). Alphen a.d. Rijn: Samsom.
BERG-ELDERING, L. VAN DEN (1986). Onderwijs en etnische ongelijkheid (Education and ethnic inequality). In J.A. van Kemenade e.a. (Eds.). *Onderwijs, bestel en beleid 2, Onderwijs en Samenleving*. Groningen: Wolters-Noordhoff.
BERG-ELDERING, L. VAN DEN (1988a). Opvoeden in verandering. Aanzet tot een interculturele pedagogiek (Raising a family in changed circumstances. An introduction to intercultural education). *Nederlands Tijdschrift voor Opvoeding, Vorming en Onderwijs*, 4(2), 54-67.
BERG-ELDERING, L. VAN DEN (1988b). *Home intervention in ethnic minority families*. Paper presented at the Annual Meeting of the American Anthropological Association, 16-20 November, Phoenix, Arizona.
BERRUETA-CLEMENT, J.R., SCHWEINHART, C.J., BARNETT, W.S., EPSTEIN, A.S. & WEIKART, D.P. (1984). *Changed lives: the effects of the Perry-Preschool program on youths through age 19*. Ypsilanti, Michigan: High-Scope Educational Research Foundation.
C.B.S. (1984). *Leefsituatie van de Nederlandse bevolking 1983* (*Quality of life survey among the Dutch population 1983*). Voorburg: C.B.S.
C.B.S. (1985). *Leefsituatie van Turken en Marokkanen in Nederland 1984* (*Quality of life survey among Moroccans and Turks 1984*). Deel 1 eerste uitkomsten. Deel 3 huishoudens en migratie. Voorburg: C.B.S.
C.B.S. (1986). *Leefsituatie van Surinamers en Antillianen in Nederland 1985* (*Quality of life survey among Surinamese and Antilleans*). Deel 1 eerste uitkomsten. Voorburg: C.B.S.
CUMMINS, J. (1984). *Bilingualism and Special Education: Issues in assessment and pedagogy*. Clevedon: Multilingual Matters.

ERICKSON, F. (1987). Transformation and school success; the politics and culture of educational achievement. In E. Jacob & C. Jordan (Eds.), Explaining the school performance of minority students. *Anthropology and Education Quarterly, 18*(4), 335-356.

ESCH, W. VAN, (1983). *Toetsprestaties en doorstroomadviezen van allochtone leerlingen in de zesde klas van lagere scholen (Performance of and advice for minority pupils in the sixth grade).* Nijmegen: I.T.S.

Ethnic-Minorities (1979). Report issued by the WRR Advisory Committee. Den Haag: Staatsdrukkerij.

EVERTS, H., GOLHOF, A., STASSEN P., & TEUNISSEN J. (1985). *Trendstudie over het onderzoek naar etnische groepen in het onderwijs (State of affairs of the research on ethnic-minority pupils in education).* Utrecht: Vakgroep Onderwijskunde, Rijksuniversiteit Utrecht.

EXTRA, G. & VALLEN, T. (1988). *Second Language acquisition in elementary school. A crossnational perspective on the Netherlands, Flanders and Federal Germany.* Paper presented at the International Workshop on "Education and cultural development of ethnic minority children", 12-14 September, Kerkrade, Netherlands.

FASE, W., & VAN DEN BERG, G. (1985). *Theorie en praktijk van intercultureel onderwijs.* (theory and practice of intercultural education). Rotterdam: Erasmus Universiteit.

FASE, W., & JONG, M.J. DE (1983). *Internationale Schakelklas. Beleidsgerichte evaluatie van het functioneren van de schakelperiode (Evaluation of the reception classes in secondary education).* Rotterdam: Vakgroep onderwijssociologie en onderwijsbeleid, Erasmus Universiteit.

FASE, W. & RISSEEUW, P. (1984). *De Internationale schakelklas: eerste halte of eindstation? Verslag van een vervolgonderzoek (Evaluation of the reception classes in secondary education, follow-up research).* Rotterdam: Vakgroep onderwijssociologie en onderwijsbeleid, Erasmus Universiteit.

HAFFMANS, M.A.F. & MAS, P. DE (1985). *De gezinshereniging van Marokkanen in Nederland, 1968-1984 (Family reunion of Moroccans in The Netherlands, 1968-1984).* Den Haag: Ministerie van Sociale Zaken en Werkgelegenheid.

JACOB, E. & JORDAN, C. (Eds.) (1987). Explaining the School Performance of Minority Students. *Anthropology and Education Quarterly, 18*(4), Special Issue.

JONG, M.J. DE (1987). *Herkomst, kennis en kansen. Allochtone en autochtone leerlingen tijdens de overgang van basis- naar voortgezet onderwijs (Origins, knowledge and opportunities. Allochthonous and autochthonous pupils from primary to secondary schools).* Lisse: Swets en Zeitlinger BV.

KLOPROGGE, J.J.J. (1989). The evaluation of the new Dutch National Education Priority Programme. *Studies in Educational Evaluation, 15*(1).

KLOPROGGE, J.J.J., VAN DER WERF, G., & TESSER, P. (1989). *Voorrang voor de gebieden? Notitie over het onderwijsvoorrangsbeleid in 1988. (Educational Priority Policy in 1988).* Den Haag: SVO.

KOOT, W., TJON-A-TEN, V. & UNIKEN VENEMA, P. (1985). *Surinaamse kinderen op school. (Surinamese children at school).* Muiderberg: Coutinho.

LOMBARD, A. (1981). *Success begins at home. Educational Foundations for Preschoolers.* Lexington, MA: Lexington Books.

LUYKX, M. (1988). *Schoolsucces van Turkse en Marokkaanse meisjes (School success of Turkish and Moroccan girls).* Utrecht: ISOR, Utrecht University.

McDermott, P.P. & Goldman, S.V. (1983). Teaching in multicultural settings. In Lotty van den Berg-Eldering, Ferry J.M. de Rijcke & Louis V. Zuck (Eds.), *Multicultural education: a challenge for teachers.* Dordrecht - Holland/Cinnaminson - U.S.A: Foris Publications.

Memorandum inzake het Minderhedenbeleid in de jaren '90 (Memorandum concerning Minority policy for the nineties) (1988).

Ministerie van Onderwijs en Wetenschappen (1984). *Kwantitatieve ontwikkelingen ten aanzien van leerlingen uit culturele minderheden in het k.o. en g.l.o. (Quantitative developments of Cumi-pupils in primary education).* Den Haag. (Unpublished)

Ministerie van Onderwijs en Wetenschappen (1987): *Cumi-raming. Raming van de aantallen leerlingen uit culturele minderheden in het b.o. en v.s.o. 1987 t/m 1993.* (Estimation of Cu-Mi pupils 1987-1993). Den Haag. (Unpublished)

Ministerie van Onderwijs en Wetenschappen (1988). *O.E.T.C.: niet apart maar samen.* Inspectierapport 27. Den Haag: Staatsdrukkerij.

Ogbu, J.V. (1987). Variability in minority school performance: A problem in search of an explanation. In E. Jacob & C. Jordan (Eds), Explaining the school performance of minority students. *Anthropology and Education Quarterly, 18*(4), 312-334.

Penninx, M.J.A. (1988). *Minderheidsvorming en emancipatie. Balans van kennisverwerving ten aanzien van immigranten en woonwagenbewoners 1967-1987 (Formation of minority groups and emancipation).* Alphen aan den Rijn: Samsom.

Sammons, P. (1988). *School effectiveness and school organization. Some findings from a recent study of junior education in the United Kingdom.* Paper presented at the International Workshop on "Education and the cultural development of ethnic minority children. 12-14 September, Kerkrade, Netherlands.

Slavenburg, J.H. (1986). *Onderwijsstimulering en gezinsactivering. Berichten summatieve evaluatie (Educational enrichment and home intervention).* Project Onderwijs en Sociaal Milieu. Den Haag: S.V.O.

Spindler, G.D. (Ed.) (1974). *Education and Cultural process: toward an anthropology of Education.* New York: Holt, Rinehart and Winston.

Spindler, G.D. (Ed.) (1982). *Doing the ethnography of schooling. Educational Anthropology in Action.* New York: Holt, Rinehart and Winston.

Tomlinson, S. (1988). *Ethnicity and educational achievement in Britain.* Paper presented at the International Workshop on "Education and the cultural development of ethnic minority children". 12-14 September, Kerkrade, Netherlands.

Tierney, J. (Ed.), (1982). *Race, migration and schooling.* London: Holt Education.

Trueba, H.T. (1988). Culturally based explanations of minority students' academic achievement. *Anthropology and Education Quarterly, 19*(3), 270-287.

Tweede Kamer der Staten Generaal (1983). *Minderhedennota (Policy-Plan for minorities).* Tweede kamer zitting 1982-1983, 16102 nrs. 20-21.

Vries, M. de (1981). *Waar komen zij terecht? De positie van jeugdige allochtonen in het onderwijs en op de arbeidsmarkt (The condition of minority youngsters in education and the labour market).* ACOM-advies. Den Haag.

Werdmölder, H. (1986). *Van vriendenkring tot randgroep. Marokkaanse jongeren in een oude stadswijk (Ethnography of a Moroccan peergroup in a marginal position).* Antwerpen: Het Wereldvenster.

7

Çiğdem Kağıtçıbaşı
Boğaziçi University, Istanbul

Child Rearing in Turkey: Implications for Immigration and Intervention

1. INTRODUCTION

This chapter deals mainly with child rearing in Turkey and its implications for adjustment in immigration. The issues involved are approached selectively. The focus is on problems of child development in the context of lower socio-economic development. The chapter also gives an account of an intervention study carried out in low-income urban areas of Istanbul to alleviate some of these problems and to foster the overall development of children. This research is discussed as an example of an intervention to break the cycle of disadvantage that also has implications for application elsewhere. It needs to be recognized that many of the problems encountered in child rearing and child development are not unique to the Turkish case but are common in contexts of low levels of socio-economic development. Therefore, in the orientation adopted here, differences in social class figure more largely than differences in culture.

Cultural differences and social class differences are often confounded in attempts to understand what accounts for the observed disparity in the educational attainments of ethnic minority children and those of the majority population. Indeed, this is a general conceptual problem in any cross-cultural analysis. A great deal of research on cross-cultural psychology (see Kağıtçıbaşı & Berry, 1989) and ethnic psychology and acculturation (Ekstrand, 1986; Berry & Annis, 1988) has emphasized cultural/ethnic variation, almost to the exclusion of variation in social class. This is possibly because ethnic diversity, introduced by immigrants, is more readily apparent in the largely middle-class societies of the Western developed world (e.g. Scandinavia and Northern Europe, England, Canada, the USA, Australia, Israel) or possibly because ethnicity and low social class standing often overlap and are therefore confounded. However, in many parts of the developing world where socio-economic stratification is sharp, variations in social class are very salient, and class analysis is more prevalent.

Clearly, there is a need to disentangle cultural (or ethnic) effects from the effects of variation in class and status, both of which may determine life-styles and hence may possibly influence psychological variables. For example, in a study of parents' values Cashmore and Goodnow (1986) found that the significant differences between the Anglo-Australian and Italian parents in Australia were differentially reduced when several indicators of socio-economic status were taken into account. This finding is similar to one on child rearing values in ten countries (Lambert, 1987). Unless relative social class standing is known, any differences obtained between samples cannot be attributed to ethnic or cultural differences. In other words, culture cannot be assumed to be the main independent variable if social class is not dealt with adequately.

Statistics and studies done all over the world clearly show that, in general, children who are socio-economically disadvantaged fall behind in academic achievement (UNICEF, 1987). This is mainly because of environmental conditions not conducive to the full development of the individual's potential. Children growing up in low-income areas are often hampered in their physical and intellectual development because of a myriad of factors, ranging from malnutrition to lack of intellectual stimulation.

2. CHILD REARING ENVIRONMENT IN TURKEY

Studies in Turkey, as well as in other societies, have pointed to low levels of environmental stimulation in low-income urban or semi-urban areas and especially in rural villages, as evident in the scarcity of toys, books and other reading materials, as well as the paucity of logical verbal reasoning and communication oriented toward the goal of supporting the child's intellectual growth and language development. This may be due, at least partially, to the limited vocabulary and verbal competence of the parents in the poor setting, with low levels of formal education. It may also be due to a lack of conscious 'child centered' and 'child development-directed' efforts to 'teach' young children, who are rather, considered uneducable until school age. Thus, in a pioneering early study in a Turkish village, Helling (1966) noted the prevalence of a parental teaching style based on demonstration, imitation, and motor learning rather than verbal reasoning. Revisiting the same village twenty years later, Helling[1] did not observe any appreciable change in this non-verbal orientation of 'teaching by doing'.

These child rearing orientations may negatively affect children's language and cognitive development. Some research, indeed, points to substantial rural-urban and socio-economic status (SES) differences in children's intellectual performance. Semin (1975) found large differences in vocabulary of middle and lower class children in Istanbul, and Ataman and Epir (1972) found that children from low-income families in Ankara formed concepts of lower level complexity compared with middle class children. In a study I conducted in and around Bursa[2] in the urban centre and rural villages, I studied the performance of fifth-grade children on the *Figure Drawing Test*. I found a clear linear relationship between the SES or level of development and intellectual performance (the level increasing in the order of most remote and least developed village, medium-level village, nearest/most developed village, urban low-income and urban middle-income areas) (Kağıtçıbaşı, 1979).

Research findings such as the above point to diversity in the degree to which the immediate environment of the child is supportive of his/her intellectual development. In Turkey this diversity is mainly based on the level of socio-economic development of the area of dwelling. A national survey was conducted on the value of children for parents (VOC), where 'the level of development' was operationalized as a complex index and the sampling framework was based on this index (Kağıtçıbaşı, 1982a).

The results of the VOCstudy showed that basic values attributed to children and therefore the 'place' of the child in the family also changes according to SES and the level of development of the area of dwelling. Specifically, utilitarian economic values (including old-age security value) are more widely attributed to children in rural and less developed areas, and psychological values of children are more prevalent in urban, developed contexts. Similarly, 'general security in old age' as an advantage of having children decreases in importance as we proceed from underdeveloped to developed areas (mentioned by all of the respondents from less developed areas; by 73 per cent of those who live in intermediately developed areas; by 61 per cent of those who lived in developed areas; and by only 40 per cent of those in the metropolitan centres). Similar results were obtained in other countries in which the cross-cultural VOCstudy was conducted[3] (Kağıtçıbaşı, 1982b, 1984).

Thus, urban-rural and socio-economic variation is important. Nevertheless, family interdependence is a general value shared by widely differing groups. This interdependence first takes the form of the child's dependence on parents and then, in old age, the parents' dependence on the grown-up offspring. It is the child's dependence rather than its independence that is valued, as is apparent from a question asking about the desired attributes of children: 60 per cent of the respondents endorsed "the child's obeying his parents" as the most (or second most) desirable attribute of a child, compared with 18 per cent who endorsed "the child's being independent and self-reliant". When this is considered together with the highly salient future desired attribute of "being good and loyal to parents", we see a home environment conducive to the socialization of familistic and communal values of mutual support rather than individualistic achievement.

What appears to happen with increased urbanization and socio-economic development is a decrease in *material* interdependencies. With better social security systems, alternative old age security resources emerge and the elderly do not have to depend on their offspring for their livelihood. In urban contexts children become more of an economic burden than an economic asset. Nevertheless, *emotional* interdependencies appear to continue, with closely-knit familial ties being highly valued and reinforced (Duben, 1982; Kağıtçıbaşı, 1985a).

Whereas on the one hand familial ties and a "culture of relatedness" (Kagıtçıbası, 1985b) provide valuable interpersonal support, dependency pressures on children may impede their competent functioning in the changing social system. This problem has been noted in research, mainly done with adolescents (e.g. Ekşı, 1982; Geçtan, 1973). It has been observed widely in the home as well as in educational settings, where dependency on and obedience to parents is encouraged to be transferred to the teacher.

A related problem concerns the development of external control in the growing child. In line with the expectations of obedience and dependency from the child, he/she grows up under the absolute authority of the parents, and especially the father (Köknel, 1970; Jaquette & Erkut, 1975). Usually, what is expected from the child is not autonomous action or decision making and carrying the responsibility for the decision, but rather obedience to the parent. Thus, the child is constantly controlled from outside, which does not allow much room or need for internal control. In the closely-knit extended family-community context, other adults, in addition to the parents, are also in close proximity to the child, and they also have the possibility and the right to control his/her behaviour.

In developmental psychology the establishment of internal control is considered to be of key importance, and toward this end, the type of discipline used in child rearing is emphasized. Specifically, frequent use of power assertion, where the parent uses his physical power to control the child, is found to lead to weak internal control and reliance on external control (e.g. Hoffman & Saltzstein, 1967). On the other hand, induction, i.e. reasoning with the child and making him aware of the consequences of his actions for others is found to develop higher internal control (Hoffman & Saltzstein, 1967; Sampson, 1976; Kohlberg, 1969).

Observations in Turkey show the prevalence of physical punishment in child rearing, especially in the traditional family set-up. Verbal reasoning with the child is not common, as mentioned earlier. Together with the close control of the child by parents and other adults, the type of discipline used in child rearing thus produces more dependency and reliance on external control. In this type of child rearing environment the child would constantly refer to others for control of his actions, acceptance, evaluation, and approval. Self-control and self- evaluation may not develop adequately.

The above problems of child rearing often originate from the objective conditions of poverty and are reflected in traditional values regarding children, child rearing orientations, and child discipline. They persist through social change and urbanization, though some changes also take place. Pressures to change exist side by side with resistance to change, especially within newly urban groups and lower urban socio-economic status groups. This produces a stressful environment for the family, especially for the mother and the child. What appears to be needed is a new synthesis in values and orientations combining communal and familial concerns with individual autonomy. In other words, traditional values of group cohesion and cooperation can be protected and maintained, but not at the cost of individual initiative and autonomy - a synthesis of the 'communal' with the 'individual'.

Obviously, such an achievement is a remote ideal for any society, and will not be pursued here any further. Rather, practical and specific contributions to the family and the child will be briefly discussed. Supporting and educating the family and especially the mother is of key importance for the overall development of the child in Turkey. When such support is available together with institutional service for intellectual enrichment to the child, the impact of such a comprehensive education can be substantial.

This is, indeed the general conclusion to be drawn from the results of numerous studies on early intervention, reviewed elsewhere (Kağıtçıbaşı, 1983). It has also generally been found that programmes that involve the parents and the family and have a community-integrating comprehensive approach are more successful than programmes involving only parent education or only work with children away from home. Short-term programmes are not as effective as follow-through programmes. Comprehensive longitudinal fostering programmes can produce sustained results; otherwise, initial gains are lost later.

Some of the 'failures' of early intervention programmes that have been reported in the literature appear to be due, at least partially, to the common practice in research and application of abstracting the child from his environment and treating him in isolation from his 'natural' setting. There is much evidence of the importance of supporting the immediate social environment of the child, and especially of helping the mother (Smilansky, 1979; Woodhead, 1985; Halpern & Myers, 1985; Lombard, 1981). In general, in preschool intervention programmes initial IQ gains are achieved with exposure to the "directive cognitive" approach (Smilansky, 1979). However, if this cognitive development is not supported by the induction of corresponding growth of the child's self-confidence, autonomy and initiative, it will not be self-sustaining after the completion of the programme. This will especially be the case if there is no fostering of the child's immediate social environment, mainly the mother, which could have provided the child with continued support. Thus, it is possible that some of the disappointing results of intervention programmes in producing lasting IQ gains or cognitive development may be due, ironically, to these programmes' preoccupation with cognitive growth.

Thus, a *comprehensive* approach to the child's welfare and education in the early years is needed; one which aims to support the total development of the child and which also incorporates service to the family and community mainly through supporting the mother. Preschool services that are conceptualized in such a comprehensive fashion can provide a supportive environment for the overall development of the child.

In Turkey, preschool services are very inadequate in quantity and quality. The need for these services is felt keenly, especially among the urban lower socio-economic groups, where more and more mothers work away from home and where mother surrogates are lacking. In 1978-80 a group of researchers, child development experts and practitioners undertook a project, directed by the author. The Turkish *Preschool Child Development and Education Project* worked in close cooperation with the Turkish Ministry of Education, aiming to study the state of early childhood development and education in Turkey, to develop working models, and to prepare material for the launching of widespread programmes (Kağıtçıbaşı, 1981). The material was designed to train the teacher and the mother to support the child's overall development. Source books for use by teachers and parents included *Child Development*, *Preschool Programmes*, *Preschool Activities*, *Cognitive Activities* and the first parent education book prepared in Turkey *Your Child and You*. These books were published in 1983 (all in Turkish) by the Ministry.

3. EARLY ENRICHMENT PROJECT[4]

In the light of research findings in various settings and the experience of the Turkish *Preschool Child Development and Education Project*, a five-year longitudinal study was undertaken, directed by the author. This study utilized a comprehensive approach involving both the preschool and the home in low-income urban areas, to foster the overall development of the child. Mother training constituted a focal part of the study. In-depth mother interviewing, home observations, mother training, and constant home support were used to enhance mothers' self confidence by positively influencing their self-image, to help them deal with child rearing problems, and to foster higher levels of autonomy, internal control, and cognitive development in their children.

This is an example of action research involving modification of some basic child rearing orientations and values to foster the overall development of the child, enabling him/her to function more efficiently in modern urban society. Emphasis is put here on the needs of children, to produce awareness in parents of these (non-material) needs. Thus, an effort is made to compensate for the environmental deprivation in the urban low-income context by enriching the non-material environment of the child.

In the present research mothers were encouraged to develop a positive self-concept and feelings of competence and efficacy, as well as specific cognitive stimulation and enrichment at home. This was done by reinforcing the existing close mother-child relationship, on the one hand, and by capitalizing on the existing communal support systems, on the other. The latter were utilized in group meetings of mothers in the community and in paraprofessional home instructions.

Of special relevance are the findings regarding autonomy and dependence. Initial interviews with mothers revealed strong needs for close ties with their children. When asked what children's behaviour pleased them most, relational behaviour, such as being good to mother, was mentioned most frequently. Together with showing affection, being obedient and getting along well with others, relational behaviour accounted for almost 80 per cent of desired behaviour in children. Further probing of other things children do that pleases mothers brought forth more expressions of relational behaviour. In contrast, autonomy, while having a low priority among desired behaviours in children, loomed large among behaviour that angered mothers. Taking the form of self assertion or not obeying, it accounted for more than half of the unacceptable behaviours. Almost all of the other undesirable behaviours of children cited by the mothers had to do with interfering with good relations. In contrast, complaint about dependence (on mother) was strikingly low (1.2%). In describing a "good child", furthermore, the mothers in the Istanbul study stressed being polite (37 per cent) and obedient (35 per cent) more than any other characteristic, being autonomous and self-sufficient again elicited a negligible response (3.6 per cent of the mothers mentioned it).

These findings are similar to earlier ones from similar closely knit societies with collective ecological settings (e.g. see Kağıtçıbaşı & Berry, 1989; Kağıtçıbaşı, 1982b, 1984) and to the results of the *Value of Children* study (Kağıtçıbaşı, 1982a) discussed before. The emphasis on relatedness is striking in these findings: individualistic separation and self-assertion are not valued by mothers.

After the initial interviewing to obtain baseline data, some of the mothers participated in a training programme for two years designed to provide them on the one hand with cognitive skills to teach their children and on the other with sensitization to the needs of the growing child[5]. This extensive parent education intervention was carried out in terms of home instruction and supportive group discussions utilizing existent close-knit communal ties and support systems. In these group discussions the existing relatedness values and behaviours such as showing physical affection, being close, helping and supporting, being good to and sensitive to the child were reinforced. However, new values encouraging autonomy in the child were also introduced, such as allowing the child to make decisions and to carry the responsibility for them, to do things on his own, etc. Care was taken to show that these new values of autonomy are not incompatible with harmonious close-knit human relatedness. After the intervention, in the fourth year of the study, the mothers' child rearing attitudes were reassessed. It was found that mothers who participated in the parent education intervention (N=90) valued autonomous behaviour in their children more than non-trained mothers (N=160) (F=12.5; p=.02). Furthermore, more than twice as many trained mothers as non-trained mothers mentioned autonomous child behaviour as pleasing them (21 per cent *vs* 9.7 per cent, chi square=6.04, df=1, p=.01). This change is remarkable, especially compared with the first year baselines. Yet, the majority of mothers in both groups continued stressing affectionate and relational behaviour in children as pleasing and otherwise demonstrated close-knit ties as reflected in their behaviour and values. Thus the trained mothers acquired a new positive orientation toward the child's autonomy while remaining as close to their children as the non-trained mothers. A synthesis of individualistic and relational values appears to have been achieved.

The few findings reported here comprise a very small part of this longitudinal study. They focus directly on autonomy. Some of the other findings have implications for individual autonomy and achievement also, such as the higher aspirations and expectations of trained mothers regarding their children's school succes and years of schooling, as well as their higher expectations of the child being able to succeed without asking for help from others (48.8 per cent *vs* 18.6 per cent of the non-trained group).

Children's behaviour showed dramatic differences between the two groups, as well, which cannot be elaborated here. Suffice it to say

that children whose mothers had training performed better than the
others in all tests and measures of intellectual performance, including school achievement (Kağıtçıbaşı et al., 1989). Thus, some of the
negative aspects of the living conditions that are not conducive to
the optimum cognitive development of children *can* be counteracted
by supporting the child's early human environment. This kind of a
holistic approach is very promising in dealing with school failure of
immigrant children in the long run.

4. IMPLICATIONS FOR IMMIGRATION AND SOCIAL CHANGE

The Turkish *Early Enrichment Project* has been described in some
detail as an example of an applied study which can change the child
rearing environment to make it more supportive of the child's overall development. This research attempted to reach toward the synthesis of the communal with the individual discussed earlier. Thus,
on the one hand it built upon and strengthened the already existing
close mother-child ties and the closely-knit relations in the community of women. On the other hand, this relatedness did not stifle the
individual mother or the child. On the contrary, the mother was em-
powered by group belongingness and support, and the child attained greater autonomy through close interaction with and attentive-
ness from the mother. Children exposed to the enrichment were
found to be less dependent, and trained mothers were found to value autonomy in children more than non-trained mothers. Thus it
needs to be noted here that individual autonomy need not be incompatible with close-knit familial communalities (Kağıtçıbaşı, 1987).
This is a key to understanding some of the main problems of adjustment and conflict in the context of immigration into Europe. The
basic family cultures are different in the sense that the individualistic
culture prevails in Europe, whereas the culture of relatedness is
prevalent in Turkey. In addition to differences in social class, economic development, education, etc., discussed before, there are differences in basic human and family relations too. This can be a real
source of conflict when, for example, the Turkish parent's strict discipline is interpreted by the social worker in Europe as a rejection of
the child or child abuse, or when the closely-knit familial relations
are labelled pathological. Such evaluation would be culture-biased in
the sense that it is based on one cultural experience (individualism
and clearcut boundaries separating persons) but is used to judge

human relational patterns in another culture. It also assumes that the pattern of the dominant family culture is normal and healthy, and therefore a different pattern must be 'deficient' and therefore must change to resemble the dominant pattern through assimilation, and in general through social change and development.

An underlying assumption shared by many accounts of modernization is that the closely-knit extended family structure goes through a process of nucleation resulting in the Western type conjugal/nuclear family (e.g. Caldwell, 1977; Goode, 1963). A main characteristic of this family, furthermore, is the independence (and separation) of its members from one another. Individual autonomy and separation of self from others with clear boundaries are, in fact, considered necessary for 'healthy' family interactions (e.g. Minuchin, 1974). The family, itself, is also separated from kin, including the older parents, and the community. Yet, what appears to happen in traditional societies like Turkey is a decrease in *material* interdependencies, but not in *emotional* interdependencies through economic development (Kağıtçıbaşı, 1986, 1987), as mentioned before.

In countries like Turkey, familial and social interactions are characterized by close interpersonal ties and interdependence. Even through family nucleation, this type of human interaction continues, penetrating into the 'modern' family pattern. Thus, there is evidence that even old parents who have independent incomes prefer to live with their adult children (or close to them) rather than by themselves, and for young adults to send their parents to old peoples' homes is considered shameful. Close emotional ties between generations persist, even though material investments are directed more toward children than toward elderly parents. The elderly are very much a part of the family as long as they live. They are functional, and they do not feel marginalized, as feelings of relatedness, rather than separateness prevail (Kağıtçıbaşı, 1982b). Thus, the shift in the vertical family interaction patterns is not necessarily toward intergenerational independence but toward continued emotional interdependence.

Support for this view comes from research conducted in Turkey with migrants from rural to urban areas (Karpat, 1976; Kongar, 1976) and on urban family-community relations, including visiting patterns (Kongar, 1972; Duben, 1982; Olson, 1982). These studies point to the pervasiveness and significance of kinship-community-neighbourhood relations among urban families, both former rural migrants and middle class urbanites, even professionals, in metropolitan centres.

Within the closely-knit family, furthermore, the expectations of obedience and dependence from the child, and expectations of loyalty and support from grown-up offspring weigh heavily on the growing person. These basic elements of the traditional child rearing values also constitute social norms and are cherished by society. Thus group (family) loyalties are often more important than individual loyalties – a commonly observed phenomenon in collectivistic societies (Kağıtçıbaşı, 1987).

Within this family context strict discipline and control are prevalent rather than permissiveness, as mentioned before. An early comparative study (Kağıtçıbaşı, 1970) established two dimensions of family emotional atmosphere: affection and control, or warmth-hostility and restrictiveness-permissiveness. Whereas more family control was found in a Turkish sample compared with an American sample, there was no difference between them in family affection. The typical Turkish family appears to be warm-restrictive, in line with the previous descriptions.

In a social context where the common pattern of family control is characterized by permissiveness, as in European society, children may perceive restrictive parental discipline as rejection. However, in a society where restrictive discipline is common, children would perceive such discipline as 'normal' and not as parental rejection. Cross-cultural research, in fact, shows that this is exacty what happens. For example, whereas in Japan and Korea strict parental discipline is perceived as a sign of parental caring and warmth, it is perceived as rejection by American and Korean American adolescents (Pettengill & Rohner, 1985; Rohner & Pettengill, 1985; Trommsdorff, 1985). The same can be expected to be the case in Turkey.

Extending from the family into the second socializing agent of children, the school, the same values and expectations prevail. Thus, strict discipline is applied by the teachers and expected by the children. Permissiveness by a teacher, therefore, may result in a noisy and disorganized class. Similarly, migrant parents often complain about the lack of emphasis on discipline in schools (e.g. Hearst, 1985) since they compare them with Turkish schools.

The implications of this situation for the international migration context are far-reaching. At the basis of these expectations is the 'social comparison process', where the child compares what he has with other children (for example whether other children also have strict parents). When the Turkish family moves into a society with different patterns of control, the family's habitual traditional strict control

becomes the 'exception' rather than the 'rule'. The child may, therefore, start to interpret it as parental rejection, as was found to be the
case for Korean Americans (Pettengill & Rohner, 1985). The negative
views of the host society people, such as social workers, further add
to the shifts in the perceptions of parental behaviour.

5. SUMMARY AND CONCLUSIONS

In this chapter some aspects of family dynamics and child rearing in
Turkey with direct implications for problems of adjustment in the
context of immigration have been discussed. It needs to be reiterated
that sweeping generalizations about ethnic and cultural differences
must be tempered by clarifications of other differentiating factors
such as the social class standing, education, and background (rural
or urban) of the people to be compared. It should be remembered
that most migrants come from backgrounds not conducive to high
academic achievement even in their countries of origin. It is possible,
however, to change the living conditions of children and to support
them in such a way that their intellectual performance increases.
This can best be done by enriching the human environment of the
child, especially the mother, so that enduring support can be provided to the child. The child's cognitive development can be supported
by such an enrichment in the formative early years, to promote
better preparation for school. For example, the potential of the
Turkish Early Enrichment model with immigrant populations in
Europe is substantial. Indeed, it is already being used in the Netherlands (van den Berg-Eldering, 1988) and will shortly be introduced
in Belgium.
The family culture of socialization also needs to be well understood
to ascertain the main causes of differences in child rearing attitudes
and behaviour between the majority society and the immigrant populations. Greater insight about what functions these different attitudes and behaviour serve would prevent the simplistic thinking
that 'different' necessarily means 'deficient'. What in fact is not functional for the overall development of the child and does not promote
successful performance needs to be well defined and should be
changed. However, it should also be recognized that several aspects
of the traditional family culture may be healthy in providing the
growing person with the fulfilment of his/her basic needs, such as
the need for relatedness.

Often, an integrationist mode striving to achieve a synthesis of the different cultural elements is more healthy and enriching than an assimilationist mode that attempts to replace the family culture of origin with that of the dominant society. It is to be hoped that psychologists and social scientists studying the problems of immigrants can help promote the enrichment.

NOTES

1 Personal communication, 1986.

2 A city in Northwestern Turkey.

3 The other VOC countries were Germany, Indonesia, Korea, The Philippines, Singapore, Taiwan, Thailand, and the U.S.A.

4 Director: Ç. Kağıtçıbaşı; co-workers: D. Sunar and S. Bekman (supported by the International Development Centre).

5 For cognitive enrichment the project utilized the Home Instruction Programme for Preschool Youngsters (HIPPY), developed by Lombard (1981).

REFERENCES

ATAMAN, J. & EPIR, S. (1972). Age, socioeconomic status and classificatory behavior among Turkish children. In L.J.C. Cronbach and P.J.D. Drenth (Eds), *Mental Tests and Cultural Adaptation.* The Hague: Mouton.

BERG-ELDERING, L. VAN DEN (1988). *Home intervention in ethnic minority families.* Paper presented at the Annual Meeting of the American Anthropological Association, nov 1988, Phoenix, Arizona.

BERRY, J.W. & ANNIS, R.C. (1988). *Ethnic psychology: Research and practice with immigrants, refugees, native peoples, ethnic groups and sojourners.* Lisse: Swets & Zeitlinger.

CALDWELL, J.A. (1977). Towards a restatement of demographic transition theory. In J.C. Caldwell (Ed), *The persistence of high fertility. Part I.* Canberra: The Australian National University.

CASHMORE, J.A. & GOODNOW, J.J. (1986). Influences on Australian parents' values: Ethnicity versus socio-economic status. *Journal of Cross-Cultural Psychology, 17,* 441-454.

DUBEN, A. (1982). The significance of family and kinship in urban Turkey. In Ç. Kağıtçıbaşı (Ed), *Sex roles, family and community in Turkey.* Bloomington, Indiana: Indiana University Press.

EKŞI, A. (1982). *Gençlerimiz ve Sorunlari (Our youth and their problems).* Istanbul: Istanbul University Publication no. 2790.

EKSTRAND, L. (1986). *Ethnic minorities and immigrants in a crosscultural perspective.* Lisse: Swets & Zeitlinger.

GEÇTAN, E. (1973). *Toplumuz bireylerinde kimlik kavrami*. (Identuty in the individuals of our society). 50. yila armagan. Ankara University, Faculty of Education Publication, 36.

GOODE, W.J. (1963). *World revolution and family patterns*.. Glencoe: The Free Press.

HALPERN, R. & MYERS, R. (1985). *Effects of early childhood intervention on primary school progress and performance in the developing countries*. Unpublished paper, Ypsilanti, Mi; High-Scope, USAID.

HEARST, S. (1985). Turkish families. In Des Storer (Ed.), *Ethnic family values in Australia*. Prentice-Hall of Australia Pty Ltd.

HELLING, G.A. (1966). *The Turkish village as a social system*. Occidental College, Los Angeles, Calif., (Unpublished Monograph).

HOFFMAN, M.L. & SALTZSTEIN, H.D. (1967). Parent discipline and the child's moral development. *Journal of Personality and Social Psychology, 5*, 45-57

JAQUETTE, D. & ERKUT S. (1975). Operative and representational social thought: Some categories of social experience in the Turkish village. *Hacettepe Bulletin of Social Sciences and Humanities, 7*(1-2), 70-92.

KAGITÇIBAŞI, Ç. (1970). Social norms and authoritarianism: A comparison of Turkish and American adolescents. *Journal of Personality and Social Psychology, 16*(3), 444-451.

KAGITÇIBAŞI, Ç. (1979). The effects of socio-economic development on Draw-a-Man scores in Turkey. *Journal of Social Psychology, 108*, 3-8

KAGITÇIBAŞI, Ç. (1981). Early childhood education and intervention. UNESCO: *Child, Family, Community*. August.

KAGITÇIBAŞI, Ç. (1982a) *The changing value of children in Turkey*. Honolulu, Hawaii: East-West Population Institute Publication: 60-E.

KAGITÇIBAŞI, Ç. (1982b) Old-age security value of children and development. *Journal of Comparative Family Studies, Special Issue, 13*, 133-142.

KAGITÇIBAŞI, Ç. (1983) Early childhood education and preschool intervention: Experiences in the world and in Turkey. In K. King & R. Myers (Eds.), *Preventing school failure: The relationship between preschool and primary education*. Ottawa: IDRC.

KAGITÇIBAŞI, Ç. (1984). Socialization in traditional society: A challenge to psychology. *International Journal of Psychology, 19*, 145-157

KAGITÇIBAŞI, Ç. (1985a) A model of family change through development: The Turkish family in comparative perspective. In I.R. Lagunes & Y.H. Poortinga (Eds.). *From a different perspective. Studies of behavior across cultures* (pp. 120-135). Lisse: Swets & Zeitlinger/Berwyn: Swets North America.

KAGITÇIBAŞI, Ç. (1985b). Culture of separateness-Culture of relatedness. 1984; Vision and Reality. *Papers in Comparative Studies, 4*, 91-9.

KAGITÇIBAŞI, Ç. (1986) Status of women in Turkey: Cross cultural perspectives. *International Journal of Middle East. Studies, 18*, 485-99.

KAGITÇIBAŞI, Ç. (1987) Individual and group loyalties: Are they compatible? In Ç. Kağıtçıbaşı (Ed.), *Growth and progress in cross-cultural psychology* (pp. 94-103). Lisse: Swets Zeitlinger.

KAGITÇIBAŞI, Ç. & BERRY, J.W. (1989). Cross-cultural psychology: Current research and trends. *Annual Review of Psychology* (in press).

KAGITÇIBAŞI, Ç. SUNAR, D. & BEKMAN, S. (1989). *Early Enrichment Project*. Ottawa: IDRC Manuscript Report

KARPAT, K. (1976). *The Gecekundu: Rural migration and Urbanization.* London: Cambridge University Press.

KOHLBERG, L. (1969). Stage and sequence: The cognitive-developmental approach to socialization. In D.A. Goslin (Ed.), *Handbook of Socialization Theory and Research.* Chicago: Rand McNally, 347-480.

KÖKNEL, Ö. (1970). *Türk toplumunda bugünün gençligi.* (*Today's youth in Turkish society*). Istanbul: Bozok.

KONGAR, E. (1972). *Izmirde Kentsel aile. Ankara (Urban family in Izmir).* Turk Sosyal Bilimler Dernegi Yayinlari A-3.

KONGAR, E. (1976). Changing roles of mothers: Changing intra-family relations in a Turkish town. In P. Peristany (Ed), *Mediterranean family structure.* Cambridge: University Press.

LAMBERT, W. (1987). The fate of old country values in a new land: A cross-national study of child rearing. *Canadian Psychology 28,* 9-20

LOMBARD, A. (1981). *Success begins at home. Educational foundations for preschoolers.* Lexington, Mass.: DC Heath.

MINUCHIN, S. (1974). *Families and family therapy.* Cambridge, Mass: Harvard Univ. Press.

OLSON, E. (1982). Duofocal family structure and an alternative model of husband-wife relationship. In Ç. Kağıtçıbaşı (Ed.), *Sex roles, family and community in Turkey.* Bloomington: Indiana University Press.

PETTENGILL, S.M. & ROHNER, R.P. (1985). Korean-American adolescents' perceptions of parental control, parental acceptance-rejection and parent-adolescent conflict. In I.R. Lagunes & Y.H. Poortinga (Eds.). *From a different perspective: Studies of behavior across cultures.* Lisse: Swets & Zeitlinger.

SAMPSON, E.G. (1976). *Social psychology and contemporary society.* (2nd ed.). New York: John Wiley & Sons, Inc.

SEMIN, R. (1975). *Okulda basarisizlik.* Istanbul Universitesi Edebigat Fakultesi Yayinlari.

SMILANSKY, M. (1979). *Priorities in education: Pre-school, evidence and conclusions.* (World Bank Staff Working Paper. No. 323). Washington, D.C.

TROMMSDORF, G. (1985). Some comparative aspects of socialization in Japan and Germany. In I.R. Lagunes & Y.H. Poortinga (Eds), *From a different perspective: Studies of behavior across cultures.* Lisse: Swets & Zeitlinger.

UNICEF (1987). *The state of the world's children.*

WOODHEAD, M. (1985). Pre-school education has long term effects: But can they be generalized? *Oxford Review of Education, 11*(2), 133-155.

8

Guus Extra and Ton Vallen
Tilburg University

Second Language Acquisition in Elementary School

A Crossnational Perspective on the Netherlands, Flanders and the Federal Republic of Germany

1. CROSSNATIONAL TRENDS

It has been estimated (e.g., Widgeren, 1975) that in the year 2000, one-third of the population under the age of 35 in urban Europe will have an immigrant background. As yet, these demographic trends have not led to a proportionally motivated emergence of crossnational studies on the education of non-indigenous ethnic minority children in European countries. Only a small number of rather diverse studies on various countries have been published.

An early collection of studies on the language and education of ethnic minority groups in the Netherlands, Belgium and the Federal Republic of Germany was published by Nelde et al. (1981). Tosi (1984) reported on some previous work in EC countries on bilingualism and education in a multi-ethnic society. Churchill (1986) examined a wide range of factors determining the process of policy making during the last two decades for the education of both indigenous and non-indigenous minority groups in OECD countries. Boos-Nünning et al. (1983) offered a comparative perspective on the education of ethnic minority children in Belgium, England, France and the Netherlands, within the framework of an evaluative study of different experimental programmes. These programmes were carried out under the auspices of the EC Ministers of Education in the cities of

Genk, Bedford, Paris and Leiden. Whereas the programmes in Bedford and Paris focused upon education in ethnic group languages and cultures, the programme in Genk related to second language instruction. Both first and second language instruction were taken into account in the Leiden programme. In the framework of this crossnational EC project, Tosi (1984) paid special attention to processes of language maintenance and shift over time within the Italian community in Bedford.

Moreover, Fase (1987) made a comparative analysis of first language education policy and facilities in six countries, in which he paid special attention to trends and controversies in the Netherlands. Meinhardt (1985) gave a rather selective perspective on German and Dutch policy on ethnic minority groups, focusing upon their social and legal status. As yet, only a few in-group reports have appeared on the position of ethnic minority children in Western Europe. Vassaf (1985) wrote an in-group essay on the social and psychological problems of Turkish children in various European countries, which was published both in German and Turkish.

In this chapter we focus upon second language acquisition by ethnic minority children in three neighbouring countries, the Netherlands, Belgium (in particular, Flanders) and the FRG. There are some obvious differences between these three countries in terms of the size and composition of ethnic minority groups (which, especially in the Netherlands, partly reflect colonial history), in the level of policy decisions on education (which in the FRG is the autonomous responsibility of the different *Länder*), and in the status of the 'national' standard language (which in Belgium is both French and Dutch, two languages that have been in conflict for centuries and whose status continues to absorb almost all public attention, probably at the cost of ethnic minority group issues). However, these differences are relatively small, when crossnational similarities are taken into account. The most important ones are listed below.

1. In all three countries similar demographic trends can be observed over time. First, an economically motivated process of migration of heads of families, especially originating from Mediterranean countries, took place. This migration related to contract workers who were expected to stay for a limited period of time. As the period of their stay gradually became longer, this pattern of economic migration was followed by a pattern of social migration of remaining families. Finally, a second generation was born in the immigrant countries and grew up with uncertainty and ambiva-

lence about whether to 'stay or go'. These demographic shifts over time are also reflected in shifts of denotation for the groups under consideration (foreign workers, migrant workers, immigrant families, and ethnic minorities, respectively), and in repeated demographic announcements by governmental authorities that their country "should not be seen as an immigrant country".

2. In all countries under consideration, most ethnic minority groups have a disadvantaged status from various perspectives. First of all, they have a low socio-economic status, determined by low levels of education and profession or employment. Moreover, their legal status is poor; the inequality of legal rights between the indigenous majority and ethnic minority groups is marked for ethnic minority groups originating from non-EC countries. Finally, the languages and cultures of the countries of origin of ethnic minority groups generally have a low status in the perception of the indigenous majority; this is especially true for ethnic minority groups originating from Islamic countries.

3. As far as the school population is concerned, and because of the demographic shifts mentioned under (1), the percentage of ethnic minority school children is higher than the percentage of ethnic minority groups in the total population of the country. When taking a closer look, however, one finds an overrepresentation of ethnic minority children in certain types of special education and an underrepresentation of ethnic minority children in higher types of secondary education (cf. Vallen & Stijnen, 1987 for the Netherlands, Hobin & Moulaert, 1986 for Flanders, and Röhr-Sendlmeier, 1986a for the FRG).

4. EC guidelines on the education of ethnic minority children were published in 1977 and came into force in 1981. Boos-Nünning et al. (1983) and Tosi (1984) discussed these guidelines from a historical perspective. The guidelines called for special attention and facilities for both L1 and L2 instruction. However, these guidelines did not result in a consensus about the weight of the two languages in the actual school curriculum. In fact, there is a top-down focus of dominant groups (e.g., national or local authorities, school principals, and majority language teachers) on L2 acquisition, most commonly in combination with a rather negative attitude towards L1 maintenance over time. On the other hand, there is a bottom-up focus of dominated groups (e.g., ethnic communities, parents, minority language teachers) on L1 acquisition and L1 maintenance over time.

5. Corresponding with the demographic shift mentioned under (1), a shift over time can also be observed in the arguments for L1 instruction for ethnic minority children. Initially, its importance derived from the prospect of return-migration to the country of origin. More recently, its importance for the development and maintenance of ethnic identity, for the purposes of intergenerational communication, and for L2 acquisition is being stressed. However, and in spite of good arguments for special L1 education, two main dilemmas arise from bilingual education for ethnic minority children only (cf. Extra, 1988a). Such programmes will inevitably lead to non-communal educational objectives for majority and minority children, and to a segregation of the two groups for at least part of the school curriculum. Moreover, pleas for bilingual education for only a part of the school population will, by definition, lead to a double learning task for some instead of all children.

6. L1 and L2 are most commonly taught by different teachers. In fact, bilingualism is seen as a desirable objective for ethnic minority children rather than as a necessary precondition for their teachers. A common characteristic of L2 teachers is that they have little, if any, command of the L1 of ethnic minority children. Typically, L1 teachers have a low L2 proficiency (although L1 teachers are usually more proficient in the two languages under consideration than L2 teachers), and a low team status within the school in terms of type of contract, number of lessons to be given, and participation in staff decisions. Moreover, ethnic minority group teachers rarely, if ever, teach majority group children.

7. Finally, there is a broad spectrum of variation in the proficiency of ethnic minority children in majority and minority languages. The common intergenerational pattern of language shift over time, observed in predominantly English speaking immigrant countries like the USA, Canada or Australia is as follows:

Interaction	Preferred language
parent to parent	minority language
parent to child	minority language
child to parent	minority + majority language
child to child	majority language

As yet, it is unclear to what degree such a pattern of language shift over time will apply to which ethnic minority groups in Western

Europe. However, although we will use the concepts of first language (L1) and second language (L2) to refer to the dominated minority language and the dominant majority language respectively, it must be borne in mind that such equations will become less obvious over time.

2. SECOND LANGUAGE ACQUISITION

2.1 *Determinants of second language acquisition*

The fact that language acquisition refers to a process of language change over time allows for two basic types of questions (cf. Extra & Vallen, 1988; Extra, 1988b): *how* are properties of the target language acquired and *how much time* does it take to acquire those properties? These questions relate to structural and temporal determinants of language acquisition respectively (see also the chapter by Strömqvist in this volume, for a discussion of determinants of language acquisition). Most commonly, the distinction between these two types of questions is only made implicitly in studies on L2 acquisition. This can be illustrated by two classic studies on adult L2 acquisition.

Klein and Dittmar (1979) developed a *Cumulative Syntactic Index* for describing the L2 German proficiency level of Italian and Spanish adult immigrants. This CSI was basically used as a tool for ordering the L2 learners in different 'stages' of acquisition (actually: different levels of accuracy, as the data were derived cross-sectionally). Moreover, Klein and Dittmar studied the correlation between L2 proficiency level (in terms of CSI) and various socio-biographical factors determining the degree of success of L2 acquisition. In fact, the CSI part of their study related to structural determinants of language acquisition, whereas the correlational part related to temporal determinants. Schumann (1978) is the author of the well-known case study of Alberto, a Puerto-Rican adult learner of English. In this longitudinal study, attention was paid to the development of interrogative, negative, and auxiliary structures over time, and to possible causes of Alberto's slow rate of learning. Schumann took the position that social and psychological 'distance' between Alberto and his surrounding Anglo environment were the primary factors impeding L2 development. Again, the developmental part of this study related to structural determinants of language acquisition, whereas the concept of 'distance' related to temporal determinants.

More recently, studies on structural *vs.* temporal determinants of L2 acquisition correspond with differences in research design as well. Structurally-oriented studies are often based on a microscopic analysis of longitudinal data on a small number of informants, resulting in a 'revival' of Leopold's (1949) classic case study approach. On the other hand, temporally-oriented studies are most commonly based on a correlational analysis of various L2 proficiency measures and non-linguistic variables of rather large groups of subjects.

Finally, it is interesting to note that temporal determinants have in fact received far more attention in studies on L2 acquisition by children or adults than in studies on L1 acquisition by children. The following factors emerge as possible explanations for these different biases:

- initial L1 acquisition takes place before and out of educational contexts; studies on L2 acquisition often focus upon the question of how education can promote language acquisition, which is most commonly taken to be a temporal question;
- far more individual variation has been observed in the rate and success of L2 acquisition than in the rate and success of L1 acquisition; L1 acquisition takes place in interaction with the primary social environment, whereas L2 acquisition can occur at different ages and under widely different conditions; large individual differences in the rate and success of L2 acquisition have led to a great interest in what makes a 'good' language learner, which – again – is most commonly taken to be a temporally determined question.

2.2 *Structural determinants*

Languages differ. This phenomenon can not only be confirmed by linguists, but is also a basic experience of all L2 learners. Until the early 1970s it was generally assumed that the structure of L2 acquisition was determined by the degree of contrast between L1 and L2. This equation of L1-L2 contrast and L2 learning characteristics was the breeding ground for the flourishing field of contrastive analysis (cf. Van Els et al., 1984). Contrastive analyses were oriented towards a description and explanation of specific similarities and differences between two (or more) languages. Such analyses were motivated and undertaken without a particular scientific interest in the actual course of L2 acquisition. Very few empirical studies were done on this process. Moreover, the concept of L2 acquisition was indissolubly related to L2 instruction. The basic premise was that L2 learners would simply learn what was taught and that they would not learn what was not taught. Deviations from the L2 norm were regarded as 'unfortunate' by-products of the learning process and they were labelled as 'errors' (see also Strömqvist, this volume).

Most commonly, these 'errors' were thought to derive from linguistic contrast between L1 and L2, and were therefore interpreted as interference phenomena. The following classical hypothesis of Weinreich (1953) was accepted unquestioningly for some twenty years: "The greater the difference between the two systems, i.e., the more numerous the mutually exclusive forms and patterns in each, the greater is the learning problem and the potential area of interference."

In fact, Weinreich formulated two hypotheses that need separate empirical confirmation: (a) the greater the distance between two languages, the larger the learning load, and (b) the greater the distance between two languages, the greater the chance of interference. The first hypothesis relates to temporal determinants of L2 acquisition, the second one to structural determinants. Moreover, the first hypothesis has a more intuitive appeal than the second one. When there are large differences between L1 and L2, the learner will have few possibilities for carrying over L1 characteristics into L2 use.

After 1970, in the wake of a growing scientific interest in the process of L1 acquisition, empirical studies started to focus upon the actual course of L2 acquisition by children or adults with different L1 backgrounds. These studies showed that equating L1-L2 contrast with L2 learning characteristics was based on false premises and that there were candidates other than L1 transfer or interference that could explain the course of L2 development. This is especially true in the case of widely different languages. All L2 learners are faced with the task of decomposing and building up a hierarchically structured system of target language skills and subskills, and when carrying out that task they rely, at least to a great extent, on universal principles. In fact, the structure of L2 acquisition is determined by a complex and interactive set of cognitive and linguistic factors. Many of these factors will relate to structural properties of the target language (e.g., the regularity, transparency, perceptual saliency or frequency of given elements in L2); these factors are commonly referred to as *intralingual* factors. Other factors will relate to structural properties of the source language (e.g., the transferability of L1 characteristics in L2 use) and are commonly referred to as *interlingual* factors.

More recently, the early approach of contrastive analysis and error analysis has been replaced by an approach in which the concept of communicative 'strategies' is central (cf. Faerch & Kasper, 1983; 1984). The basic question in this approach is how L2 learners overcome communicative problems caused by lack of standard target language means. Derived from various proposals in the literature, the following taxonomy of strategies can be presented.

1.   Avoidance strategies
2.   Achievement strategies
      2.1.   Verbal strategies
              2.1.1. Intralingual strategies
                     - Overextension
                     - Approximation
                     - Circumscription
                     - Innovation
              2.1.2. Interlingual strategies
                     - Transfer, Transliteration
                     - Code-switching, Borrowing
                     - Foreignizing
              2.1.3. Interactive strategies
                     - Direct appeal for assistance
                     - Indirect appeal for assistance
      2.2.   Non-verbal strategies
              - Gestures
              - Facial expressions

'Avoidance' strategies will lead to an underrepresentation or even non-occurrence of L2 elements (e.g., words, morphological endings, syntactic constructions) in a given data base. L2 learners may avoid the use of specific L2 elements, for various reasons. Most research in this area has focused upon learners' assumptions about lack of similarity between L1 and L2. Such assumptions may lead to the avoidance of L2 elements different from or similar to L1 elements. The first type of avoidance is commonly based on awareness of contrast between L1 and L2 that is conceived as 'difficult'. The opposite type of avoidance is based on 'disbelief' of actual linguistic similarity.

Intralingual strategies are based on an exploitation of already available knowledge of the target language (L2), whereas interlingual strategies are based on an exploitation of previous knowledge of other languages (including L1). Van Els et al. (1984) listed a number of factors that influence the probability of occurrence of L1 transfer to L2 use. Interactive strategies are most commonly based on native/non-native speaker interaction. They often surface as direct or indirect metalinguistic comments of non-native speakers like "What do you say?" or "I don't know whether X is the right word".

2.3 *Temporal determinants*

In section 2.1. it was already mentioned that large individual differences have been observed in the rate of L2 acquisition and the level of L2 proficiency ultimately reached. In cases of L2 acquisition by members of ethnic minority groups, this rate is largely determined by the 'distance' between minority and majority group members (cf. Schumann, 1978; Lalleman, 1986). The following survey gives an overview of various distance factors that have been considered in the literature.

Distance factor	Examples
Communicative distance	Type and degree of oral and written contact
Social distance	Social status, profession
Economic distance	Position on the labour market, income
Legal distance	Civil status, electoral status
Linguistic distance	Typological status, language prestige
Cultural distance	Cultural norms and values
Religious distance	Adherence, e.g., Islam *vs.* Christianity
Demographic distance	Group size (influenced by birth rate or migration surplus) and group cohesion (influenced by group spread and interethnic marriages)

The common assumption is that little distance between minority and majority group members will lead to relatively rapid acquisition of the majority language (L2). However, it is difficult to predict the exact weight of the various factors mentioned above. Moreover, reverse effects will show up. Rapid L2 acquisition may also reduce the distance between the two groups.

Temporally-oriented studies on L2 acquisition are most commonly based on correlational analyses of specific linguistic and non-linguistic variables. In studies on L2 acquisition by ethnic minority children, most attention has been paid to variables of language contact and socio-cultural orientation. Such factors were operationalized on the basis of more or less structured interviews, questionnaires, or attitude scales. The language of investigation in these studies was most commonly the majority language, rarely the minority language. Informants were the children themselves, their parents and/or classroom teachers.

The obvious importance of L2 contact for the success of L2 acquisition does *not* imply that within the educational context of elementary schools an L2-only approach for ethnic minority children would yield the best results in terms of L2-oriented educational achievement. Actually, such "submersion" programmes have resulted in widespread academic failure among ethnic minority children. This failure has been observed in various countries where a dominant majority language was taught to dominated minority children, e.g., in English-only programmes for Hispanic children in the USA or in Swedish-only programmes for Finnish children in Sweden (cf. Skutnabb-Kangas, 1983) as well as in majority language oriented programmes in EC countries.

Two arguments in support of upgrading the status of ethnic minority children's L1 in at least the initial stages of the school curriculum were derived from these negative experiences:

1. ethnic minority children's motivation for L2 acquisition will increase, if the school makes room for their linguistic and cultural backgrounds;
2. the level of L2 proficiency that ethnic minority children attain is partially a function of the level of L1 proficiency that these children have acquired at the time when intensive exposure to L2 begins.

Cummins (1979) calls the second hypothesis the 'interdependency' hypothesis. Moreover, with respect to defining 'success' of L2 acquisition, Cummins (1980) made a distinction between "basic interpersonal communicative skills" (BICS) and "cognitive academic language proficiency" (CALP). BICS was thought to relate primarily to surface fluency in social talk, CALP to decontextualized literacy and metalinguistic awareness. In Cummins's opinion, it would take much more time to acquire CALP than to acquire BICS. Because there were problems in clearly operationalizing and distinguishing between these two aspects of L2 proficiency, Cummins (1983) reformulated his dichotomy in terms of a model with two dimensions, each based on a continuum: context-embedded *vs.* context-reduced communication, and cognitively demanding *vs.* undemanding tasks. Apart from new ambiguities in defining these different dimensions, it remains unclear in which contexts they are used and how they are acquired (cf. Noack, 1987). Cummins's ideas, however, played an important role in the topic discussed in the following section.

3. DIDACTIC APPROACHES AND MODELS OF LANGUAGE TEACHING

Schools, individual teachers, and governmental authorities (although so far mostly tacitly) adopt different theoretical and didactic stances regarding language teaching in multilingual settings.

3.1 Didactic approaches

According to Trudgill (1983), it is possible to distinguish three different points of view on language teaching of children whose mother tongue or home language (L1) is different from the majority language or school language (L2). In this respect it does not matter whether L1 is an indigenous or a non-indigenous language variety.

The first approach can be described as leaving L1 'out in the cold' or even eliminating L1. In this approach, traditionally rather common in Western Europe, teachers prevent the child from speaking his L1 at school. L1 features are commented on and corrected as much as possible. The prestige variety, in most cases the standard language of the country of residence, is the exclusive medium of instruction and target language. In the most extreme version of this approach, L1 is considered as an inferior language or even as no language at all; this has negative influences on the cognitive level of the children as well. The logical consequence of such a 'deficit-inspired' attitude is L1 rejection in the classroom and compensatory monolingual L2 education as a didactic solution (cf., e.g., Bereiter & Engelmann, 1966). Linguists and many others involved in L2 acquisition and teaching believe this approach to be wrong for a number of linguistic, psychological, social, and, perhaps most importantly, practical reasons. Trudgill (1983, p. 74) stated: "It is wrong because it does not and it will not work." History has clearly shown that if minority children have difficulties in school because their L2 proficiency is insufficient, the solution cannot be found in eliminating their L1.

The second approach aims at linking up L1 and L2. In the literature it has often been called the bidialectal or bilingual approach (though in our opinion, this is at least partly a misconception). This viewpoint has been adopted by many linguists who support Labov's difference-hypothesis concerning language variation, and by a much smaller group of educationalists. According to this point of view, individuals have a natural right to continue using L1 at home or with friends and in many circumstances and specific lessons at school. But this approach also advocates that the primary and ultimate goal of language education is that minority language speakers are taught the majority language as a school language, because it is the most important language of social mobility in the country of residence. Minority and majority languages are treated as distinct entities and the differences between them are illustrated, discussed and pointed out as interesting facts. The role of L1 in education is primarily considered as a helpful tool for accomplishing the transition from L1 to L2. Therefore, L1 should not be treated as an inferior language, but as a medium for introducing children into school and for facilitating L2 acquisition. Moreover, in most cases L1 is used and receives attention in the first years of schooling, but ultimately there is only room for L2.

The third approach aims at stimulating and maintaining L1 at school. It is an emancipatory point of view based on the concept that minority language varieties have both an intrinsic and social value. This position implies an upgrading of L1 in the classroom, not only in the initial stages of education but during the whole course of the school curriculum. Within this conception both L1 and L2 are to be taught at school in such a way that at the end of their school career children have a functional competence in two languages. Furthermore, a threshold level of L1 proficiency is considered to be a necessary condition for attaining sufficient L2 proficiency. This approach appears to be obtaining increasing support from linguists and psychologists, but not from educationalists, teachers, and policy makers.

In our opinion, the present situation could be improved if governments would provide a well considered but flexible framework for both first and second language teaching, based on a clear and consistent educational and language policy. Such a policy should be inspired by recent scientific findings of linguists and educationalists, on the one hand and, on the other hand, by a realistic estimation of the social conditions and possibilities for change in the country in question. School boards should adapt this framework to the specific situation in their schools, and present their ideas and decisions in annual curriculum plans. Finally, individual teachers should implement these plans within the specific conditions of their own classrooms.

However, most West European countries have hardly begun to develop a consistent policy and legislation for first and second language teaching. The status of the respective national or standard languages seems to be so high or self-evident that formulating an educational policy on the basis of insights into language diversity is not accorded any priority, or is even prohibited. It cannot be expected that school boards and individual teachers alone will develop approaches that take into account all the conditions mentioned above. As long as the present unsatisfactory situation continues, teachers will remain in doubt about their daily language teaching practice. Experts within this field should cooperate with policy makers to develop an adequate educational policy on both first and second language teaching.

3.2 Models of language teaching

In relation to the didactic approaches mentioned above, four different models for language teaching in multilingual settings can be distinguished (see also Extra & Vermeer, 1984; Extra & Verhoeven, 1985). Figure 1 gives an overview of the main differences between these models.

Figure 1: Four basic models for language teaching of minorities
Horizontal axis: stage of education (class 1-n)
Vertical axis: amount of attention paid to L1 and/or L2

Monolingual Education	A L1 Segregation	B L2 Assimilation
Bilingual Education	C L2 / L1 Transition	D L2 / L1 Maintenance

Model A (segregation) and model B (assimilation) aim at monolingual education, models C and D (transition and maintenance, respectively) at bilingual education.

Within a segregation programme only the minority language (L1) functions as a school subject and as medium of instruction; children are not taught the majority language (L2). In fact, this language model is primarily found in educational programmes oriented towards the separation of ethnic minority children, anticipating upon their return to their country of origin. The reverse holds for model B (assimilation): only L2 is allowed and there is no place for L1. Within this model a distinction should be made between a *submersion* and an *immersion* approach (cf. Skutnabb-Kangas, 1982; Belke, 1986).

In a submersion programme, minority children who speak a low-status L1 are forced to accept education in a high-status L2, which is the native language of most of their classmates and teachers. Most commonly, the teacher has no proficiency in the minority language. The L2 submersion model is most frequently used in Western Europe, especially in educational settings with relatively low concentrations of ethnic minority children.

In an immersion programme, majority children who speak a high-status language variety are voluntarily taught by means of a minority language which is a foreign language for all children in the classroom. The teacher speaks both languages and there is no danger of the majority language being substituted for the minority language – an additive language acquisition context (Lambert, 1978). In Canada, immersion programmes have been successful for English speaking students accepting a French immersion teaching condition. As far as we know, no immersion programmes have been carried out in the Netherlands, Flanders and the FRG for ethnic minority children – only submersion programmes.

In a transitional L1/L2 model, L1 is mainly used to facilitate a pedagogically responsible transition from L1 to L2 in education. Minority languages are primarily considered as media for introducing minority children into the majority middle class school system, especially in the light of L2 acquisition in the first years of elementary schooling. If possible, education starts with L1; L2 is usually introduced simultaneously or somewhat later. In most cases L1 is not taught as a school subject within the regular curriculum, but is mainly used as a medium of instruction whenever necessary and possible. Only a few lessons of L1 instruction are given per week and only minority children participate. After a relatively short period the L1/L2 approach is replaced by a 'second language only' approach, because L2 proficiency is the ultimate and primary goal of education. The transitional model is often advocated in educational settings with relatively high concentrations of minority language speakers. Also, some parents of minority children prefer such an approach.

Within a maintenance or language shelter model, minority children participate in a bilingual programme in which from the start to the end of the school curriculum both L1 and L2 function as school subjects and are used as a medium of instruction. The maintenance model is frequently advocated by minority groups themselves and by those linguists and psychologists who see the maintenance and development of L1 either as a goal in itself or as a necessary condition for successful L2 acquisition. Within the Netherlands, Flanders and the FRG, the Dutch Frisians are the only language minority group that have succeeded in turning this demand into effective legislation (cf. Extra, 1988c).

During the last ten years there has been a lively debate about the advantages and disadvantages of monolingual versus bilingual education. From these discussions it emerged that it is much clearer what is meant by monolingual than by bilingual education. Advocates of the first option always plea for monolingual L2 education (assimilation in terms of submersion), never about monolingual L1 education. With respect to bilingual education, an explicit choice between model C (transition) and model D (maintenance) is insufficiently recognized and even less frequently made.

Within the framework of the 1977 EC guidelines on the education of ethnic minority children, all member states are advised to provide L2 instruction in a way that takes into account the children's specific conditions and needs. Moreover, the member states should take measures to ensure adequate training of L2 teachers and, in coordination with the regular educational programme, to facilitate education in the languages and cultures of the countries of origin.

In the next three sections we will discuss basic aspects of Dutch, Flemish and German language education policy in the light of both the EC guidelines and the four models of language teaching mentioned. We will also give a short state-wise overview of a number of studies on L2 acquisition, especially those studies taking into account the role of L1 with respect to L2 acquisition.

4. THE NETHERLANDS

4.1 Legislation and facilities

Dutch education is primarily based on freedom of denomination, according to Article 23 of the Constitution. This implies the right of any individual or group of individuals to found a school, appoint a school board and teachers, and organize instruction according to a particular denomination, if at least 50 potential pupils for such a school can be recruited and maintained. Any school can expect full financial support from the government if it operates within the legal margins of, e.g., the number and type of subjects to be taught, teacher qualifications, and examination standards. In this way and over many decades, Catholic, Protestant and nondenominational schools were founded and given government support. Most recently, the first Islamic and Hindustani schools have been added to this pluriform system on the basis of the same constitutional right, though this development has been received rather reluctantly by both local and national authorities.

The fact that in educational policy the Netherlands is conceived of as a multi-ethnic and multilingual society, has led to a number of legislative measures and facilities in this respect since 1980 (see the chapter of Eldering in this volume, for an extensive overview). In the 1960s and 1970s, Dutch governmental policy was unclear and mainly oriented to the return of recent immigrant groups to their countries of origin; by definition, all measures had a temporary character (Kroon & Vallen, 1989). In the early 1980s, two important governmental reports and a number of governmental circulars were published in which the permanent character of recent immigration was recognized (e.g., Ministerie van Onderwijs & Wetenschappen, [Ministry of Education and Science] 1981; Ministerie van Binnenlandse Zaken, [Ministry of Home Affairs] 1983). In the 1981 document of the Ministry of Education and Science three major topics related to language diversity and language teaching:
- Education should contribute to eliminating the disadvantaged position of ethnic minority groups in society and education by means of special facilities for teaching Dutch as a second language;
- Education should take into account the identity of ethnic minority groups by means of teaching the language and culture of their countries of origin;
- Education should contribute to the development of a multi-ethnic society by means of intercultural education.

Since the publication of the 1981 policy document, a number of governmental notes and circulars have paid attention to education in first language and culture and intercultural education, but no governmental publication has been devoted to second language teaching. Moreover, the conceptual change of Dutch policy on ethnic minority groups has led to an important and central renewal in the most recent version of the Elementary Education Act of 1985. Article 9, Paragraph 3 states: "Education takes as a point of departure that pupils grow up in a multicultural society." Meanwhile a similar article came into existence in the Secondary Education Act.

In spite of the language diversity in the Netherlands in both indigenous and non-indigenous minority groups, only a few sections in Dutch educational legislation deal with language teaching in a multilingual society (cf. Vallen & Stijnen, 1987). Regulations for indigenous minority languages (dialects and Frisian) have already been in existence for a relatively long period of time and have, for instance, led to Frisian having the relatively advantageous position of being a mandatory school subject in all elementary schools in the province of Friesland since 1980.

The most recent version of the Dutch Elementary Education Act dates from 1980 and came into force in 1985. In order to facilitate the transition and adaptation to Dutch education, the law allows the languages of the countries of origin of ethnic minority pupils to be used as a medium of instruction (cf. Eldering in this volume). These language varieties may also be taught as an optional school subject, but only under certain restrictive conditions:

- The proper school authorities may decide to make instruction in the language and culture of the country of origin part of the curriculum, but this option does not exist for all ethnic minority children (for curious reasons it does not, for instance, for Chinese, Surinamese, and Antillean children).
- Classes with this type of instruction may also be attended by pupils from other schools, if this type of instruction is unavailable at their schools.
- Ethnic minority children are only required to attend instruction in the language and culture of their country of origin, if their parents wish them to do so.
- Of the time spent on this type of instruction (with a maximum of 5 hours per week), at most 2.5 hours are considered to be part of the minimum number of hours of instruction required for elementary school pupils per week (Vallen & Stijnen, 1987).

There are a number of differences in the Elementary Education Act's treatment of Frisian as an indigenous minority language on the one hand, and its treatment of non-indigenous minority languages on the other (cf. Extra, 1988c). These differences seem to be based ultimately upon political rather than psychological, linguistic or educational criteria. Although there are many more speakers of ethnic minority languages than speakers of Frisian, and although there is much more empirical evidence on educational problems in the former case, only Frisian has achieved the status of a mandatory school subject.

In secondary education there are even more restrictions on L1 instruction of ethnic minority children than in elementary education (cf. Extra, 1986). The first legislation was not enacted until 1987. Apart from restrictions similar to those in elementary schools, so far only Turkish and Moroccan pupils can take L1 lessons at secondary level as a non-mandatory school subject. The number of hours permitted and opportunities for examination are still under discussion.

Although the Ministry of Education and Science declared L2 instruction to be an issue of central importance in its 1981 policy plan, there is still no legislation on this. In all elementary schools, complex counts take place every year, in which individual pupils are 'weighted' on the basis of their social and ethnic backgrounds. Ethnic minority children with a low socio-economic status count for 1.9, while a modal Dutch pupil counts for 1. The total score of a school determines the number of teaching hours of a school, and indirectly the number of teachers working in that particular year (see the chapter by Eldering in this volume). However, school boards are autonomous in deciding for what purposes these teaching hours are used. Therefore, hours 'earned' by ethnic minority children are not always spent on them. As far as Dutch as a second language is taught, this generally takes place in small groups separated from the other classmates. However, for the time being most ethnic minority children in elementary schools attend regular Dutch classes and obtain language instruction within a submersion assimilation model.

4.2 *Studies on second language acquisition*
Although the number of studies on L2 acquisition by ethnic minority children in the Netherlands has increased substantially during the last decade, they still form a modest proportion of the Dutch research on ethnic minority groups at large. Some major reasons for this were given by Extra and Vallen (1988). So far, most studies have concentrated on the acquisition of L2 Dutch by Turkish and Moroccan children. Little has been done on adult second language acquisition or on other ethnic groups. Various approaches have been chosen with respect to period of observation (longitudinal *vs.* cross-sectional research), number of informants (case-studies *vs.* larger groups of subjects), and type of data (natural observations *vs.* elicited data and tests). Extra and Vallen (1985, 1988) and Extra, Van Hout and Vallen (1987) have given an overview of Dutch second language acquisition research and presented the outcomes of a number of projects (cf. also

Appel, 1986). Only a small number of projects have provided results on the relationship between L1 and L2 acquisition of ethnic minority children. Given the focus of this volume, in this section we will restrict ourselves to the latter type of projects.

In a longitudinal study, Appel (1984) compared the acquisition of Dutch by 24 Turkish and Moroccan children (age 6-12) participating in an experimental transitional bilingual programme under the auspices of the EC, in which a considerable amount of L1 instruction was given in the initial stages of the school curriculum, with the results of research on the L2 acquisition of 33 Turkish and Moroccan children in ordinary (submersion) school classes. He concluded that L1 teaching did not harm or hinder L2 acquisition, even although less time was spent on L2 instruction in the experimental programme. According to Appel, L1 instruction might even stimulate and create conditions facilitating L2 acquisition. Moreover, from the evaluative study by Boos-Nünning et al. (1983) of the Leiden experiment it emerged that children, parents and teachers were rather positive about the experimental approach. This held for members of both majority and minority groups.

Teunissen (1986) did a similar study on the effects of an experimental bilingual-bicultural educational programme for Turkish and Moroccan children in the first and second grades of elementary schooling in the city of Enschede. However, whereas the Leiden study focused upon recently immigrated children, the Enschede study was carried out with children born in the Netherlands. The experimental group of Turkish children was compared with a control group participating in a monolingual-monocultural submersion programme on the basis of a number of language tests and tests on other school subjects. In a few cases the experimental group had better scores (not only on language tests); in most cases, however, the scores of the two groups were similar. On the basis of a confrontation of the experimental and control groups with paired pictures of Dutch and Turkish stereotypes, it was also observed that the experimental group had developed a more 'balanced' attitude towards the two respective cultures than the control group. Teunissen's results point in the same direction as those of Appel. His main conclusion was that simultaneous bilingual-bicultural programmes for young ethnic minority children would represent a viable solution for many educational problems.

Verhoeven (1987) compared the results of literacy acquisition in an L2 submersion context with those of literacy acquisition in two transitional programmes. About 100 Turkish and 40 Dutch children took part in his study. In addition, the results of two small-scale experiments in transitional literacy instruction were examined. Compared with the children in the submersion programme, the children in the transitional classes tended to obtain better literacy results in L1, whereas the L2 literacy results of the two groups were very similar. Moreover, the transitional approach tended to encourage a more positive orientation towards ethnic background and a stronger appreciation of literacy in general. The latter result was also regarded as evidence for the suitability of a transitional approach.

Similar results were reported in earlier studies on indigenous minority children with a non-standard Dutch background; time spent on L1 in education (and consequently a smaller amount of time spent on learning the L2 majority language) did not harm the standard Dutch proficiency level. Wijnstra (1976; 1980) demonstrated that this was also true for Frisian children; Kuijper et al. (1983) demonstrated this for children who spoke Limburg dialect.

Finally, it should be pointed out that the above-mentioned results of L1/L2 research stem from projects with a highly experimental status. Van den Berg-Eldering (1986) has stated that the long-term effects of such programmes should be studied more thoroughly. As yet, it is unclear whether there are differences in Dutch L2 proficiency between ethnic minority children who have or have not received L1 instruction within the provisions of current legislation. However, the type of L1 instruction stipulated in the legislation is not functioning optimally in the Netherlands in many schools and has therefore been under constant review.

5. FLANDERS

5.1 Legislation and facilities

More than ten years after the acceptance of the EC guidelines mentioned in section 1 above, neither the central Belgian government nor the Flemish authorities have succeeded in turning these guidelines into structural legislation. Although there is in fact no legislative basis for L1 or L2 instruction for ethnic minority children in Flanders, the government has published a number of circulars which give possibilities for these types of instruction and allow for financial support of experiments on this under certain, mostly restrictive, conditions (see also Roosens's contribution in this volume).

Compared with the Netherlands, there are some important differ-

ences with respect to public and scientific attention to ethnic minority issues. In the Netherlands, politicians frequently participate in the
public debate about such issues; in Belgium/Flanders this is rare. At
both the national and the Flemish level there is still no official and
public policy document dealing with the education of ethnic minority groups (the first document on ethnic minority education was due
to be published in the autumn of 1988). One reason for this might be
that ethnic minority groups in Belgium are concentrated in a few
areas and in Brussels. Therefore, their problems might be considered
more as regional or local issues than as an issue deserving national
attention.

The few research projects and other work to introduce educational
innovations for L1 and L2 instruction of ethnic minority children in
Flanders were mainly initiated by social scientists, especially anthropologists and psychologists (e.g., Roosens 1972; 1982). Jaspaert and
Vallen (1986) suggested that the absence of Flemish linguists in this
domain might stem from their traditional and strong involvement
with the already complex indigenous multilingual situation; perhaps
it cannot be expected that a nation carrying a heavy burden of language frustration for so many centuries would have a strong interest
in the language problems of newly arrived immigrant citizens. Nevertheless, Flemish linguists with their sensitivity to issues of language and inequality could make an important contribution to
research on ethnic minority language and education.

Recent overviews of facilities for L1 and L2 instruction for ethnic
minority children in Flanders have been given by Hobin and Moulaert (1986) and Degraeve (1988). At most Flemish schools ethnic
minority children participate in L2 submersion programmes. However, elementary schools with a minimum of ten ethnic minority
children are allowed to set up additional intensive L2 instruction
within the regular school curriculum for a maximum of three hours
per week, but only if these children have had less than three years of
Flemish elementary education. Additional (unemployed) teachers
(for instance, for intensive L2 instruction), can also be provided on
the basis of the B.T.K. (Bijzonder Tijdelijk Kader) system. Within this
latter regulation, facilities are only given to schools with more than
30 per cent ethnic minority children.

In Flanders only Dutch is the official language of instruction in education. Therefore, L1 instruction was originally given outside the
regular school curriculum. However, since the early 1980s specific
regulations have made it possible for other languages to be used in

elementary education. Facilities for L1 instruction (as well as multi-cultural activities) within the regular curriculum are provided by the framework of 'Elkaar Ontmoetend Onderwijs' (EOO), an experimental, relatively short-term programme of action which started in 1982-1983 under the auspices of the Belgian Ministry of Education. The EOO programme was based on the experiences with the EC pilot projects carried out in the Province of Limburg during the period 1976-1982. The EOO experiment was originally set up for three years, but was extended and modified in 1985. In 1988, it has been extended for another three-year period. Generally speaking, there are four options for L1 instruction in elementary (and nursery) education within the most recent proposals for the EOO framework:
- ethnic minority children have four hours of L1 instruction per week in the first grade of elementary education (and in nursery school), three hours in the second grade, and two hours in the third grade;
- ethnic minority children have a maximum of 18 hours monthly of L1 instruction during the total period of elementary education (six years), with a maximum of four and a minimum of two hours per week;
- the bilingual-bicultural experiment of Foyer Brussels, which allows a maximum of 14 hours of L1 instruction per week in the first grade of elementary education (and in nursery school) and twelve hours in the second grade. In higher grades the first option has to be chosen;
- in nursery classes with more than 70 per cent ethnic minority children speaking the same L1, a maximum of ten hours of instruction in L1 per week is allowed. For the other ethnic minority children in those classes the first model has to be used.

Most schools participating in the EOO experiment prefer the first option. All L1 teachers are appointed and paid by the authorities in their countries of origin, in contrast with the situation in the Netherlands where all L1 teachers work under the jurisdiction of, and are paid by the Dutch government.

Apart from the three national regulations mentioned above, there are a number of local and regional initiatives that aim to improve the educational situation of ethnic minority children, especially in cities and regions with high concentrations of ethnic minority groups (e.g., Antwerp, Gent, and Brussels, and the Province of Limburg).

Summarizing the Flemish situation, it has to be concluded that all measures concerning L1 and L2 instruction have a temporary character and are very unclear about facilities and conditions (see Roosens in this volume). Not surprisingly, this is a source of frustration for many teachers and school boards.

5.2 Studies on second language acquisition

As mentioned before, little substantial research has been carried out in Flanders. Some work has been done at Antwerp University and more recently (on L2 reading proficiency) at the Free University of Brussels by van de Craen and Humblet. Apart from a number of contemplative contributions (e.g., Verdoodt, 1977; van Molle & Rosso, 1978) and numerous internal papers, nearly all publications relate to the education of ethnic minority children in elementary schools. This holds especially for the experiments with bicultural education in the Province of Limburg (EG-Pilootexperiment, 1982; Haesendonckx, 1980) and the Foyer Project in Brussels (e.g., Foyer, 1983, Foyer-Stuurgroep, 1985; 1986). Further information on L2 acquisition of ethnic minority children in Flanders was given by Seghers and van den Broeck (1978), Rosiers and Moors (1979a,b), Gailly and Leman (1982), Spoelders et al. (1985), and Heyerick (1985). Other Flemish publications on ethnic minority issues have given a general overview in which linguistic considerations emerged only incidently (e.g., Martens & Moulaert, 1985). The same holds for a number of extensive studies on specific ethnic groups (e.g., Leman, 1982; Cammaert, 1985).

With respect to the relationship between L1 and L2 proficiency, some evaluative findings of the EC pilot project in Genk (Limburg) and the Foyer project (Brussels) should be mentioned. Whereas the evaluation of Boos-Nünning et al. (1983) of the Genk project was quite unclear in this respect, test results of Haesendonckx (1980) showed that a substantial amount of attention for L1 in the participating schools had no negative consequences for the children's L2 proficiency. Spoelders et al. (1985), Smeekens and de Smedt (1987) and Leman (1987) reported on the transitional bicultural Foyer project. L1 played a major role (third option, cf. section 5.1.) especially in nursery school and the first two grades of elementary school. Evaluative studies of the language-oriented components of the Foyer model by Lemmens and Jaspaert (1987), Jaspaert and Lemmens (1989), and Leman (1987) did not show substantial differences in L2 proficiency between the Foyer children and a control group of children participating in regular Brussels schools. This last conclusion is especially interesting, because in the Brussels context most ethnic minority children learn Dutch not as a second but rather as a third language. At home they speak their native language, outside their families they are most commonly socialized in French, and at school they learn Dutch. In sum, the Flemish bicultural experiments provide similar results about the relationship between L1 and L2 acquisition as the Dutch experiments in Leiden and Enschede.

6. FEDERAL REPUBLIC OF GERMANY

6.1 Legislation and facilities
In the same year (1981) that the Dutch government recognized that the Netherlands is a multicultural society, the German government stated that the FRG is not an immigrant country (Belke et al., 1986). Obviously, this governmental position has an impact on ethnic minority issues in the FRG. For a general discussion of educational policy on ethnic minority children in the FRG we refer to the chapter by Boos-Nünning and Hohmann in this volume.
Educational policy on L1/L2 teaching of ethnic minority children in the FRG differs between the *Bundesländer*, because each state has autonomy in educational legislation. Common concepts have been pursued in various 'recommendations' at conferences of the ministers of culture (*KMK-Empfehlungen*). Röhr-Sendlmeier (1986a) has given an annotated survey of these recommendations since 1952. The status of L1 education in the various states was discussed in a synopsis of KMK resolutions in *Deutsch Lernen* 1 (1983). In 1983, the following regulations on L1 education existed (cf. Damanakis, 1983):

State	Hours p.week	German supervision/ payment	L1 compulsory subject	Minimum of particip.
Baden-Württemberg	5-8	no	no	12
Bayern	5	yes	no	12
Berlin	5-8	no	no	–
Bremen	5	no	no	–
Hamburg	4-6	no	no	–
Hessen	3-5	yes	yes	12
Niedersachsen	5	yes	no	8
Nordrheinl.Westfalen	5	yes	no	15
Rheinland-Pfalz	5	yes	no	8
Saarland	5	no	no	15
Schleswig-Holstein	5	no	no	–

In some states L1 curriculum development and L1 teacher supply and payment are the responsibilities of German authorities, whereas in other states these responsibilities are left to the embassies of the countries of origin, often in extra-curricular hours.

There is a major controversy about the issue of 'national' *vs.* 'regular' classes for ethnic minority children. In national classes ethnic minority children are segregated from German children and other ethnic minority children on the basis of a specific L1 background, whereas in regular classes ethnic minority children are taught together with German children of a similar age level. The 1971 KMK called segregated national classes or schools illegitimate and made a strong plea for regular education. In practice, however, the different states kept pursuing different goals, focusing upon integration of ethnic minority children in the German school system, remigration to the country of origin (especially in Bayern and Baden-Württemberg), or a more or less ambivalent combination of both. Integration was aimed at by education in 'preparatory' classes which might take some years. In these classes part of the curriculum was given in separate instruction (especially instruction in L2 German and ethnic group language instruction), whereas other subjects were taught in 'integrated' classes (especially music, gymnastics, handicrafts, and other general subjects). One of the problems of these 'preparatory' classes was that they could actually keep ethnic minority children separated from their German peers for many years.

The 1977 KMK recommendations showed a change of strategy with respect to the controversy of national *vs.* regular classes: "Es geht darum, die ausländischen Schüler zu befähigen, die deutsche Sprache zu erlernen, und die deutschen Schulabschlüsse zu erreichen sowie die Kenntnisse in der Muttersprache zu erhalten und zu erweitern. Gleichzeitig sollen die Bildungsmassnahmen einen Beitrag zur sozialen Eingliederung der ausländischen Schüler für die Dauer des Aufenthaltes in der Bundesrepublik Deutschland leisten. Ausserdem dienen sie der Erhaltung ihrer sprachlichen und kulturellen Identität" (page 3).

The importance of both L1 and L2 education was now taken into account. As regards L1 education, the goal of developing a cultural identity took over the former goal of preparing for remigration. This last goal was central to the Bayern and Baden-Württemberg concept of national classes and has been severely criticized (cf., e.g., Boos-Nünning, 1981; 1983a). Most of the criticism was based on ideological rather than empirical grounds. However, Oomen-Welke (1985) gave a detailed ethnographic report on national Turkish and Greek elementary classes in Baden-Württemberg, where L2 was taught for 6-7 hours a week by German teachers. Oomen-Welke observed that the classes were well supplied in terms of equipment and learning materials, the L2 proficiency level of L1 teachers was good, there was good pupil attendance, discipline and role-bound behaviour of girls and boys, and an achievement-oriented attitude of both teachers, pupils and parents towards this type of 'national' education. Moreover, less stigmatization based on poor L2 proficiency was observed than in regular classes. However, one main problem, inherent to segregated instruction remained unsolved. Exchange of experiences between minority and majority peer groups is a crucial condition for the development of interethnic understanding and solidarity, and for the development of L2 competence (see also Molfenter, 1986). Even in 'national' classes with dedicated L1 and L2 teachers, this lack of exchange can hardly be compensated for. Viewed from this perspective, national classes cannot be a bicultural alternative for regular classes, because bicultural education can only flourish in interaction between children from different linguistic and cultural backgrounds. Apart from affirmative legislation in rather conservative states like Bayern and Baden-Württemberg, the pressure for L1 education stems primarily from concerned ethnic minority groups. The well-known *Memorandum zum Muttersprachlichen Unterricht in der BRD* (cf. *Deutsch Lernen* 1, 1983) was preponderantly edited by ethnic minority associations from various source countries. This Memorandum presented arguments and goals for bilingual education, and for special curriculum development and teacher training. Along similar lines, Damanakis (1983) and Boos-Nünning (1983b) made pleas for L1 education. Critical comments upon the Memorandum were given by Götze (1983) and Liebe-Harkort (1983).

The Greek community in the FRG is particularly in favour of Greek national schools or at least classes (cf. Zografou, 1981). Greek parents are commonly organized in Greek associations which strongly pursue these goals. Damanakis (1987) studied the educational viewpoints of the parents of Greek children. These parents have high aspirations regarding the schooling of their children. They want their children to get good marks at German schools and to follow higher types of secondary education, preferably in Greece. Moreover, they are most commonly in favour of national classes in which L1 is both a subject and an intermediate language, L2 is a separate subject, and music and handicrafts are offered in integrated classes with German children. These needs not only stem from the aspiration of higher education in Greece, but also from the fear of alienation from the Greek language and culture, from the desire of future remigration, and from the generally low educational success of ethnic minority children in regular German classes.

The preference for national classes actually shows that the 'regular' school system has failed on three counts: to integrate ethnic minority children in mainstream education, to solve their educational problems, and to stimulate their aspirations.

6.2 Studies on second language acquisition

Many studies on the acquisition of L2 German by ethnic minority children link up with the traditional approach of contrastive analysis and error analysis (cf. Kuhs, 1987). Given this linkage, it is no surprise that in most of these studies, source language related transfer was thought to be a prime characteristic of L2 development (cf., e.g., Meyer-Ingwersen et al., 1977).

Some studies focused exclusively upon the oral or written L2 German of ethnic minority children from one particular L1 background (often Turkish or Serbo-Croatian), whereas other studies took a comparative perspective by also taking into account:

1. the L2 German of other ethnic minority children with a different L1 background (e.g. Pfaff, 1980);
2. the ethnic group language (L1) use of the same ethnic minority children (e.g. Stölting et al., 1980; Baur, 1986);
3. the L1 German of German children (e.g. Thieroff, 1986; Apeltauer, 1987).

Many developmental characteristics were observed that were common to all children learning German as L1 or L2, especially in type (1) and type (3) studies. A survey of some of these studies was given by Röhr-Sendlmeier (1986b). Such common developmental characteristics indicate that universal principles related to target language guide the process of L2 acquisition rather than principles of transfer related to source language (see also section 2.2). Insofar as evidence of L1 influence in L2 use could be found, it showed up more in the domains of lexicon and phonology than in those of syntax or morphology.

Most studies focused upon descriptions of utterance level, whereas only a few studies took conversational and/or interactional dimensions into account. Moreover, most studies had a cross-sectional rather than a longitudinal design. Here, we only mention two studies, focusing upon structural and temporal determinants of L2 acquisition respectively.

Pienemann (1981) did a longitudinal case study on the initial acquisition (during one year) of L2 German by three eight-year-old Italian girls. The focus of the study was on methodological aspects of L2 acquisition research, illustrated by an analysis of order of acquisition of syntactic categories in affirmative sentences. Pienemann found many developmental features that were independent of L1 background and age of the L2 learners; the data were compared with those on other child and adult learners of German.

Röhr-Sendlmeier (1985) did a study on elicited L2 use of 26 Turkish first and second grade children at two points of measurement (nine-month interval). The same receptive and productive tests were used in a control study of 19 German children of similar age and socio-economic status. Moreover, Röhr-Sendlmeier conducted standardized interviews (in German) with the Turkish children, their parents, and their teachers. The factors that determined L2 learning success were the degree and length of contact with native German (both oral and written German, used by both children and adults, within and outside school contexts), the level of education and L2 proficiency of the children's parents, and the children's attitudes towards their stay in the FRG. However, no statistical correlation was found between the children's L2 proficiency level and their orientation towards Turkish-Islamic culture, family support of educational achievement, housing conditions, or family connections with Turkey.

With respect to L2 acquisition in an educational context, it took some time before the concept of 'Deutsch als Zweitsprache' became generally accepted in the field of L2 German instruction. Originally, in conformity with the more established field of professional training for the teaching of German abroad, 'Deutsch als Fremdsprache' was used for denoting the field of L2 instruction, and many curricular concepts were borrowed from the discipline of foreign language teaching (cf. Pienemann, 1981).

Hohmann (1976) made an early attempt to fulfil the needs of German teachers of ethnic minority children; a third reprint of the book he edited appeared in 1980. One of its main contributions was written by Reich (1976), who discussed goals and methods of L2 instruction, and procedures for the evaluation of L2 textbooks. Neumann and Reich (1977) published an annotated survey of themes that German teachers of Turkish children should be familiar with; however, their treatment of L2 learning problems was heavily based on contrastive analysis rather than on empirical data on L2 development. More recently, Rückert (1985) and Ucar (1984) discussed a number of shortcomings in the preparation of professional L2 teachers.

Part of the L2 curriculum is the availability of valid tests for measuring the level of L2 proficiency in various stages of the school career. Luchtenberg (1984) gave a detailed report on the quality of ten language proficiency tests for ethnic minority children; eight tests related to L2 proficiency, whereas two tests related to both L1 and L2 proficiency. Large variation was observed in target groups, test objectives, test contents, test methods, test duration, and test instruction. Little attention was given to pupils' self-evaluation of L2 proficiency, and to the measurement of communicative competence and cultural background knowledge (*Landeskunde*). Luchtenberg made an urgent plea for the development of better tests for measuring both L1 and L2 proficiency; moreover, such tests should derive from specified educational objectives rather than vice versa.

7. DISCUSSION AND RECOMMENDATIONS

Most ethnic minority children in the three countries discussed participate in L2 submersion programmes and most educational facilities and measures for this specific group of pupils have a temporary character. The problems with this type of approach emerge quite clearly from the less successful school careers of many first and second generation ethnic minority children.

In all three countries under consideration, ethnic minority children grow up in contact with both majority and minority language use. However, a biased interest can be observed in evaluating their language proficiency. Monolingual majority children are taken as the point of reference and ethnic minority children's language proficiency is most commonly discussed in terms of deficiency rather than difference. Along similar lines, ethnic minority children's bilingualism is more frequently seen as a handicap than as a resource. Within educational contexts, L1 is seen at the utmost as instrumental in promoting the process of L2 acquisition. Such a perspective also leads to a biased conception of 'educational success'. This notion refers most commonly to L2-related educational achievement and rarely, if ever, to L1 progress.

Given these commonalities, there is a need for more international cooperation in the field of bilingualism and bilingual education.

Such cooperation should relate to various areas of research and curriculum development. At least the following areas of cooperation should be given priority:

1. survey studies on home language use of ethnic minority groups; what language varieties are actually used and what intergenerational patterns of shift can be observed within and between different ethnic minority groups?
2. studies on attitudes of different majority and minority groups (e.g., children, parents, teachers) towards the acquisition and maintenance of ethnic group languages;
3. longitudinal studies on L1/L2 acquisition of ethnic minority children within and outside educational contexts (cf. Kagitçibasi and Eldering in this volume);
4. evaluative studies on experimental bilingual education programmes for ethnic minority children in which L1 has a prominent status in at least the initial stages of the school curriculum;
5. development of diagnostic instruments for measuring the type and degree of L1/L2 proficiency of ethnic minority children in different stages of the school curriculum;
6. specification of objectives and content of bilingual education programmes;
7. development and evaluation of course materials for both L1 and L2 instruction;
8. development and evaluation of teacher training programmes preparing for bilingual education.

Apart from cooperation in the areas of research and curriculum development, a common revision and elaboration of the EC guidelines (1977) for L1/L2 education should be aimed at. Apart from a renewal of arguments in favour of bilingual education for ethnic minority children (cf. Vallen & Stijnen, 1987), some inspiration for policy makers could be derived from Swedish legislation on education for ethnic minority groups and Dutch legislation on the teaching of Frisian. The following affirmative guidelines for bilingual education might be considered (cf. Extra, 1988c):

1. The local school boards should provide special facilities for majority and minority language instruction for ethnic minority children.
2. The school boards should make yearly announcements of the existence and importance of both types of instruction. This information should be disseminated in oral and written form (both in

majority and minority languages) among all relevant ethnic minority groups within the school board's recruitment area.

3. Ethnic minority children should be entitled to a sophisticated diagnosis of their level of proficiency in both the minority and majority language. The local school board should be responsible for providing the opportunity and guaranteeing the quality of such a bilingual diagnosis.

4. On the basis of quantitative and qualitative needs, the school boards should define the contours of a coherent educational programme for ethnic minority children.

5. The various parts of the programme should be carried out by qualified and interactive teachers.

6. Schools with special majority and minority language instruction should be eligible for extra facilities on the basis of quantitative and qualitative needs.

7. Exemption from the obligation to offer special majority and minority instruction should only be rendered by law:
   a. after evidenced lack of need for special majority language instruction.
   b. after evidenced lack of interest in special minority language instruction.

REFERENCES

APELTAUER, E. (1987). Indikatoren zur Sprachstandbestimmung ausländischer Schulanfänger. In E. Apeltauer (Ed.), *Gesteuerter Zweitspracherwerb. Voraussetzungen und Konsequenzen für den Unterricht.* München: Hueber Verlag, 207-232.

APPEL, R. (1984). *Immigrant children learning Dutch. Sociolinguistic and psycholinguistic aspects of second-language acquisition.* Dordrecht/Cinnaminson: Foris.

APPEL, R. (Ed.) (1986). *Minderheden: taal en onderwijs.* Muiderberg: Coutinho.

BAUR, R. (1986). Kann der Zweitsprachenerwerb "gesteuert" werden? Perspektiven der Zweitsprachendidaktik. *Deutsch Lernen, 1,* 31-50.

BELKE, G. (1986). Schulpolitische Voraussetzungen und sprachdidaktische Konsequenzen einer zweisprachigen Erziehung. *Diskussion Deutsch, 90,* 379-388.

BELKE, G., CHRYSAKOPOULOS, C., KROON, S., LUCHTENBERG, S., OOMEN-WELKE, I., POMMERIN, G. & REICH, H. (1986). Planung mehrkultureller Erziehung. *Diskussion Deutsch, 90,* 424-438.

BEREITER, C. & ENGELMANN, S. (1966). *Teaching disadvantaged children in the preschool.* Englewood Cliffs: Prentice-Hall.

BERG-ELDERING, L. VAN DEN (1986). Onderwijs en etnische ongelijkheid. In J.A. van Kemenade et al. (Eds.), *Onderwijs: bestel en beleid 2. Onderwijs en Samenleving.* Groningen: Wolters-Noordhoff.

Boos-Nünning, U. (1981). Muttersprachliche Klassen für ausländische Kinder. Eine kritische Diskussion des bayrischen "Offenen Modells". *Deutsch Lernen, 2*, 40 ff.

Boos-Nünning, U. (1983a). Fördern die muttersprachlichen Klassen in Bayern die Zweisprachigkeit ausländischer Schüler? *Ausländerkinder, 13*, 52 ff.

Boos-Nünning, U. (1983b). Kulturelle Identität und die Organisation des mutter-sprachlichen Unterrichts für Kinder ausländischer Arbeitsnehmer. *Deutsch Lernen, 2*, 3-14.

Boos-Nünning, U. & Hohmann, M. (1988). *The educational situation of migrant workers' children in the Federal Republic of Germany.* Paper presented at the International Workshop on 'Education and Cultural development of ethnic minority children', Kerkrade, Netherlands, 12-14 September.

Boos-Nünning, U., Hohmann, M., Reich, H. & Wittek, F. (1983). *Aufnahmeunter-richt, Muttersprachlicher Unterricht, Interkultureller Unterricht.* München: Olden-bourg Verlag.

Cammaert, M. (1985). *Grens en transgressie in de wereld van de Berbervrouw.* Leuven: Universitaire Pers.

Churchill, S. (1986). *The education of linguistic and cultural minorities in the OECD Countries.* Clevedon: Multilingual Matters.

Cummins, J. (1979). Linguistic interdependence and the educational development of bilingual children. *Review of Ecucational Research, 49,* 2, 222-251.

Cummins, J. (1980). The construct of language proficiency in bilingual education. In J. Alatis (Ed.), *Current issues in bilingual education.* Washington: Georgetown University Press, 81-103.

Cummins, J. (1983). Language proficiency and academic achievement. In J. Oller (Ed.), *Issues in language testing research.* Rowley, Mass.: Newbury House, 108-129.

Damanakis, M. (1983). Muttersprachlicher Unterricht für ausländische Schüler. *Deutsch Lernen, 2,* 15-47.

Damanakis, M. (1987). Bildungsvorstellungen griechischer Eltern. *Deutsch Ler-nen, 1,* 22-53.

Degraeve, M. (1988). *Onderwijsmaatregelen in verband met de opvang en de begelei-ding van migrantenleerlingen.* (Unpublished paper).

E.G.-Pilootexperiment (1982). *Pedagogische opvangvormen voor migrantenkindere n in het basisonderwijs.* Hasselt: Provincie Limburg (2 vols.).

Eldering, L. (1988). *Ethnic Minority children in Dutch schools. Underachievement and its explanations.* Paper presented at the International Workshop on 'Educa-tion and Cultural development of ethnic minority children', Kerkrade, Nether-lands, 12-14 September.

Els, Th. van, Bongaerts, Th., Extra, G., Os, Ch. van & Janssen-van Dieten, A. (1984). *Applied linguistics and the learning and teaching of foreign languages.* Lon-don: Edward Arnold.

Extra, G. (1986). De positie van etnische groepstalen in het voortgezet onderwijs. *Levende Talen, 407,* 32-37.

Extra, G. (1988a). Over taal gesproken. Overheidsbeleid inzake taalonderwijs aan etnische minderheidsgroepen. *Samenwijs, 6,* 216-219.

Extra, G. (1988b). Processes of language change over time. A linguistic perpec-tive on ethnic minority research in The Netherlands. In F. Aarts & Th. van Els (Eds.), *Dutch contributions to linguistics.* Washington: Georgetown University Press (to appear).

EXTRA, G. (1988c). Ethnic minority languages versus Frisian in Dutch primary schools. A comparative perspective. *Journal of Multilingual and Multicultural Development* (to appear).

EXTRA, G. & VALLEN, T. (Eds.) (1985). *Ethnic minorities and Dutch as a second language.* Dordrecht/Cinnaminson: Foris.

EXTRA, G. & VALLEN, T. (1988). Language and ethnic minorities in The Netherlands. In F. Coulmas & J. Stalpers (Eds.), *The sociolinguistics of Dutch. Topic issue of International Journal of the Sociology of Language, 73,* 85-110.

EXTRA, G. & VERHOEVEN, L. (1985). Tweetaligheid en tweetalig basisonderwijs. *Pedagogische Studiën, 62(1),* 3-24.

EXTRA, G. & VERMEER, A. (1984). Minderheidstalen in het basisonderwijs. *Levende Talen, 389,* 101-109.

EXTRA, G., HOUT, R. VAN & VALLEN, T. (Eds.) (1987). *Etnische minderheden: taalonderzoek, taalonderwijs, taalbeleid.* Dordrecht/Providence: Foris.

FAERCH, C. & KASPER, G. (Eds.) (1983). *Strategies in interlanguage communication.* London: Longman.

FAERCH, C. & KASPER, G. (1984). Two ways of defining communication strategies. *Language Learning, 34,* 45-63.

FASE, W. (1987). *Voorbij de grenzen van onderwijs in eigen taal en cultuur. Meertaligheid op school in zes landen verkend.* Den Haag: SVO.

FOYER (Ed.) (1983). *Four years bicultural education in Brussels.* Brussel: Foyer vzw.

FOYER-STUURGROEP (Ed.) (1985). *Vier jaar Foyer-Bicultureel te Brussel.* Brussel: Foyer vzw.

FOYER-STUURGROEP (Ed.) (1986). *Vijf jaar Foyer-Bicultureel te Brussel.* Brussel: Foyer vzw.

GAILLY, A. & LEMAN, J. (Eds.) (1982). *Onderwijs, taal- en leermoeilijkheden in de immigratie.* Leuven: Acco.

GÖTZE, L. (1983). Die Rolle der Muttersprache beim Zweitspracherwerb. Anmerkungen zum "Memorandum zum Muttersprachlichen Unterricht". *Deutsch Lernen, 2,* 48-60.

HAESENDONCKX, M. (1980). *Bi-cultureel onderwijs aan gastarbeiderskinderen in het eerste leerjaar als antwoord op de vervreemding van hun cultuur.* Malle: De Sikkel.

HEYERICK, L. (1985). Problemen van migrantenkinderen en hun leerkrachten in het Vlaams basisonderwijs. In A. Martens & F. Moulaert (Eds.), *Buitenlandse minderheden in Vlaanderen-België.* Antwerpen/Amsterdam: De Nederlandsche Boekhandel, 103-113.

HOBIN, V. & MOULAERT, F. (Eds.) (1986). *Witboek integratiebeleid inzake migranten in Vlaanderen-België.*

HOHMANN, M. (Ed.) (1976). *Unterricht mit ausländischen Kindern.* Düsseldorf: Schwann.

JASPAERT, K. & LEMMENS, G. (1989). Linguistic evaluation of Dutch as a third language. *International Journal of the Sociology of Language* (to appear).

JASPAERT, K. & VALLEN, T. (1986). Karakteristieken van sociolinguïstisch minderhedenonderzoek in Nederland en Vlaanderen. *Gamma, 10(3),* 325-338.

KAGITÇIBASI, Ç. (1988). *Child rearing in Turkey. Implications for immigration and intervention.* Paper presented at the International Workshop on 'Education and Cultural development of ethnic minority children', Kerkrade, Netherlands, 12-14 September.

KLEIN, W. & DITTMAR, N. (1979). *Developing grammars. The acquisition of German syntax by foreign workers.* Berlin: Springer.

KROON, S. & VALLEN, T. (1989). Ethnische Minderheiten und Sprachunterricht in den Niederlanden. *Diskussion Deutsch* (to appear).

KUHS, K. (1987). Fehleranalyse am Schülertext. In E. Apeltauer (Ed.), *Gesteuerter Zweitspracherwerb. Voraussetzungen und Konsequenzen für den Unterricht.* München: Hueber Verlag, 173-205.

KUIJPER, H., STIJNEN, S. & HOOGEN, J. VAN DEN (1983). *Onderwijs tussen dialect en standaardtaal. Onderzoek in en beschouwingen over de innovatiefase van het Kerkradeproject.* Nijmegen: Nijmegen University.

LALLEMAN, J. (1986). *Dutch language proficiency of Turkish children born in The Netherlands.* Dordrecht: Foris.

LAMBERT, W. (1978). Psychological approaches to bilingualism, translation and interpretation. D. Gerver & H. Sinaiko (Eds.), *Language interpretation and communication.* New York: Plenum Press.

LEMAN, J. (1982). *Van Caltanissetta naar Brussel en Genk.* Leuven: Acco.

LEMAN, J. (Ed.) (1987). Taal- en cultuurgevoelig onderwijs voor immigrantenkinderen. In *Cultuur en Migratie (2).* Brussel: Cultuur en Migratie vzw.

LEMMENS, G. & JASPAERT, K. (1987). *Evaluatie van het Nederlands in het Foyer-bicultureel onderwijsproject.* Tilburg: Department of Language & Literature (internal Foyer evaluation report).

LEOPOLD, W. (1949). *Speech development of a bilingual child. A linguist's record.* Evanston: Northwestern University Press.

LIEBE-HARKORT, K. (1983). Muttersprachenunterricht, ein Problem der Integration. Zum "Memorandum zum Muttersprachlichen Unterricht". *Deutsch Lernen, 2,* 61-70.

LUCHTENBERG, S. (1984). Sprachstandsdiagnoseverfahren für ausländische Kinder und Jugendliche. Ein kritischer Vergleich. *Deutsch Lernen, 1,* 25-41.

MARTENS, A. & MOULAERT, F. (Eds.) (1985). *Buitenlandse minderheden in Vlaanderen-België.* Antwerpen/Amsterdam: De Nederlandsche Boekhandel.

MEINHARDT, R. (Ed.) (1985). *Ausländerpolitik und interkulturelle Arbeit mit ethnischen Minderheiten in den Niederlanden und der Bundesrepublik Deutschland. Texte zum Vergleich.* Oldenburg: Universität.

MEYER-INGWERSEN, J., NEUMANN, R. & KUMMER, M. (1977). *Zur Sprachentwicklung türkischer Schüler in der Bundesrepublik.* Kronberg: Scriptor.

MINISTERIE VAN BINNENLANDSE ZAKEN (1983). *Minderhedennota.* Den Haag: Staatsuitgeverij.

MINISTERIE VAN ONDERWIJS EN WETENSCHAPPEN (1981). *Beleidsplan culturele minderheden in het onderwijs.* Den Haag: Staatsuitgeverij.

MOLFENTER, E. (1986). Erfahrungen in einer zweiten türkischen Nationalklasse. Ein Lehrerbericht. *Diskussion Deutsch, 90,* 402-412.

MOLLE, P. VAN & ROSSO, S. (1978). Taal in immigratie, taal in liquidatie? *Kultuurleven, 4,* 319-320.

NELDE, P., EXTRA, G., HARTIG, M. & VRIENDT, M. DE (Eds.) (1981). *Sprachprobleme bei Gastarbeiterkindern.* Tübingen: Gunter Narr.

NEUMANN, U. & REICH, H. (1977). *Türkische Kinder, Deutsche Lehrer.* Düsseldorf: Schwann.

NOACK, B. (1987). Erwerb einer Zweitsprache: je früher, desto besser? Über die Chancen sprachlicher Integration von türkischen Gastarbeiterkindern. *Deutsch Lernen, 3*, 3-33.

OOMEN-WELKE, I. (1985). Innenansicht einer Türkenklasse. Erfahrungen und Reflexionen aus der Arbeit in einem "nationalen Modell". *Deutsch Lernen, 2*, 3-45.

PFAFF, C. (1980). Incipient creolization in "Gastarbeiterdeutsch". An experimental sociolinguistic study. *Studies in Second Language Acquisition, 3*, 165-178.

PIENEMANN, M. (1981). *Der Zweitspracherwerb ausländischer Arbeiterkinder.* Bonn: Bouvier Verlag.

REICH, H. (1976). Zum Unterricht in Deutsch als Fremdsprache. In M. Hohmann (Ed.), *Unterricht mit ausländischen Kindern.* Düsseldorf: Schwann 149-184.

RÖHR-SENDLMEIER, U. (1985). *Zweitsprachenerwerb und Sozialisationsbedingungen.* Frankfurt: Lang.

RÖHR-SENDLMEIER, U. (1986a). Die Bildungspolitik zum Unterricht für ausländische Kinder in der BRD. Eine kritische Betrachtung der vergangenen 30 Jahre. *Deutsch Lernen, 1*, 51-67.

RÖHR-SENDLMEIER, U. (1986b). Stand der Forschung zum Zweitsprachenerwerb ausländischer Schüler. *Lernen in Deutschland, 2*, 40-45.

ROOSENS, E. (1972). *Cultuurverschillen en etnische identiteit.* Brussel.

ROOSENS, E. (1982). Etnische groep en etnische identiteit. Symbolen of concepten? In J. van Amersfoort and H. Entzinger (Eds.), *Immigrant en samenleving.* Deventer: Van Loghum Slaterus, 99-122.

ROOSENS, E. (1988). *Success and failure: an open question.* Paper presented at the International Workshop on 'Education and Cultural development of ethnic minority children', Kerkrade, the Netherlands, 12-14 September.

ROSIERS, M.C. & MOORS, A. (1979a). Aperçu général sur les problèmes de l'enseignement aux enfants migrants et proposition d'une solution basée sur un enseignement inter-culturel. In *L'action éducative dans un environnement multiculturel.* Liège: Université de Liège, 123-135.

ROSIERS, M.C. & MOORS, A. (1979b). Enquête sociale concernant l'opinion des parents d'enfants suivant l'enseignement à tendance bi-culturelle. In *L'action éducative dans un environnement multiculturel.* Liège: Université de Liège, 136-141.

RÜCKERT, G. (1985). *Untersuchungen zum Sprachverhalten türkischer Jugendlichen in der BRD.* Pfaffenweiler: Centaurus.

SCHUMANN, J. (1978). *The pidginization process. A model for second language acquisition.* Rowley, Mass.: Newbury House.

SEGHERS, J. & BROECK, J. VAN DEN (1978). Bilingual education programs for the children of migrant workers in the Belgian Province of Limburg. *International Journal of the Sociology of Language, 15*, 77-84.

SKUTNABB-KANGAS, T. (1982). Some prerequisites for learning the majority-language. A comparison between two different conditions. *OBST, 22*, 79-91.

SKUTNABB-KANGAS, T. (1983). *Bilingualism or not.* Clevedon: Multilingual Matters.

SMEEKENS, L. & SMEDT, H. DE (1987). Nederlands in Brussel: tweede taal of vreemde taal? In G. Extra, R. van Hout & T. Vallen (Eds.), *Etnische minderheden: taalverwerving, taalonderwijs, taalbeleid.* Dordrecht/Providence: Foris, 85-94.

SPOELDERS, M., LEMAN, J. & SMEEKENS, L. (1985). The Brussels Foyer bicultural education project: socio-cultural backgrounds and psycho-educational language assessment. In G. Extra and T. Vallen (Eds.), *Ethnic minorities and Dutch as a second language.* Dordrecht/Cinnaminson: Foris, 87- 104.

STÖLTING, W. (1980). *Die Zweisprachigkeit jugoslawischer Schüler in der Bundesrepublik.* Wiesbaden: Harrassowitz.

STRÖMQVIST, S. (1988). *Perspectives on second language acquisition in Scandinavia.* Paper presented at the International Workshop on 'Education and Cultural development of ethnic minority children', Kerkade, the Netherlands, 12-14 September.

TEUNISSEN, F. (1986). *Eén school, twee talen.* Utrecht: Utrecht University.

THIEROFF, H. (1986). Linguistische Analyse von Filmnacherzählungen deutscher und türkischer Schüler. *Deutsch Lernen, 4,* 32-70.

TOSI, A. (1984). *Immigration and bilingual education.* Oxford: Pergamon Press.

TRUDGILL, P. (1983). *Sociolinguistics: an introduction to language and society.* Harmondsworth: Penguin.

UCAR, A. (1984). Defizite in der Lehrerausbildung aus der Sicht eines Schulpsychologen. In H. Essinger and A. Ucar (Eds.), *Erziehung in der multikulturellen Gesellschaft.* Baltmannsweiler: Schneider, 219-233.

VALLEN, T. & STIJNEN, S. (1987). Language and educational success of indigenous and non-indigenous minority students in The Netherlands. *Language and Education. An International Journal , 1* (2), 109-124.

VASSAF, G. (1985). *Wir haben unsere Stimme noch nicht laut gemacht. Türkische Arbeiterkinder in Europa.* Felsberg: Res Publicae.

VERDOODT, A. (1977). *Les problèmes des groups linguistiques en Belgique.* Leuven: Peeters.

VERHOEVEN, L. (1987). *Ethnic minority children acquiring literacy.* Dordrecht /Providence: Foris.

WEINREICH, U. (1953). *Languages in contact. Findings and problems.* The Hague: Mouton.

WIDGEREN, J. (1975). *Migration to Western Europe. The social situation of migrant workers and their families.* UN/SOA/SEM/60/WP2.

WIJNSTRA, J. (1976). *Het onderwijs aan van huis uit friestalige kinderen.* Den Haag: Staatsuitgeverij.

WIJNSTRA, J. (1980). Education of children with Frisian home language. *Applied Psychology, 29,* 43-60.

ZOGRAFOU, A. (1981). *Zwischen zwei Kulturen. Griechische Kinder in der Bundesrepublik.* Frankfurt am Main: Institut für Sozialarbeit und Sozialpädagogik.

9

Sven Strömqvist

University of Göteborg

Perspectives on Second Language Acquisition in Scandinavia[1]

1. INTRODUCTION[2]

In this chapter, I first spell out some theoretical points of departure and point out some pertinent problems and dilemmas (section 2). Second, I give a bird's eye perspective on the research situation in Scandinavia, notably Sweden, from the early 1970s to the late 1980s. Also, I make a few remarks on the public debate as well as on educational policy (section 3). Third, I suggest a few guidelines for future research (section 4).

Needless to say, my overview is not meant to be exhaustive. My purpose is to indicate main streams of ideas, attitudes and approaches and to examine some of their theoretical underpinnings. Although it may otherwise be motivated, I will not be concerned here with, for example, the most applied types of research, such as feasibility studies or testing and assessment procedures, nor will I deal with the demographic aspects of multilingualism in post-war Scandinavia. I will concentrate on research on the acquisition of Swedish, Norwegian, and Danish as second languages in Sweden, Norway, and Denmark, respectively. For more information, see Eliasson (1979), Wande (1980; 1987), Bratt-Paulston (1982), Allwood et al. (1982), Viberg (1984b), Gustavsson (1988b).

2. BACKGROUND

2.1 *Some theoretical points of departure*

Perspectives on language acquisition
Any theory of language acquisition, whether first or second language acquisition, should be able to say something about the nature of the acquisition process. The acquisition process, in its turn, presupposes something to be acquired, namely a language, and any theory of language acquisition therefore presupposes a theory of the nature of the language to be acquired. In what follows, I will discuss these two main aspects of a theory of language acquisition in somewhat greater detail.

Facts and factors. First, let us state a few general facts of language acquisition, which from previous research experience we know to hold true for both L1 and L2 learners:
1. The acquisition process is determined by several different factors in interaction and the relative weight of a given factor may vary with different stages or phases of acquisition.
2. All domains of a language are not worked at simultaneously by a learner. Rather, the learner devotes his energy to them in a selective fashion, and they are acquired with different speed and ease.
3. The individual variation in both structure and speed of acquisition is considerable.

Thus, any theory of language acquisition should be compatible with these three facts.
As to the determinants of language acquisition, we can distinguish the following main types of factors:
a. Biological factors
b. Activity factors
c. Properties of the language to be acquired
d. The learner's previous knowledge and experience (for L2 acquisition, notably properties of L1)
e. The time and motivation the learner devotes to the acquisition task.

The language acquisition of any learner is thus determined by an interaction of factors belonging to these five types. I assume that the reader is familiar with these determinants, and I shall here restrict myself to briefly commenting upon the first two of them. Hypotheses on the nature of our inborn capacity for language acquisition are extremely hard to test empirically. In this context suffice it to say that there is no evidence to suggest that the human being is not biologically equipped to deal with the task of acquiring two or more languages.

As to activity factors, the language of a learner's social environment is primarily accessible through particular activities in which the language is used (and secondarily accessible through descriptions of the language). Since different activities require partly different bits and pieces of language, in different types of activity the learner will receive the stimulation of partly different aspects of the language to be acquired. The activity factor has been conceptually clarified and placed in a pivotal position in the analysis of spoken interaction in general and in L2 acquisition in particular by various authors, notably by Allwood (e.g., 1985; 1988a).

As to the relative weight of factors (a) and (b) in development, biological factors provide a variable that is very dynamic in early stages of ontogeny and more static in later stages, whereas activity factors provide a variable that is potentially dynamic throughout all stages of development.

The relative weight of factors (b) – (e) were explored by Extra et al. (1988) in a study of lexical development in adult second language learners. All of these four factors were controlled in the design of the study, and the results proved to suggest the following 'default' hierarchy determining the linguistic performance of a learner (where '>' stands for 'more powerful determining factor than' and 'TL' and 'SL' stand for 'Target Language' and 'Source Language' respectively):

$$\text{TL properties} > \frac{\text{time}}{\text{actvity}} \quad \text{type} > \text{SL properties}$$

The default character of this hierarchy means that a search for explanations for the learner's linguistic performance should proceed from left to right rather than the other way around, unless there are clear indications to the contrary. This means, in effect, that, as a rule, SL properties becomes a potentially valuable explanatory factor only when the other factors in the hierarchy above have failed to apply (Extra et al., 1988).

N.B. The hierarchy above is valid only in relation to a theoretical question of the following type (that is, 1):

1. Why does the learner construct his utterance in the way he does?

In relation to question 2 below, by contrast, the hierarchy should be constructed the other way around, in order to be valid:

2. Why does the learner deviate from the target language norm in the way he does?

We will return to some implications of these two questions in the following sections.

Perspectives in modelling language development. Let us now consider two ways of modelling or thinking about language acquisition or language development; two perspectives that are closely related to questions 1 and 2 above. I will henceforth refer to them as the 'development perspective' (cf. question 1) and the 'deviation perspective' (cf. question 2) (cf. the 'ascending' versus 'descending' approach in Deutsch and Budwig's (1983) terminology):

1. The development perspective: the learner's language development consists of the learner organizing and reorganizing his language in interaction with his social environment.
2. The deviation perspective: the learner's language development consists in the learner reducing the gap between his performance and a given target norm – a gap which is assumed to be maximal at the start of development

Note, in particular, that the deviation perspective models the language development in an individual with reference to a normatively determined target state not yet attained by the individual, whereas the development perspective does not make reference to factors beyond the state in which the individual actually is (cf. Lindblom et al. (1984) and the notion of a self-organizing system). Or, to put it in a different fashion, the deviation perspective guides us to think about acquisition in terms of what the learner cannot (yet) do, whereas the development perspective guides us to think about acquisition in terms of what the learner can do.

The two perspectives supplement each other in the sense that (1) offers a superior descriptive and explanatory view on the individual's development, and (2) highlights the norm the learner has to orient himself towards in order to become a fullfledged member of the linguistic community (cf. our discussion of pedagogical aspects in a later subsection). The two perspectives are seldom spelled out explicitly in acquisition studies, and it should be noted that the deviation perspective is in many studies an important covert perspective. Interestingly enough, there is a tendency to give preference to the development perspective in studies of first language acquisition, whereas many studies in second language acquisition show a strong bias towards the deviation perspective. We will return to this difference in preference for perspective in the following section.

The two perspectives, however, may come into conflict. Thus, for example, on the basis of a longitudinal case study of the development of reference to person in first language acquisition, Strömqvist (1988) demonstrates that a developmental change from a cognitively less sophisticated to a cognitively more sophisticated use of a term can result in an increase in error types. Whereas it is clear from the development perspective that the child in such a case has made a significant step forward, the increase in error types makes the child's language deviate more from the target norm than previously, something which, according to the deviation perspective, suggests that the child's language is deteriorating.

Consider, further, two types of theories about the nature of a language, which I will refer to as 'more-or-less theories' and 'either-or theories' respectively:

1. More-or-less theories: according to theories of this kind, a language is something vague; consequently, it becomes problematic to delimit all elements of one language from all elements of another language.
2. either-or theories: for any utterance, an either-or theory of a language makes it possible to determine whether or not the utterance belongs to the language in question.

Influential either-or theories of languages have notably been formulated in the chomskyan tradition (see, e.g., Chomsky, 1965). In that tradition any utterance can be judged as '+/- grammatical' or '+/- acceptable' according to a set of explicit criteria for grammaticality or acceptability. A famous more-or-less theory, by contrast, was formulated by Wittgenstein (1953), according to whom a language is seen as a number of "language games". These games are interrelated by family resemblance, which is to say that for a language game to belong to a certain family, it is only required that the particular game shares at least some property with any other game belonging to the family in question.

Now, if we couple the deviation perspective with an either-or theory of the language to be acquired, we are forced to model language acquisition in a very counterintuitive fashion. Thus, for example, the acquisition of a language will be possible only through a sudden leap, since as long as the learner deviates from the target language norm in some way, he is necessarily outside that language.

If, however, we couple the development perspective with a more-or-less theory of the language to be acquired, we will not run into con-

tradicions when we argue that a language can be acquired by and
by, or that a learner can have acquired a language a little, although
not fully.

Note, further, in the special case of second language acquisition, that
an either-or theory of the learner's L1 and L2 can have important
(and peculiar) consequences for a theory of the structure of development. Thus, if the learner's performance is judged (by the researcher) to be distinct from both the learner's L1 (source language) and
his L2 (target language), the problem arises as to what language the
learner is speaking. In the tradition of Selinker (1972), we are invited
to solve this problem by postulating a so-called interlanguage.

This solution, however, creates a new problem. What status as a language does the postulated interlanguage have? Can this language be
unique to the individual learner? How can we determine when the
learner expands a given interlanguage and when he switches to
another? In many respects, the notion of an interlanguage may be
more of a method for the researcher than a linguistic reality.

On the relation between first and second language acquisition

Social and attitudinal differences. A child acquiring his first language is
from very early on already considered a member of its surrounding
social environment. An adult L2 learner, by contrast, is faced with
gatekeeping attitudes in his new social environment: he can be let in
into the new community or kept outside. If we want to let someone
in, we tend to focus on similarities, if we want to keep him outside,
we tend to focus on differences. These differences in attitudes and
relations, which typically hold between the social situations of first
and second language learners, may well account for some of the
typical differences in acquisition career between L1 and L2 learners,
such as, for example, the fact that the relative proportion of L1 learners who reach fullfledged L1 competence is far greater than the relative proportion of L2 learners who reach fullfledged L2 competence.
Moreover, these social and attitudinal differences may prove to have
an explanatory value, when we consider typical differences in
preference perspective in research on first and second language
acquisition (see further below).

Differences in acquisition structure. An important question is whether
the acquisition structure is similar or different for first and second
language acquisition and why it is similar or different. In order to

answer this question, however, we must qualify it in several ways.

First, an important qualification is when the second language enters the life of the learner. McLaughlin (1978) argues that three years is a crucial age: if the second language is introduced before three years of age, the acquisition will be similar to that of a first language, whereas if it is introduced after the age of 3, it is likely that it will be different.

Second, it is important to qualify what aspect or part of a language we consider, when we make the comparison. Thus, if we consider, for example, unbound anaphora, these are present from early on in adult second language acquisition, whereas they emerge only in a later phase of first language acquisition (cf. Strömqvist, 1986). An important part of an explanation for this asymmetry lies in the cognitive difficulty of the anaphoric device; it is a mechanism for discourse cohesion which requires hierarchization and thematization strategies, and these strategies are easily accessible to an adult with a thorough experience of a first language but their acquisition requires much effort for a child learning his first language.

Further, if we consider gender in Swedish, it is obvious that adult second language learners have difficulties in acquiring this domain (Extra et al., 1988), whereas first language learners show a relatively 'error-free' acquisition of the same domain (Plunkett & Strömqvist, in preparation). Andersson (in preparation), who investigates the acquisition of gender in children acquiring Swedish as a second language, finds a tendency to relatively error-free acquisition in children below three years of age and greater difficulty and variability in children around five years of age. This finding supports McLaughlin's suggestion that three years is probably a critical age.

Third, it is important to qualify how the L1 and L2 results that are being compared have been attained. The results are often produced under different theoretical foci and this can decrease the validity of the comparison. Below, I will discuss this question further.

Differences in preference for research perspectives. As mentioned earlier, there is a tendency in studies of first language acquisition to give preference to concepts and approaches associated with what I referred to as the development perspective, whereas many studies in second language acquisition show a bias towards the deviation perspective and associated concepts. This difference in preference for research perspective shows up in several ways and I shall briefly consider three of them here.

First, there is a strong tradition in L1 research to study hypotheti-

cally universal patterns in language acquisition. Perhaps the strong-
est reason for this is an influence from cognitive psychology coupled
with nativist assumptions: language acquisition is explored as a win-
dow onto a set of cognitive processes which are assumed to be
present in all (normal) human beings. In L2 acquisition research, by
contrast, there is a strong tradition to focus on particular patterns,
namely the particular structures of the learner's L1 and L2 as well as
the interference patterns resulting from mismatches between the
two.

This focus on language-particular patterns in the L2 acquisition process may be reinforced by the whorfian tradition of exploring differences between languages as indicative of differences in thinking and
concept formation (see e.g. Whorf, 1956). Thus, one could argue with
Whorf, that the Swedish way of specifying the containment relation,
namely by the preposition *i* (e.g., "i skogen" [in the wood]) represents a different way of conceptualizing the relation than the Finnish
way, which is by means of a case ending, *-ssV* (e.g. "metsä-ssä" [in
the wood]). In L1 acquisition research, by contrast, the very same difference between Swedish and Finnish would typically be explored as
evidence of hypotheses as to what the syntactic and morphological
(as distinct from the semantic) properties of languages contribute to
the acquisition structure. Thus, the Swedish and Finnish counter-
parts of 'in the wood' would be analysed under the assumption that
precisely the content side of the different expressions remains
constant (cf. notably Slobin, 1973; 1986).

Second, a difference in preference for research perspective shows up
in relation to learner 'errors'. Clearly, the concept of 'error', in the
first place, is constructed according to a deviation perspective. The
usefulness of 'errors' for making inferences about the acquisition
process, however, is recognized in both L1 and L2 acquisition
research, although to a more limited extent in L2 than in L1 acquisition research (see notably Corder, 1967). In L1 research, errors tend to
be interpreted as a sign of creativity and as indicative of where the
learner is going in his development (see, e.g. Bowerman, 1982).
Furthermore, the phenomena under discussion are usually conceptualized as generalizations (rather than errors) by the L1 acquisition
researcher, thus reinforcing the development perspective. In L2 research, by contrast, the concept of error prevails and the cases in
point are often interpreted as indicative of where the learner comes
from (namely, his L1 background). The deviation perspective is
further reinforced by concepts such as, e.g., interference, suggesting

that the learner's L1 is a disturbing – rather than a helpful – factor in his L2 acquisition process.

Third, there is a tendency to analyse the L2 learner's utterances and communicative doings as compensatory strategies, a concept which suggests that the learner's expressive capacity is somehow impaired.

An important implication of the difference in preference perspective discussed above is that there are several pattern gaps to be filled in both L1 and L2 acquisition research, in order to obtain a richer picture of both first and second language acquisition.

A pedagogical perspective. Let us briefly consider the learner's development from a pedagogical point of view also. Basically, the pedagogue has three main concerns, which I will refer to as a descriptive aspect, a normative aspect, and a didactic aspect:

1. The descriptive aspect: what state is the learner in?
2. The normative aspect: what is the nature of the state that we want the learner to be in (that is, the target state)?
3. The didactic aspect: how can we make it easier for the learner to move from where he/she is (this presupposes the descriptive aspect) to where we want him/her to be (this presupposes the normative aspect).

The focus of pedagogical concern is, of course, on the third aspect. In relation to the two aspects presupposed by the didactic one it should be observed, however, that in educational contexts there is usually much more emphasis on the normative aspect than on the descriptive one. In effect, there is a bias in educational contexts towards the deviation perspective on language acquisition/learning.

2.2 Some problems and dilemmas

In the former section a few theoretical problems related to first and second language acquisition were discussed. In this section I shall consider a few problems and dilemmas of a more practical and political nature, namely:

a. Language difference – language deviance – language deficit.
b. Bilingualism – exception or rule, handicap or resource?
c. Integration versus segregation.
d. The fear of linguistic and cultural contamination.
e. Explanations and ideologies

These five problem areas are more or less interrelated and I will therefore discuss them together rather than singly.

For an L2 learner in Sweden, Norway or Denmark, the learner's L1 will be a minority language and his L2 a majority language. How will his linguistic situation be perceived and utilized by the majority community? Will it be seen as different, as deviant or as deficient? Will the learner be perceived as a resource or as a handicap for the majority community? In trying to account for his success or failure to learn the majority language, will the majority community make reference primarily to his linguistic and cultural background or to the interaction between the learner and his new socio-cultural environment?

If we consider the relation between the learner's L1 and his L2, the majority community will, as a rule, not perceive it in terms of a set of descriptive categories which are valid for any language in the world, but rather in terms of how his L1 deviates from his L2 (the majority language). This will lead to a very linguocentric perspective on the learner's L1 in particular and on the linguistic variation in the world in general. Thus, for example, in relation to Swedish as the linguocentric point, the difference between, say, Turkish and Farsi will come out in terms of how they differ in their deviations from Swedish.

Furthermore, if we consider the acquisition process of an individual second language learner, this process is likely to be compared with the acquisition process of first language learners in the monolingual majority community. This comparison is likely to produce a picture of deviating, perhaps even deficient, development in the L2 learner. The fallacy rests, among other things, on the (tacit) assumption in the majority community that monolingual development in an individual constitutes the normal case. A quick look at the global situation in the world, however, demonstrates that multilingual development in the individual is the rule and not the exception. (A comparison of adult L2 learners with L1 learners is further complicated by the fact that there are virtually no studies of the continued L1 development in adults.)

In short, the majority community produces the norms and standards according to which the linguistic situation of the L2 learner is defined as deviant or deficient, and these norms and standards ought to be modified according to norms and standards of the minority communities in question, in order to be adequate.

It is, however, a question of great political delicacy whose language and whose norm should be officially legitimized or sanctioned (cf. Mey, 1985).

It may, furthermore, be a matter of debate in the majority community whether the goal of the L2 acquisition is to make the learner convert to the majority language or whether the goal is that he should develop a bilingual (multilingual) competence. The latter goal rests, crucially, on the condition that the community functionally motivates the individual to develop and maintain a multilingual competence (cf. Boyd, 1985). Unless the community can produce this condition, bilingualism can be a handicap both for the individual and the community.

In this context the dilemma of integration versus segregation is actualized. Allardt (1987) argues that, on a societal level, a certain degree of segregation of a minority from the majority community is necessary, in order for the minority to survive. This creates a persistent dilemma, more precisely a value conflict: "... it is an important value that linguistic minorities can survive and continue to exist. It requires some degree of segregation, but to avoid segregation is also an important value. Accordingly, in all policy related to bilingualism there is a kind of value conflict between the aim of minority survival and the aim of avoidance of segregation." (Allardt, 1987, p. 49.)

In educational contexts a similar conflict is present. Immigrant children in Sweden are often offered school training in their L1, especially during the first years in school. This is done in order to strengthen the children's first language. At the same time, however, this procedure can easily have the effect of segregating the immigrant children from their Swedish peers: the immigrant children as well as the Swedish children may be led to believe that they are unable to communicate and cooperate, only because the immigrant children have not yet mastered the Swedish language. Indeed, the segregation of immigrant children in school contexts can operate to reinforce hostility between groups of Swedish children and groups of immigrant children (see Allwood, 1988).

Another conflict exists between, on the one hand, the promotion of crosscultural and crosslinguistic communication and, on the other hand, the fear of cultural and linguistic contamination. Using bits and pieces of the linguistic resources available, in the special case under discussion the learner's L1 and L2, in the learning process as well as in crosscultural communication (everyday encounters) is a natural and creative thing to do (see, e.g., Burling, 1981). It is, however, typically not perceived in this way; on the contrary, communicative mixtures and blends of this sort are usually looked upon with indignation by the linguistic gatekeepers of the majority community,

who have learnt to use terms such as, for example, 'interference' or
'false friends'. (One may ask why we do not care to talk about cases
of successful transfer from L1 to L2 as 'true friends'?) Indeed, it is an
explicit main goal of the Swedish Academy to work upon the 'purity
and grandeur' of the Swedish language, a goal which is hardly
promoted if language switching, language blend, false friends and
other interference phenomena are let loose in crosscultural communication. To preach the slogan that all linguistic and cultural
minorities should have the same freedom to bloom as long as they
do not interfere with each other or, most importantly, with the majority language and culture, by no means provides a solution to this
conflict; it is simply equivalent to suggesting linguistic and cultural
apartheid.

In the former section I claimed that language acquisition is determined by an interaction of several factors, some of which are social and
some of which can be reduced to the individual. From a scientific
point of view, it can be methodologically sound to focus on one of
these determining factors, in order to see how far it can be pushed
before it collapses in an explanatory model. Outside the scientific
context, however, such an attempt can easily be associated with prejudice. Thus, for example, an attempt to reduce explanatory factors
behind second language acquisition to properties of the individual
learner will easily associate with the extreme view that, say, a Latin-
American immigrant in Sweden cannot learn to speak Swedish
properly, because he/she is Latin-American. The sound instinct must
be to look for explanations in the interaction (in a broad sense) between the learner and his social environment.

3. DEBATE, RESEARCH, AND EDUCATIONAL POLICY

In this section I will give a brief orientation of views on second language acquisition as evidenced in the debate, research, and educational policy in Scandinavia, mainly Sweden. My focus will be on research.

3.1 The debate
The debate (that is, the more public debate) on second language acquisition in Sweden and Scandinavia has mainly concerned the linguistic situation of immigrant children and the rights of linguistic
minority groups. The debate, as a rule, has had several political un-

dertones, and it is often difficult to trace the ultimate motivation of an argument.

What has given the Swedish and Scandinavian debate much of its flavour are the controversies around the concept of *semilingualism*. This concept was introduced in the 1960s by Hansegård in a series of lectures on the linguistic situation on the Swedish side of the Torne Valley. Hansegård pointed out that many children in this area were under the pressure of learning both Swedish and Finnish in addition to their own dialect. According to Hansegård, these children were *halvspråkiga* (semilingual), that is, they had not mastered either their first or their second language (see, e.g, Hansegård, 1968).

The linguistic situation in Tornedalen was further investigated by Loman (1974). Loman is very sceptical about Hansegård's claims, and argues that it is extremely difficult to measure linguistic competence and that claims about semilingualism must therefore be viewed with caution. Also, Loman criticizes Hansegård for pointing out linguistic factors *per se* rather than social factors as the prime determinants of the children's problematic situation.

In the 1970s, the debate on the specific situation in the Torne Valley was generalized to the situation of immigrant children, notably by Toukomaa, who studied the situation of Finnish immigrant children in two Swedish towns, Göteborg and Olofström (see, e.g., Toukomaa, 1977). Toukomaa argued that the children, who were of school age, were less proficient in Finnish than Finnish children in Finland and that they were less successful in school than Swedish children. Toukomaa found this to be particularly true for those children who were in their early school years; older children performed better. On the basis of this finding, Toukomaa argued that you can acquire a second language only after having acquired your first language to a sufficient degree.

The concept of semilingualism in general and Toukomaa's argumentation in particular were reinforced in several articles by Skutnabb-Kangas (see, e.g., Skutnabb-Kangas & Toukomaa, 1976; Skutnabb-Kangas, 1981). The idea of strengthening the first language of immigrant children as a prerequisite to their successful acquisition of a second language (the majority language) also gained support in a project, *Fisk-projektet*, where Finnish immigrant children received all their initial school training in Finnish (see Hansson, 1980).

In general, however, the doctrine of second language acquisition only after first language acquisition, has very weak support and it has been heavily criticized in the Swedish context too, notably by

Ekstrand, who argues that contrary to Toukomaa's claim, second language acquisition is facilitated by bringing in the second language at the earliest stage possible (see, e.g. Ekstrand, 1978).

The concept of semilingualism as well as the procedures and norms by which children's linguistic proficiency is measured have also been subjected to critical discussion, notably by Martin-Jones and Romaine (1987), who argue, *inter alia*, that "language assessment procedures need to be grounded in community based norms" (1987: 101), that is, in the norms of the local community in which the children (learners) engage in everyday interaction. Thus, it seems hardly relevant to compare Finnish children in a bilingual situation in Sweden with Finnish as a minority language to Finnish children in Finland, as Toukomaa did. The need to study minority group norms that deviate from the national standards sanctioned by the source or target country of the migrant children is further discussed by Boyd (1988). What status should these norms be given in relation to early school training, importantly writing? Boyd argues that it is important to consider which norm is more likely to promote the survival of the linguistic variety spoken by the minority in question.

Furthermore, the notion of semilingualism and its use in the debate is discussed by Öhman (1981), who argues that the label *halvspråkighet* in many contexts is used to stigmatize immigrant children and define them as outcasts.

For a more detailed critical discussion of the Swedish debate see Wande (1977), Bratt-Paulston (1982), and Allwood et al. (1982: 228-242).

3.2 Research

In this section I shall give a brief orientation about research – mainly linguistic – on second language acquisition and closely related areas in Scandinavia in the 1970s and 1980s. The reference list at the end of this chapter contains several relevant titles, but for reasons of space I will here describe only a few projects and studies in somewhat greater detail.

In Sweden, research in the 1970s was much inspired by the method of error analysis outlined by Corder (1967) and the concept of interlanguage by Selinker (1972). Error analysis and contrastive typology provided an important point of departure for Hammarberg and Viberg in their project *Svenska som målspråk* (Swedish as a target language; SSM). This project was concerned with aspects of language structure and language use that represent learning problems for adult immigrants who study Swedish as a second language. Aspects of lexical structure, morphology and basic syntax were studied in a functional perspective. Combining error analysis with typological studies, the SSM project established a typological profile of Swedish and related it to the major immigrant languages in Sweden. The project also produced a systematized collection of examples of authentic errors. The input to the error analyses were mainly compositions written by adult students in Swedish classes at various levels of proficiency (see, e.g., Hammarberg & Viberg, 1977; 1979).

A similar project within the domain of phonetics was Gårding's and Bannert's *Optimering av svensk uttalsundersvisning* (Optimal teaching of Swedish pronunciation). The aim of this project was to improve the teaching of Swedish pronunciation to adult immigrants, to suggest pedagogical priorities, and to specify a basic prosody (i.e. rhythmic and prosodic patterns) as well as a basic pronunciation of segmental features. Special attention was given to prosody. In a broader perspective, the project contributed to the integration of a theory of (foreign) accent within a theory of linguistic variation in general (see Gårding & Bannert, 1979; Bannert, 1979; 1980).

Other studies which deal with contrastive analysis or error analysis within the domain of phonology include Eliasson (1978), Toutati (1987), Hammarberg (1988).

As to the concept of interlanguage, this was seized upon in the Swedish context first and foremost by Hyltenstam (e.g. 1978), who places universals and markedness relations rather than linguistic particulars at the centre of the analysis. In his dissertation (1978) Hyltenstam deals with the acquisition of negation, interrogative structures, and subject-verb inversion (in declaratives after sentence-initial non-subjects) in Swedish by adult second language learners. He finds that the variety of Swedish, or 'interim language', spoken by his subjects is characterized by many variable rules. For example, some learners variably place the negation before and after the finite verb (and this variation is not random in Swedish). Hyltenstam also found that his adult subjects showed a similar, regular route of acquisition, independently of differences in background, notably knowledge of other foreign languages or, to some extent, differences in Source Language (the only significant background variable was length of education). More precisely, the learners proceeded from the structurally simple to the structurally more complex, where the simple was characterized by unmarked categories and the complex by marked categories. The data underlying the study were elicited by means of cloze tests. In the 1980s, Hyltenstam has developed some of the ideas from his dissertation further, notably in a study of pronominal copies in relative clauses (pronominal copies are not permitted in Swedish) in second language acquisition (1984; cf. also Hyltenstam, 1982).

The research situation in the 1980s is characterized by a new wave of studies, focusing on developmental processes (rather than normative target states) and spoken language and interaction (rather than samples of written text, e.g., compositions). Importantly, the preoccupation with the L2 learner's first language is supplemented with an ecological perspective, focusing various aspects of the interaction between the learner and his social environment. Studies of non-tutored acquisition emerge, as well as descriptive studies of classroom communication (as distinct from normative suggestions as to how language teaching should be conducted). Also, there are studies of nonverbal aspects of crosscultural communication. In the 1980s there is, furthermore, expanding research in Denmark and Norway on the acquisition of Danish and Norwegian as second languages, mainly along the lines of the contrastive, TL-oriented approach.

Several of the new tendencies mentioned above are present in the project Ecology of Adult Language Acquisition (EALA), a joint international project involving five European countries, among them a Swedish research group (project leader: Jens Allwood). The Swedish team studied non-tutored acquisition of Swedish by Finnish and Spanish speaking Latin-American immigrants with a low education. The following linguistic and communicative domains were studied longitudinally in relation to a broad range of activity types recurring over time: Understanding and misunderstanding (see, e.g., Allwood & Aberlar, 1985; Dorriots, 1986; Strömqvist, 1983, 1987b; Voionmaa, 1983); Feedback processes (see Allwood, 1988a, 1988c); Lexicon (see Allwood & Ahlsén, 1986; Broeder & Voionmaa, 1986; Extra et al., 1988); Reference to space and Reference to time (see, e.g., Ahlsén, 1988); and Thematic structure (see, e.g., Strömqvist, 1986).

In the EALA project, Allwood's research group had the main responsibility for the study of feedback processes. The function of feedback expressions (such as *ja* (yes), *nej* (no), *mm* (aha), *va* (what), etc.) is to signal contact (continued interaction), perception (of verbal and nonverbal signals), understanding, and attitudinal reaction. Feedback is therefore essential to interaction management and the understanding process. By implication, it is also crucial to language acquisition, since the learner has to communicate in order to learn. In the project, the acquisition of feedback expressions as well as the learner's use of feedback as an instrument for language acquisition were studied. To study the acquisition of feedback expressions, a theory of feedback mechanisms in Swedish as well as in the other source and target languages of the project had to be constructed (see Allwood, 1988b), because no such theory or description was available (something which testifies to the written language bias in linguistics).

One of the findings was that even at an early phase of acquisition the learners had internalized a small number of types of feedback expressions which they used very frequently and in a highly multifunctional and often vague way. As time went by and they internalized more types of feedback expressions, they tended to use feedback expressions in a functionally more clearcut way. There was also a modest overall decrease in the relative frequency of feedback items over time. These findings suggest, among other things, that feedback plays an important role in all phases of second language acquisition, but perhaps most importantly in early phases.

Some of the theoretical questions in the EALA project are expanded upon in a follow-up project, *Vuxnas andraspråksinlärning* (Adult second language acquisition, project leader: Sven Strömqvist). So far, two studies have emerged from this project: a case study of U-shaped development as evidenced in discourse cohesion and speech planning and monitoring processes (Strömqvist, 1987a) and a comparative study of the development of discourse cohesion, based on experimental evidence from child L1 and adult L2 learners and a group of control subjects (adult L1) (Strömqvist et al., 1988).

Another project that shows similarities with the EALA project, is *Språkutveckling och undervisningsmodeller* (Language acquisition and teaching models, SUM; project leader: Åke Viberg). The SUM project differs from the EALA project mainly in that it studies tutored language acquisition. Also, SUM has a greater number of learner subjects, but a more narrow range of activity types and fewer encounters with each subject. In the SUM project, four linguistic domains are studied, namely the structure of the noun phrase (see, e.g., Axelsson, 1985; Axelsson & Viberg, 1985); sentence syntax (see, e.g. Bolander, 1987, 1988); interaction patterns and communicative strategies between teacher and pupils (see Lindberg, 1988); and lexicon.

The activity-specific premises to communication and second language acquisition in the classroom are subjected to investigation in descriptive studies, notably by Håkansson (1987) and Gustavsson

(1988a). Gustavsson presents and discusses findings from the project *Kummunikationsformer i språkundervisningen* (Forms of communication in language teaching). The empirical material for his study consists of eight dyadic lessons of Swedish as a second language in grades 4-6 of the Swedish comprehensive, compulsory school.

As material for comparison, the pupils, 10-12 year old boys from the Middle East, also participate in two non-didactic conversations around tasks defined by the research team, one together with the teacher of Swedish, and one together with a class-mate. Gustavsson finds important differences in dialogue processes – concerning dynamics, coherence and fluency – between different activities within the confines of a lesson. One of the most important results is that the teacher's interactional dominance seems to be systematically related to the content of lesson activities: the more focus on language *per se* (and the less on topics related to other school subjects or to the children's experience outside school), the fewer opportunities for talking are offered to the pupil by the teacher and the fewer opportunities are also taken by the pupil, when he is actually offered any.

Similar patterns of interactional dominance are also observed by Andersson and Nauclér in studies of spoken interaction between adults and children in multilingual nursery school settings (these studies were part of the projects *Hemspråket i förskolan* (Home language at nursery school) and *Minoritetsbarns andraspråksinlärning i förskolan* (School language acquisition by minority children at nursery school)). Andersson and Nauclér find, among other things, that the children's role in conversations where the adult has an explicitly pedagogical purpose becomes very limited: such conversations are, basically, adult monologues with short replies thrown in by the children. By contrast, child-child conversations are, as a rule, found to be very symmetrical: the participants have the same possibilities of determining the design and content of the conversation. Also, the structure of the child-child conversations is more varied than that of conversations between children and adults (see, e.g., Andersson & Nauclér, 1987; Nauclér & Andersson, 1988).

Early childhood bilingualism is also studied by Arnberg (1979; 1981), who analyses language and communication in mixed-lingual families.

In the 1980s there appear, at the same time, new studies in the tradition of contrastive typological analysis with Swedish as TL. Most importantly, Viberg (1981) presents studies of three semantic fields, namely verbs of cognition, perception, and emotion. Viberg (1984a) further extends his contrastive lexicological investigation to verbs of physical contact.

The semantic field approach was also pursued in the project Anthropological linguistics (project leader: Jens Allwood), for example, in a study of Swedish fear vocabulary (Hirsch, 1979) and a study of metaphorical usage of colour terms (Kos-Dienes, 1982). The project Anthropological linguistics also contributed crosscultural studies of gestures ranging over a large set of content categories, such as, for example, 'yes', 'no', 'come here!', 'I don't know' and others (see Allwood, 1979).

An important sociolinguistic study is contributed by Boyd (1985) who investigates the current situation and future prospects of immigrant minority languages in Sweden by looking at patterns of language choice among second generation immigrant young people. The results of this study suggest that language shift is in progress in the groups under investigation. In a new project, Variation and change in language contact, Boyd is studying language contact between minority languages and majority languages in Scandinavia.

Furthermore, the vernacular of second generation immigrants in a multicultural/multilingual setting, a suburb of Göteborg, is being studied by Day (in preparation; cf. also Kotsinas, 1988).

As to the expanding research in Norway and Denmark, I shall briefly mention a few projects and studies.

In Norway, the following projects are in progress: *Tilegnelse av to språk hos innvandrerbarn: hemmende og fremmende faktorer* (The acquisition of two languages in immigrant children; project leader: Arne Svindland) (see also Tenfjord, 1983); *Laereboktypologi og laerebokhistorie* (A typology and history of textbooks; project leader: Anne Hvenekilde); The code differentiation process in the discourse of children acquiring two languages simultaneously (project leader: Elizabeth Lanza; see Lanza, 1986); *Kommunikajson og kommunikasjonsstrategier blant finske nyinnvandrar i aust-Finnmark* (Communication and communicative strategies among Finnish immigrants in East Finnmark; project leader: Ernst Hakon Jahr); *Håndbok i norsk intonasjon (for laerere i norsk som andrespråk)* (A manual for Norwegian intonation (for teachers in Norwegian as a second language); project leader: Thorstein Fretheim). For contrastive analyses (combined with error analyses) of Norwegian as a second language, see further Hvenekilde (1980); Andenaes and Golden (1980). See also Andenaes (1984).

Among projects on second language acquisition in Denmark we find *Studier i dansk som andetsprog* (Studies in Danish as a second lan-

guage) and *På vej mod en andetsprogspaedagogik* (Towards a second
language pedagogy; project leader: Jens Normann Jörgensen);
Invandrerdansk – spontan sprogtilegnelse hos voksne invandrere (Immigrant Danish – spontaneous language acquisition in adult immigrants; project leader: Inger Jacobsen); *Progressionen i invandreres
tilegnelse af dansk syntaks* (The progression in the acquisition of
Danish syntax by immigrants; project leader: Anne Holmen). See
also Jörgensen (1983) and Jacobsen (1984).

In the Danish research context, one should, of course, also mention
the important general work on strategies and processes in second
language acquisition and interlanguage communication by Claus
Faerch and Gabriele Kasper (see, e.g. Faerch & Kasper, 1983; 1987).

3.3 Educational policy

Swedish as a second language is taught both in comprehensive, compulsory school, and in the form of special courses for adult immigrants. It should be observed that, as a rule, it is precisely the contrastive analysis of Swedish as a target language combined with
error analysis that has been seized upon in these educational contexts (note, that the concept of error analysis is here almost exclusively constructed within a deviation framework). Also, the concept
of semilingualism has played an important role as a vague and
dubious point of reference for judgements of language deficiency.
The communication-oriented, ecological perspectives typical of
research in the 1980s, however, are, as yet, almost absent.

There are many possible reasons for this bias. One is that error analysis is easily assimilated to a traditional classroom paradigm where
the teacher fulfills his role importantly by correcting errors. Another
reason may be a drive in the majority community to maintain its
identity by defining certain types of linguistic varieties as deviant or
even deficient. (In this context, it may be observed that the term
'pronunciation clinic' has been used to refer to a set of pedagogical
means for helping immigrants to 'wash away' their foreign accent,
something which invites us to think of the linguistic deviations
under discussion in pathological terms.)

The lack, in educational contexts, of communication-oriented,
ecological perspectives on second language acquisition and bilingualism is alarming. A focus on the question why the learner deviates from the target language in the way he does and a concomitant
deviation perspective on second language acquisition can easily increase the risk of segregation and of conflicts between children of the

majority community and minority group children. The need for an increased understanding of processes in crosscultural communication as well as models for positive crosscultural contacts cannot be underestimated. Also the traditional focus on language *per se* in language teaching can be counterproductive (cf. Gustavsson, 1988a). Instead, a broader and deeper understanding of how language is anchored in a cultural context of activities, beliefs and values is needed (cf. also Allwood (1981a; 1985).

Ways to meet these needs may be to work more with the cultural variation and the conflicts that are actually present in the individual classroom and to integrate crosscultural perspectives and, wherever adequate, language teaching (in the majority language as well as in the minority language(s)) with school subjects that are traditionally not thought of as linguistic, such as, e.g., mathematics (see Kilborn, 1988) or music (see Tagg, 1988). For a more detailed, crossdisciplinary discussion of these question, see Strömqvist & Strömqvist (1988).

In order to achieve this, it is necessary for teachers to obtain a more thorough knowledge of the ecology and complex processes of language acquisition, language maintenance and bilingualism in their training. It is most important that not only second language teachers or minority language teachers receive such a training, but that teachers of the majority language as a first language receive it as well. At present, there is a trend (again, most probably manifesting the drive in the majority community to preserve its identity) for minority language teachers to be often blamed for imperfect command of the majority language, whereas teachers in the majority language are never blamed for the fact that, as a rule, they have no command or knowledge at all of the minority language(s). (Note furthermore, in this connection, that the Swedish educational system offers the individual school the opportunity to have Swedish as a second language as a compulsory school subject, whereas the home languages of the minority children are only offered as optional subjects.)

To counterbalance this bias, it would in many respects be better to offer the teacher of the majority language, training in the relevant minority language(s) than to offer him special training in the art of teaching the majority language as a second language. Among other things, it would offer that teacher the opportunity (privilege) of obtaining first-hand experience of learning (as distinct from teaching) a language. Many of those who are carried away by the deviation perspective on acquisition have their language learning experience behind them.

4. Conclusions and Suggestions for Further Research

Research on second language acquisition conducted in Scandinavia, notably in Sweden, over the last two decades has experienced a change in perspective. Important aspects of this change consist of a move away from the question of why the learner deviates from the target language norm in the way he does and the concomitant deviation perspective on language acquisition to the question of why the learner constructs his utterances in the way he does and the concomitant development perspective (see section 2). This change in perspective enables a more thorough understanding of how an individual acquires a second language. Within the domain of education, however, this change in perspective has not yet taken place. It is my contention that such a change is also crucial in educational contexts and in society at large, if we are to handle the conflicts and meet the demands of a rapidly changing multilingual and multicultural society.

As to guidelines for future research, three main types of aspects or problem areas worthy of consideration can be distinguished, namely:

a. Conceptual clarification.
b. Studies of the acquisition process.
c. Philosophy and sociology of science.

Clearly, these three aspects or areas are interrelated. Empirical investigation (b) presupposes a conceptual basis (a) for the selection of observations as well as for the interpretation of the observations. Furthermore, in order to supervise the research activity, the researcher has to have an understanding of the factors which determine that activity (c).

More specifically, we have observed how ill-defined concepts, such as, for example, semilingualism, have decreased rather than increased our understanding of a speaker's linguistic knowledge and proficiency as well as of the acquisition process. At the same time, we have observed some of these concepts to have acquired a high status in the public debate and also in educational contexts. These observations highlight the need for a well defined conceptual basis for the study of (second) language acquisition as well as the need for a better understanding of what factors determine the career of an idea in spheres internal as well as external to the scientific community. (Here, the philosophy and sociology of science may prove helpful.) Hopefully, a better understanding of these determinants will also make it easier to bridge communication gaps between researchers and, for example, (political) decision-makers, teachers, or counsellors.

Furthermore, it is important to investigate how the concepts employed for describing and interpreting second language acquisition and multilingualism are constructed in different cultures, especially, of course, in the source and target cultures relevant to the individual study. It can be expected, for example, that the construction of linguistic concepts in a culture will be dependent on the degree to which that culture uses written language. Similarly, bilingualism, semilingualism and related concepts can be expected to be constructed in different fashions depending upon whether multilingualism is the normal or abnormal case in the culture in question. An empirical investigation of these issues could be pursued along the lines of, for example, empirical semantics formulated by Naess (see, e.g., Naess, 1953).

If the research is a joint venture between scholars from different disciplines or different cultures, it is also important to clarify in what ways the members of the project themselves differ in how they conceptualize the problem areas under study and how they differ in their ways of using descriptive and explanatory terms.

As to the study of the acquisition process, there is a strong need for descriptive studies of second language acquisition from what we have termed a "development perspective". Here, the new wave of communication – and ecology – oriented studies characteristic of the 1980s (see section 3) has a great potential, from both a theoretical and a practical point of view. In order to pursue research along these lines, crossdisciplinary cooperation is needed, in particular between linguistics, anthropology, sociology and psychology.

Finally, in view of the complexity of the area of second language acquisition and the many biases of perspective, it is essential to safeguard an instrument for evaluating different models, theories and proposals concerning second language acquisition. As an input to such an instrument or metatheory one would need an integrated theory of first and second language acquisition and a fair portion of philosophy and sociology of science.

NOTES

1 This study was carried out with support from The Swedish Research Council for the Humanities and Social Sciences (HSFR), grant no. F 369/87

2 I want to express my thanks to Jens Allwood, Anders-Börje Andersson, Dennis Day, Lotty van den Berg-Eldering, Guus Extra, Lennart Gustavsson, and Kerstin Nauclér for valuable discussions and comments on earlier versions of my text. Needless to say, I alone am responsible for the text I now present to the reader.

REFERENCES

AHLSÉN, E. (1988). Referensstrategier i svenskan hos afatiker och andraspråksinlärare. In P. Linell et al. (Eds.), *Svenskans beskrivning 16*, University of Linköping, Dept. of Communication Studies, 63-75.

ALLARDT, E. (1987). The ecology of bilingualism. In E. Wande, et al. (Eds.) *Aspects of bilingualism*. Acta Universitatis Upsaliensis, Studia Multiethnica Upsaliensia, 2, 351-372.

ALLWOOD, J. (1979). *Antropologisk lingvistik – en projektbeskrivning*, PAL 1, University of Göteborg, Dept. of Linguistics.

ALLWOOD, J. (1981). Svenska kommunikationsmönster – finns det? In *Vad är svensk kultur?* PAL 9, University of Göteborg, Dept. of Linguistics.

ALLWOOD, J. (Ed.) (1985). *Tvärkulturell kommunikation*. PAL 12, University of Göteborg, Dept. of Linguistics.

ALLWOOD, J. (Ed.) (1988a). *Feedback processes*. Final Report in the project Ecology of Adult Language Acquisition, European Science Foundation.

ALLWOOD, J. (1988b). Om det svenska systemet för språklig återkoppling. In P. Linell et al. (Eds.), *Svenskans beskrivning 16,*. University of Linköping, Dept. of Communication Studies, 89-106.

ALLWOOD, J. (1988c). Vuxnas språkinlärning. In K. Hyltenstam & I. Lindberg (Eds.), *Svenska som andraspråk*, University of Stockholm, Dept. of Linguistics.

ALLWOOD, J. & ABELAR, Y. (1985). Lack of understanding, misunderstanding, and adult language acquisition. In G. Extra & M. Mittner (Eds.) *Studies in second language acquisition by adult immigrants*. Tilburg: Tilburg University Press, 27-55.

ALLWOOD, J. & AHLSÉN, E. (1986). Lexical Convergence and Language Acquisition. In Ö. Dahl (Ed.), *Papers from the Ninth Scandinavian Conference of Linguistics*, University of Stockholm, Dept. of Linguistics, 15-26.

ALLWOOD, J., MacDOWALL, M. & STRÖMQVIST, S. (1982). *Barn, språkutveckling och flerspråkighet*. Expertrapport för Socialstyrelsen, delutredning i SOU, 43.

ALLWOOD, T. (1988). Invandrarbarns möte med skolan. In S. Strömqvist & G. Strömqvist (Eds.), *Kulturmöen, kommunikation, skola.*. Stockholm: Norstedts, 224-231.

ANDENAES, E. (1984). Norsk som andrespråk: bakgrunn, forskning og forskningsbehov, in K. Hyltenstam & K. Maandi (Eds.), *Nordens språk som målspråk. Forskning och undervisning.* University of Stockholm: Dept of Linguistics, 61-78.

ANDENAES, E. & GOLDEN, A. (1980). *Norsk som fremmedspråk. En sammenliknende analyse av trekk ved skriftlig norsk hos arabiske, pakistanske og tyrkiske elever i Osloskolen.* Hovedoppgave, Universitetet i Oslo: Nordisk Institutt.

ANDERSSON, A.-B. (in preparation). *Second-language learners' acquisition of gender in Sweden,* University of Göteborg, Dept. of Linguistics.

ANDERSSON, A.-B. & NAUCLÉR, K. (1987). *Språkmiljö och språkinlärning.* SPRINS-rapport 38, University of Göteborg, Dept. of Linguistics.

ARNBERG, L. (1979). Language strategies in mixed nationality families, *Scandinavian Journal of Psychology, 20,* 105-112.

ARNBERG, L. (1981). *Early childhood bilingualism in the mixed lingual family.* Linköping Studies in Education, Dissertations No 14.

AXELSSON, M. (1985). *The acquisition of markers of definiteness in Swedish as a second language.* Scandinavian Working Papers on Bilingualism 4, University of Stockholm, Dept. of Linguistics.

AXELSSON, M. & VIBERG, A. (1985). *Inlärning av species och lexikal struktur. En undersökning med instruktionstest.* SUM Report 2, University of Stockholm, Dept. of Linguistics.

BANNERT, R. (1979). *Ordprosodi i invandrarundervisningen.* Praktisk Lingvistik 3, University of Lund, Dept. of Linguistics.

BANNERT, R. (1980). *Svårigheter med svenskt uttal: inventering och prioritering.* Praktisk Lingvistik 5. University of Lund, Dept. of Linguistics.

BOLANDER, M. (1987). *"Man kan studera inte så mycket." Om placering av negation och adverb i vuxna invandrares svenska.* SUM Report 5, University of Stockholm, Dept. of Linguistics.

BOLANDER, M. (1988). Is there any order? On word order in Swedish learner language. *Journal of Multilingual and Multicultural Development,.*

BOYD, S. (1985). *Language survival: A study of language contact, language shift and language choice in Sweden.* Gothenburg Monographs in Linguistics 6, University of Göteborg, Dept. of Linguistics.

BOYD, S. (1988). Texanska – ett hemspråk? In S. Strömqvist & G. Strömqvist (Eds.), *Kulturmöten, kommunikation, skola.* Stockholm: Norstedts, 95-112.

BOWERMAN, M. (1982). Starting to talk worse: Clues to language acquisition from children's late speech errors. In S. Strauss (Ed.) *U-shaped behavioral growth.* London: Academic Press.

BRATT-PAULSTON, Ch. (1982). *Swedish research and debate on bilingualism – A report to the National Board of Education.* Stockholm: Skolöverstyrelsen.

BROEDER, P. & VOIONMAA, K. (1986). Establishing word-class distinctions in the vocabulary of adult language learners – a crosslinguistic perspective. In Ö. Dahl (Ed.), *Papers from the Ninth Scandinavian Conference of Linguistics,* University of Stockholm, Dept. of Linguistics, 74-85.

BURLING, R. (1981). Black English, blandspråk and halvspråkighet. In E. Ejerhed & I. Henrysson (Eds.), *Tvåspråkighet.* University of Umeå, 39-48.

CHOMSKY, N. (1965). *Aspects of the theory of syntax.* Cambridge, Mass.: M.I.T. Press.

CORDER, P. (1967). The significance of learner errors. *International Review of Applied Linguistics, 5,* 161-170.

DAHL, Ö. (Ed.) (1986). *Papers from the Ninth Scandinavian Conference of Linguistics,* University of Stockholm, Dept. of Linguistics.

DAY, D. (in preparation) *The vernacular of second generation immigrants in a multi-cultural/multilingual setting*, University of Göteborg, Dept. of Linguistics.

DEUTSCH, W. & BUDWIG, N. (1983). *Form and function in the development of possessives*. Papers and Reports on Child Language Development Vol 22. Stanford University: Dept. of Linguistics, 36-42.

DORRIOTS, B. (1986). *How to succeed with only fifty words – analysis of a role-play in the frame of adult language acquisition*. Gothenburg Papers in Theoretical Linguistics 52, University of Göteborg, Dept. of Linguistics.

EKSTRAND, L.H. (1978). *Unpopular views on popular beliefs about immigrant children*. Paper presented at the symposium "Sociopersonal adjustment of immigrant children in European and North-American Schools", Munich.

ELIASSON, S. (1978). Theoretical problems in Scandinavian contrastive phonology. In J. Weinstock (Ed.) *The Nordic languages and modern linguistics, 3*, Austin, Texas: The University of Texas at Austin, 217-243.

ELIASSON, S. (1979). A bibliography of Swedish contrastive linguistics and error analysis. *Nordic Journal of Linguistics, 2*, No. 2.

EXTRA, G., STRÖMQVIST, S., VAN HOUT, R., BROEDER, P. & VOIONMAA, K. (1988). *Processes in the developing Lexicon*, Final Report in the project Ecology of Adult Language Acquisition, European Science Foundation.

FAERCH, C. & KASPER, G. (Eds.) (1983). *Strategies in interlanguage communication*. London: Longman.

FAERCH, C. & KASPER, G. (Eds.) (1987). *Introspection in second language research*. Clevedon: Multilingual Matters.

GUSTAVSSON, L. (1988a). *Language taught and language used. Dialogue processes in dyadic lessons of Swedish as a second language compared with non-didactic conversations*. Linköping Studies in Arts and Science 18, University of Linköping, Departments of Theme Research.

GUSTAVSSON, L. (1988b) Språkvetenskaplig forskning om svenska som andraspråk, in K. Hyltenstam & I. Lindberg (Eds.), *Svenska som andraspråk*, University of Stockholm, Dept. of Linguistics.

GÅRDING, E. & BANNERT, R. (1979). *Projektrapporter: optimering av svenskt uttal*. Praktisk Lingvistik 3, University of Lund, Dept. of Linguistics.

HÅKANSSON, G. (1987). *Teacher talk. How teachers modify their language when addressing learners of Swedish as a second language*. Travaux de l'Institut de linguistique de Lund 20. Lund: Lund University Press.

HAMMARBERG, B. (1988). *Studien zur Phonologie des Zweisprachenerwerbs*. Stockholmer Germanistische Forschungen 38. Stockholm: Almqvist & Wiksell.

HAMMARBERG, B. & VIBERG, Å. (1977). *Felanalys och språktypologi. Orientering om två delstudier i SSM-projektet*. SSM Report 1, University of Stockholm, Dept. of Linguistics.

HAMMARBERG, B. & VIBERG, Å. (1979). *Platshållartvånget, ett syntaktiskt problem i svenskan för invandrare*. SSM Report 2, University of Stockholm, Dept. of Linguistics.

HANSEGÅRD, N. E. (1968). *Tvåspråkighet eller halvspråkighet?* Stockholm: Aldus.

HANSSON, G. (1980). Modersmålsklasser och övergångsmodeller. *Invandrare och minoreteter, 3*, 6-8.

HIRSCH, R. (1979). *Swedish fear vocabulary*. PAL 4, University of Göteborg: Dept. of Linguistics.

HVENEKILDE, A. (Ed.) (1980). *Mellom to språk. 4 kontrastive språkstudier for laerere*. Oslo: Cappelen.

HYLTENSTAM, K. (1978). *Progress in immigrant Swedish syntax. A variability study.* University of Lund, Dept. of Linguistics.

HYLTENSTAM, K. (1982). Markedness. language universals, language typology and second language acquisition. In C. Pfaff (Ed.), *Proceedings from the 2nd European Workshop on Cross-Linguistic Second Language Acquisition Research.* Rowley, Mass.: Newbury House.

HYLTENSTAM, K. (1984). The use of typological markedness conditions as predictors in second language acquisition: the case of pronominal copies in relative clauses. In R.W. Andersen (Ed.), *Second Languages: a cross-linguistic perspective.* Rowley, Mass.: Newbury House.

HYLTENSTAM, K. & MAANDI, K. (Eds.) (1984). *Nordens språk som målspråk. Forskning och undervisning.* University of Stockholm: Dept. of Linguistics.

JACOBSEN, I. (1984). Dansk som målsprog – undervisning, laereruddannelse, forskning. In K. Hyltenstam & K. Maandi (Eds.), *Nordens språk som målspråk. Forskning och undervisning.* University of Stockholm: Dept. of Linguistics, 79-89.

JÖRGENSEN, J.N. (1983). Fremmedarbejderbörns danske orförråd, en sociolingvistisk undersögelse. In *Proceedings from the Fifth International Conference of Nordic Languages and Linguistics*, August

KARLSSON, F. (Ed.) (1983). *Papers from the Seventh Scandinavian conference of linguistics*, University of Helsinki, Dept. of Linguistics.

KILBORN, W. (1988). Är matematikens språk interkulturellt? In S. Strömqvist & G. Strömqvist (Eds.), *Kulturmöten, kommunikation, skola.* Stockholm: Norstedts, 198-209.

KOS-DIENES, D. (1982). *Om färgtermernas symboliska användning*, PAL 4, University of Göteborg, Dept. of Linguistics.

KOTSINAS, U.-B. (1988). Rinkebysvenskan – en dialekt? In P. Linell et al. (Eds.), *Svenskans beskrivning 16*, University of Linköping, Dept. of Communication Studies.264-278.

LANZA, E. (1986). Språkdifferensiering hos småbarn som tilegner seg to språk samtidig. In P.E. Mjaavatn & L. Smith (Red.), *Barnespråk – om normal og avvikende språkutvikling.* Universitetet i Trondheim, NAVF's Senter for barneforskning, 150-173.

LINDBERG, I. (1988). *Om kommunikation i andraspråksundervisningen.* SUM Report 4, University of Stockholm: Dept. of Linguistics.

LINDBLOM, B., MACNEILAGE, P. & STUDDERT-KENNEDY, M. (1984). Selforganizing processes and the explanation of phonological universals. In B. Butterworth, B. Comrie & Ö. Dahl (Eds.), *Explanations for language universals.* Den Haag: Mouton, 181-203.

LINELL, P., ADELSWÅRD, V., NIKSSON, T. & PETTERSON, P. (Eds.) (in press) *Svenskans beskrivning 16*, University of Linköping, Dept. of Communication Studies.

LOMAN, B. (1974). Till frågan om tvåspråkighet och halvspråkighet i Tornedalen. In B. Loman (Ed.) *Språk och samhälle 2. Språket i Tornedalen.* Lund: Gleerup, 43-79.

MARTIN-JONES, M. & ROMAINE, S. (1987). Semilingualism: A halfbaked theory of communicative competence. In E. Wande et al. (Eds.), *Aspects of bilingualism.* Acta Universitatis Upsaliensis, Studia Multiethnica Upsaliensia 2, 87-104.

McLAUGHLIN, B. (1978). *Second-language acquisition in childhood*. Hillsdale, N.J.: Lawrence Erlbaum.

MEY, J.L. (1985). *Whose language? – A study in linguistic pragmatics*. Amsterdam: John Benjamins.

NAUCLÉR, K. & ANDERSSON, A.-B. (1988). Invandrarbarns språkmiljö i förskolan. In S. Strömqvist & G. Strömqvist (Eds.), *Kulturmöten, kommunikation, skola*. Stockholm: Norstedts, 113-132.

NAESS, A. (1953). *Interpretation and preciseness. A contribution to the theory of communication*. Oslo.

ÖHMAN, S. (1981). Halvspråkighet som kastmärke. In *Att leva med mångfalden*. Stockholm: Liber, 189-197.

PLUNKETT, K. & STRÖMQVIST, S. (in preparation) *The Acquisition of Scandinavian Languages*. Hillsdale, NJ: Lawrence Erlbaum.

SELINKER, L. (1972). Interlanguage. *International Review of Applied Linguistics, 10*, 209-231.

SKUTNABB-KANGAS, T. & TOUKOMAA, P. (1976). *Teaching migrant children their mother tongue and learning the language of the host country in the context of the sociocultural situation of the migrant family*. Tampere: Dept of Sociology and Social Psychology, Research Report 15.

SKUTNABB-KANGAS, T. (1981). *Tvåspråkighet*. Lund: Liber.

SLOBIN, D. I. (1973). Cognitive prerequisites for the development of grammar. In C.A. Ferguson & D.I. Slobin (Eds.) *Studies of Child Language Development*. New York: Holt, Rinehart and Winston.

SLOBIN, D.I. (1986). Crosslinguistic evidence of the languagemaking capacity. In D.I. Slobin (Ed.), *The Crosslinguistic Study of Language Acquisition (Vol. 1)*. Hillsdale, N.J.: Lawrence Erlbaum.

STRÖMQVIST, S. (1983). Lexical search games in adult second language acquisition. In F. Karlsson (Ed.), *Papers from the Seventh Scandinavian conference of linguistics*, University of Helsinki, Dept. of Linguistics, 532-555.

STRÖMQVIST, S. (1986). On the development of reference and information structure – an asymmetry between child L1 and adult L2 acquisition. In Ö. Dahl (Ed.), *Papers from the Ninth Scandinavian Conference of Linguistics*, University of Stockholm, Dept. of Linguistics, 292-304.

STRÖMQVIST, S. (1987a). *Chaotic phases in adult second language acquisition: part of a work schedule?* Workshop on Strategies in Language Learning, Second International Congress of Applied Psycholinguistics, Kassel, July 27-31, 1987.

STRÖMQVIST, S. (1987b). Gaze Aversion, Code-Switching, and Search Activities in Route Descriptions by Six Adult Language Learners. In E. Wande, J. Award, B. Nordberg, L. Steensland & M. Thelander (Eds.), *Aspects of bilingualism*. Acta Universitatis Upsaliensis, Studia Multiethnica Upsaliensia 2, 351-372.

STRÖMQVIST, S. (1988). Svenska i ett ontogenetiskt perspektiv. In P. Linell, V. Adelswård, T. Niksson & P. Petterson (Eds.), *Svenskans beskrivning 16*, University of Linköping, Dept. of Communication Studies, 457-474.

STRÖMQVIST, S. & STRÖMQVIST, G. (Eds.) (1988). *Kulturmöten, kommunikation, skola*. Stockholm: Norstedts.

STRÖMQVIST, S., DAY, D. & LÖVFORS, M. (1988). *The development of discours cohesion – experimental evidence from child L1 and adult L2 acquisition*. Paper presented at the 11th Scandinavian Conference of Linguistics, Joensuu, August, 29-31.

TAGG, Ph. (1988). Musiken som kommunikationsform. In S. Strömqvist & G. Strömqvist (Eds.), *Kulturmöten, kommunikation, skola*. Stockholm: Norstedts.

TENFJORD, K. (1983). *Systematisk variert tilfeldig. Ein kontrastiv analyse av mellomspråket til ei gruppe vietnamesiske ungdomar*. Hovedoppgave, Universitetet i Bergen: Nordisk Institutt.

TOUKOMAA, P. (1977). *Om finska invadrarelevers språkutveckling och skolframgång i den svenska grundskolan*. Stockholm: EIFO, Arbetsdepartementet.

TOUTATI, P. (1987). *Structures prosodiques du suédois et du français*. Travaux de l'Institut de linguistique de Lund, 21. Lund: Lund University Press.

VIBERG, Å. (1981). *Studier i kontrastiv lexikologi: en typologisk och kontrastiv jämförelse av tre semantiska fält i svenskan: perceptionsverb – kognitiva predikat – emotiva predikat*. University of Stockholm, Dept. of Linguistics.

VIBERG, Å. (1984a). Fysiska kontaktverb i svenskan. En skiss. In *Svenskans beskrivning 14*, University of Lund, Dept. of Scandinavian Languages, 174-185.

VIBERG, Å. (1984a). Forskning kring svenska som målspråk: grammatik och ordförråd. In K. Hyltenstam & K. Maandi (Eds.), *Nordens språk som målspråk. Forskning och undervisning*. University of Stockholm, Dept. of Linguistics, 3-45.

VOIONMAA, K. (1983). On interpersonal power and its relation to second language acquisition. In F. Karlsson (Ed.), *Papers from the Seventh Scandinavian conference of linguistics*. University of Helsinki, Dept. of Linguistics, 556-567.

WANDE, E. (1977). Hansegård är ensidig. *Invandrare och minoriteter*, 3-4, 44-51.

WANDE, E. (1980). Den svenska tvåspråkighetsdebatten under 1970-talet – en argumentationsanalys. In *Rapport från projektet Sverige – multietniskt samhälle*. Uppsala, University of Uppsala, Faculty of the Humanities, bil. 3:23.

WANDE, E. (1987). Aspects of multilingualism: an introduction. In E. Wande, J. Award, B. Nordberg, L. Steensland & M. Thelander (Eds.), *Aspects of bilingualism*. Acta Universitatis Upsaliensis, Studia Multiethnica Upsaliensia 2.

WHORF, B.L. (1956). *Language thought and reality*. Cambridge (Mass.): M.I.T. Press.

WITTGENSTEIN, L. (1953). *Philosophische Untersuchungen (Philosophical Investigations)*. Oxford: Basil Blackwell.

10
Pam Sammons
Inner London Education Authority

School Effectiveness and School Organization

1. INTRODUCTION

- Does the particular school attended by a child make a difference?
- Will a child's progress in reading or writing be similar wherever she or he is taught?
- Are some schools more effective than others?

These are just three of the questions, often posed by parents and educators, which have recently stimulated researchers to investigate how much difference there is between the most and the least effective schools. Curiously, traditional educational research carried out in Britain and in North America has failed to address these important questions. This was probably because social scientists, such as Coleman et al. (1966) and Jencks et al. (1972), had argued that home background factors, including social class and economic status, were much more influential on a child's development than school. They reasoned that because the differences between families were much greater than those between schools, families were likely to exert the greater influence. Whilst it is undoubtedly true that an economically advantaged family – with comfortable housing, healthy diet, and time for stimulating educational experiences, contrasts starkly with an economically disadvantaged one – with inadequate, overcrowded or even a lack of permanent housing, poor diet and little time or money for educational experiences, it is also true that schools vary a great deal. The problem for researchers is how to tease out the effects of families from the effects of schools.

Two groups of research studies – one in the United States and one in Britain – have begun to address this issue. In the United States, a group of researchers including Weber (1971), Summers and Wolfe (1977), Brookover et al. (1978, 1979), Edmonds (1979a, 1979b), Good (1979), and Goodlad et al. (1979), have been active in challenging the view that the influence of school can only be trivial. In Britain a group of researchers (see Reynolds, 1985) concerned with analysing school differences has carried out a number of pioneering studies designed to separate out the effects of home and school. Notable amongst the British group have been a study of Welsh secondary schools (Reynolds, 1982) and a study of twelve inner city secondary schools (Rutter et al., 1979). This latter study – written up in a book entitled *Fifteen thousand hours; secondary schools and their effects on children* – was important because it developed a methodology to evaluate the effectiveness of schools *after* having taken account of the characteristics of the students entering those schools.

Although these studies attracted methodological criticism, their impact was to encourage other researchers to develop suitable techniques (see Aitkin et al., 1981a, 1981b; Gray, 1981) and appropriate methods of analysis (Goldstein, 1980, 1984) to address this important issue in a more sophisticated way. A recent American review of the area of school effectiveness (Purkey & Smith, 1983) demonstrated that such studies have succeeded in identifying a number of common factors. In other words, researchers have managed to develop generally accepted ways of answering the questions listed at the beginning of this chapter.

Writing about British research into school effectiveness in 1985 David Reynolds made the following claim. "Because of its direct policy relevance and its general interest to parents and others, there is no doubt that people undertaking school effectiveness research have raised very high expectations of themselves in the wider community. Many have hoped – and are still hoping – for blueprints of the effective or high achieving school or for clear visions of what makes the effective teacher, so that practice can be directly improved."(Reynolds, 1985, p. 10.)

This chapter examines how far a recent piece of school effectiveness research has progressed towards fulfilling such expectations.

2. THE VALUE OF SCHOOL EFFECTIVENESS RESEARCH

The question of school effectiveness is of great relevance to head-teachers, teachers and policy makers, as well as to parents and, of course, to pupils themselves. It is clearly of critical importance to those concerned with the provision of education, both nationally and locally, because of their responsibilities for monitoring the quality of the service provided to the community, and improving educational standards.

Edmonds has stated that the major aim of schools should be *educational excellence*, which he defined as follows: "Educational excellence means that students become independent, creative thinkers, learn to work cooperatively and so on." He made a particular point of emphasizing student mastery of basic skills because he felt that teachers who were not successful in promoting basic skills were unlikely to be able to cope with the more demanding task of achieving excellence[1]. Goodlad (1984) has also proposed a variety of different goals for education. These include:

– adademic development;
– intellectual development;
– vocational goals;
– social, civic and cultural goals;
– personal goals.

All who accept the need to strive for educational excellence, and the importance of the different goals noted above, must be interested in the findings of research which attempts to increase our understanding of how schools influence their pupils, and what promotes their progress and development. Such research of course has a special relevance to those concerned with monitoring the education and progress of children from different ethnic backgrounds and raising standards of achievement.

In my view, neither the results of North American, nor those of British research into school effectiveness, provide a ready-made blueprint for instant effective education. However, they do have an important contribution to offer educators because a careful examination of the findings of school effectiveness research offers the right *framework* for evaluating the performance of schools. It is argued that these results help to provide much of that thorough knowledge of the *mechanisms and processes* that affect children's educational outcomes which is a prerequisite for action to improve outcomes. From this knowledge appropriate strategies for school and teacher self-evaluation can be developed. Such self-evaluation provides the necessary foundation for planning school improvement programmes, and provides educators with a methodology to monitor whether improvement is actually occurring.

In this chapter the main focus of attention is on the findings of a study of junior education, the *Inner London Education Authority's Junior School Project* (JSP). There are several reasons for looking at this study in some depth.

- It is the largest piece of school effectiveness research undertaken to date either in the UK or in North America.
- It examined a much broader range of children's educational outcomes than previous studies.
- The results support and confirm many earlier findings about school effectiveness.
- The results also extend our knowledge of what contributes to effectiveness in several important ways.
- In contrast to most previous studies, it examined both factors to do with the school as a whole and those to do with teachers' classroom practices, and shows how these relate to pupils' outcomes.
- The study was only recently completed, and therefore its findings may be less well known than those of earlier pieces of research.

Although the JSP was set up to study the junior years of schooling which cover the age-range seven to eleven, many of the results are of relevance to those working with older students (secondary) and younger children (infants). It is interesting to note the similarities between the JSP findings and those produced by other research including that concerned with secondary schools. These links are discussed in some detail by Mortimore et al., 1988.

3. THE JUNIOR SCHOOL PROJECT

The project began in September 1980 when a cohort of nearly 2000 seven-year-olds entered their junior classes, and concluded four years later when the students transferred to secondary school. The study was longitudinal, following a complete age-group of pupils, and examined their progress and development throughout the whole period of time they received junior education. The children attended a stratified random sample of 50 schools in inner London, selected from the 636 primary schools existing within the Inner London Education Authority's juridiction. The sample proved to be representative both of schools and of pupils in the area served by the ILEA[2]. (A description of the pupil sample is provided in Appendix 1.)

3.1 Aims

The project was designed to produce a detailed description of the pupils, teachers and of the curriculum and organization of schools in an inner city area, and to investigate the progress and development of an age-group of children. It attempted to answer three major questions.

1. Are some schools more effective than others in promoting children's learning and development, when account is taken of variations in the students' backgrounds?
2. Are some schools more effective than others for particular groups of children (for girls or boys, for those of different social class origins, or different racial backgrounds)?
3. If some schools are more effective than others, what factors contribute to such positive effects?

The research was conducted by an interdisciplinary group of researchers and experienced primary teachers who worked together as a team for four years. In my view it was crucial to the success of the project that teachers were involved both in the design of the study and some of the research instruments, as well as in working directly with the schools in the sample as field officers.

3.2 Information about pupils, schools and teachers

In order to answer the research questions noted above, information was collected on three major topics: children's background characteristics; their learning and development; and school characteristics. These represent measures of the pupil *intakes* to schools; measures of pupils' *educational outcomes*; and measures of school and classroom *processes*.

The characteristics of the pupil *intakes* to the 50 sample schools were measured. Detailed information was obtained for each child about sex, age, social, ethnic, language and family background; preschool and infant experiences; and initial attainments at entry to junior school. These data were needed so that the research design could establish the impact of such background factors on children's later attainments, progress and development; take into account differences between schools in their intakes; quantify the relative importance of school compared with background as influences upon pupils; and explore the effectiveness of schooling for different groups

224   *Sammons*

(e.g. boys or girls; those of different socio-economic backgrounds; those of different ethnic origins). Unless *full* account is taken of differences between schools in the intakes they receive, comparisons of the educational outcomes of children attending different schools are invalid and liable to be misleading, because of the failure properly to compare 'like' with 'like'. (See the discussion of this issue by Gray, 1981; Goldstein, 1984; or Gray & Jones, 1985.)

One of the advantages of the JSP research is that it focused on collecting data about each child individually. This meant that when schools' effects on pupils were investigated, it was possible to identify and separate those which were due to the particular school attended from those which were due to background factors.

The second set of information related to pupils' learning and development. To take account of the diversity of aims and curricula of primary education a wide range of outcomes was examined.

Cognitive or academic outcomes
It was considered desirable for the study to focus on more than attainment in 'basic skill' areas, important though these are. So, in addition to reading and written mathematics, the children's practical maths skills and visio-spatial skills were examined. Creative writing was assessed using measures which included the quality of language and ideas, as well as more technical aspects such as length, legibility and punctuation (see Strachan & Sammons, 1986). To broaden the assessments of language, children's oracy or speaking skills were also studied. The oracy assessments focused on the ability to communicate effectively, and children were not penalized for using non-standard English (see Gorman & Hargreaves, 1985).

Non-cognitive or social outcomes
Of equal interest were the non-cognitive or social outcomes of education which tend to have been neglected in previous studies of school differences. Information was obtained about pupils' attendance; their behaviour in school; their attitudes to school and to different types of school activities; and their self-concepts (including their perceptions of themselves as learners) in school.

Learning environment
The third set of information related to the characteristics of the schools, their organization, and numerous aspects of the learning environment experienced by pupils. Field officers also made detailed

observations and kept extensive notes of teachers and pupils in the classroom setting. The sorts of organizational and management factors about which information was collected are listed below.
- Aims & philosophy of school.
- Aims & philosophy of class teachers.
- Organization of school & policies.
- Rewards & punishments (school).
- Organization of classrooms.
- Curriculum.
- Structure of teaching.
- Rewards & punishment (class).
- Teacher-pupil communication.
- Support services.
- Books & resources.
- School appearance.
- Classroom appearance.

The methods used to collect the school and classroom process data included: interviews (with headteachers, deputy headteachers, class teachers, special needs teachers and parents); observations (of individual pupils and teachers in the classroom setting over a three-year period, and of the school environment); and questionnaires (with headteachers, deputy headteachers, teachers and pupils).

The parents of children in the sample in eight of the 50 schools were also interviewed, using interviewers speaking the parents' home language. This was done to find out about the parents' view of their child's education and school, and to establish their involvement with the school and with the child's learning at home (see Sammons et al., 1985; and Varlaam et al., 1985, for details of the parents study).

3.3 Measuring school effects
The analysis of all these data was complex, and extensive use was made of sophisticated statistical techniques. In essence, however, the strategy adopted was simple. The intention was to find out what impact schools had on their pupils' progress and development, once account was taken of their attainment at entry to junior school, and of the influence of age, sex and other background factors. It was possible to analyse pupil progress because the project was longitudinal. By studying the progress of individual pupils, account could be taken of the very different levels of skill possessed by children at entry to junior school. For each child, therefore, her or his initial attainment at entry was the baseline against which progress during

later years was measured. Multi-level methods of analysis were employed for these purposes. These are described in detail in the technical appendices to the research (Mortimore et al., 1986).

The impact upon pupils' educational outcomes was the criterion we used for evaluating school effectiveness. In the view of the research team this is the most valid way of comparing schools. We sought, therefore, to establish their effects – whether positive of negative – upon the children who attended them.

3.4 The influence of background factors

Children included in the Junior School Project sample were drawn from a wide variety of backgrounds (see Appendix 1). Some lived in families which were advantaged in material terms, while others were living in very difficult circumstances. Such differences in circumstances can have a considerable impact upon pupils' educational outcomes (see Essen & Wedge, 1982, or Sammons et al., 1983, for example). Within the ILEA area there is growing evidence that the incidence of disadvantage is increasing (see Hunter et al., 1985).

Educational research has frequently demonstrated that social background and income are good predictors of cognitive attainments among primary pupils (see reviews by Rutter & Madge, 1976, or Mortimore & Blackstone, 1982). Family variables – such as size and birth order – also appear to be related to educational outcomes (see Marjoriebanks, 1979).

Differences in achievement amongst pupils of primary age have also been found to be associated with sex, differences usually being found in favour of girls at this stage (see APU, 1981, 1982).

The strength of differences due to race has been debated extensively in recent years, and evidence of under-achievement by children of some ethnic minority backgrounds is a cause for serious concern (see Essen & Ghodsian, 1980; Rampton, 1981; Swann, 1985; Eggleston et al., 1985; Mabey, 1985).

Tomlinson (see chapter 2 in this volume) provides a very useful summary of the issues surrounding ethnicity and educational achievement in Britain. Research undertaken elsewhere in Europe has also demonstrated the existence of under-achievement of ethnic minority children in a variety of different school systems. Eldering (see chapter 6 in this volume) reviews the situation in Dutch schools and discusses competing explanatory models for such under-achievement.

It should be stressed, that, although differences in achievement have been identified for children of different social class, sex or ethnic groups, the *causes* of such differences are seldom clear (see Mortimore, 1983). Moreover, although there is evidence that such factors are related to cognitive attainment, their relationship to progress has rarely been studied. In addition, little attention has been paid to variations in the non-cognitive outcomes of education for different groups of pupils.

In furtherance of the ILEA's commitment to a policy of Equal Opportunities, the JSP investigated the strength of differences in a variety of cognitive and non-cognitive outcomes resulting from social class, sex and race. Attention was also paid to variations in these outcomes according to age (a factor which has been neglected in many studies) because this may be an area of educational disadvantage not always recognized in the classroom[3].

The aim of the analyses of these factors was to establish their impact on the eduational prospects of children from different backgrounds. Particular care was paid to the relative progress made by children from particular groups when account was taken of attainment at entry into junior education.

Strong relationships between background factors (especially age, social class and low income, sex and race) and children's attainments and development and, to a lesser extent, their progress during the junior years were identified by the project. Full account, therefore, had to be taken of these relationships before schools' effects on their pupils could be examined.

In order to illustrate the significance of factors relating to pupils' background as influences upon their educational outcomes, some examples of differences related to sex and ethnic background are given. These results demonstrate why it is necessary to take full account of the sorts of intakes schools receive, in any study of school effectiveness. Furthermore, identifying such differences in achievement and development is a necessary first step in developing appropriate strategies to promote equal opportunities in education.

3.5 Ethnic differences

Relationships between ethnic background, pupils' fluency in English and their attainment and progress in the various cognitive and non-cognitive areas were investigated in the same manner as were the effects of age, social class background, and sex.

Cognitive outcomes

Results of analyses of the effects of ethnic background and fluency in

English upon reading attainment at entry to junior school indicated that both factors were highly significant (p<0.0001). Thus, children who were not fully fluent in English (according to their class teacher's assessment) obtained markedly lower reading scores than those who were fully fluent. The effect of being a beginner, or at the second stage of fluency in English, was a reduction in reading scores by between 14 and 23 raw points (in relation to the overall mean of 46).

The effects of ethnic background were more complicated. Even where fluency in English and other background factors had been controlled, certain Asian groups performed differently from others. For example, those who spoke Gujerati performed better than average in the reading test, whilst those speaking Punjabi had poorer reading attainment[4]. Children of Caribbean, Greek and Turkish family backgrounds obtained lower reading scores than those of English, Scottish, Welsh or Irish (ESWI) backgrounds. (For example, the average raw score of the Caribbean group was 40.5, that for the ESWI group was 47.9.) Those of Chinese family backgrounds (a very small group of only 17 in all) had higher scores than those of all other ethnic groups, when all other background factors had been taken into account.

In both the second year and the third year reading assessment, ethnic background and fluency in English remained highly significant. Therefore, there was no evidence that the impact of these factors decreased over the junior years. For reading attainment, the pattern of initial differences remained fairly stable over time.

Relationships between ethnic family background, language fluency and childrens' progress in reading over three years were also explored. It was found that both factors had a statistically significant impact upon progress. Children of Caribbean background and those of Asian background made significantly poorer progress than other groups, even when account was taken of initial attainment. Children who were not fully fluent in English at entry to junior school also made significantly poorer progress in reading over the three years than other children.

The poorer progress of minority ethnic groups in reading supports the results of previous research (see Rampton, 1981 or Mabey, 1985) which indicated that the gap in attainment between English and Caribbean children increases over time. Amongst the present sample, however, it also appears that Asian children as well as Caribbean children made poorer progress in reading over the junior years. The size of these differences are given in Table 1.

Table 1: Effects of Ethnic Background and Fluency in English upon Reading Progress over Three Years*

	Adjusted Deviations Effect in Raw Score Points Upon Third Year Attainment
Caribbean	– 3.4
Asian	– 4.5
Incomplete fluency in English	– 3.7

N = 1101
Overall mean raw score = 53.8

* Analyses were undertaken at the individual level and adjusted for all background factors (including age, sex, social class, low income, initial attainment, test reliability and the clustered nature of the sample). Due to the small sample of Asian pupils it was not possible to examine separately the *progress* of different language sub-groups.

For mathematics attainment at entry, analyses also identified highly significant relationships with ethnic background and with fluency in English. Again, there was variation in the achievements of different sub-groups of Asian children. Those who spoke Bengali tended to have lower scores than those who spoke Gujerati (a difference of 5.5 raw points compared with a mean of 24.3). Children who were of Caribbean and of Turkish origins also tended to obtain lower scores (2.6 and 1.5 points respectively below the mean). A consistent pattern of differences between the different ethnic groups in mathematics attainment was also identified in analyses of assessments in later years. Thus, as a group, in the summer of year three, Caribbean children's attainments were 4.5 points below the mean of 26.8 raw points, and Turkish and Greek children were nearly two points below the mean. In contrast, Gujerati-speaking Asian pupils (a small group) scored nearly three points above the mean. This pattern of ethnic differences was very similar to that identified in the first year. Although the gap in mathematics attainment remained marked throughout the junior years for children of different ethnic backgrounds or with different levels of fluency in English, there was no evidence of an ethnic or fluency effect on progress in mathematics. Controlling for initial attainment, neither Caribbean or Asian children made significantly poorer progress than their ESWI peers. This result is important because it indicates that differences in the performance of children from different ethnic backgrounds did *not* increase over the junior years in mathematics, in contrast to the results for reading.

There was no significant relationship between ethnic background and writing performance in the first year in terms of quality or length. In contrast, fluency in English, as might be expected, was significantly highly related to both length and quality of writing. In the summer of the third year, however, it was found that ethnic background was related significantly to the length of writing, with the various Asian groups, those of Caribbean and those of Turkish backgrounds tending to produce shorter pieces of work. There were, however, no significant differences between ethnic groups in terms of the quality of ideas and language expressed in their written work. Again, fluency in English was related significantly to quality, but no longer had an independent impact upon length of writing.

Interestingly, a qualitative analysis of the content of the children's writing showed no evidence of racist attitudes or racial stereotyping. This does not necessarily mean that they did not exist, or that the children were unaware of such attitudes. However, racial issues were not found to be reflected in their writing (see Bunch, 1984).

When progress in the quality of writing was analysed, no relationship was found with ethnic backgrounds, although the effects of fluency in English just reached significance (p<0.04). Thus, taking account of first year writing quality, children who were not fully fluent in English made slightly poorer progress over the three years than did children who were fully fluent (by around half a point on the ten point quality scale). For progress in the quantity written over three years (controlling for lenght of first year writing), it was found that ethnic background did not have a statistically significant effect.

These results indicate that, in terms of quality of writing, ethnic background was not related to attainment or to progress during the junior years. This is in contrast to the findings for reading and for mathematics attainment. As might be expected, however, children not fluent in English are disadvantaged in attainment and progress in writing as well as in reading and mathematics.

The oracy assessments used in the JSP were designed to judge the communicative effectiveness of children's speech activities, and assessors did not penalize pupils who used non-standard English. Results from the analyses indicated that ethnic background was *not* related to performance in any of the five scales used to assess oracy. Somewhat surprisingly, fluency in English (as rated by teachers) was not related to pupils' performance in the assessment of speaking skills. The reason for this may be due to an improvement in pupils' abilities to speak English over the junior years (the fluency assessment was made in the first year of junior school, whereas the oracy assessments took place in the fourth year). Alternatively, the ability to use standard English forms may be more closely related to reading achievement than to oral skills.

Teachers' assessments of pupils' ability

At each assessment, a higher percentage of English, Scottish, Welsh and Irish than of other pupils were assessed by their class teachers as of above average ability, and a smaller percentage as of below average ability. Thus in the second year, 32 per cent of the ESWI group were rated as above average, compared with 25 per cent of the Asian and under 20 per cent of the Caribbean group.

Class teachers' ability ratings were found to be related strongly to children's attainments in reading, writing and mathematics. Individual analyses of ability ratings, once other background factors (including sex, age and father's social class) and attainment in these three areas had been controlled, indicated that ethnic background was *no longer related* to ability ratings. This finding suggests that teacher under-expectation is unlikely to explain the ethnic difference in pupils' attainment and progress identified amongst the sample.

Non-cognitive outcomes

Overall, there was a higher incidence of behaviour difficulties in school (according to class teachers' assessments) amongst the Caribbean than amongst other groups. Thus, using the criterion of being assessed highly in terms of the behaviour scale (where a high score signifies greater difficulties) in two or more of the three years, nearly 20 per cent of Caribbean, compared with 12 per cent of Asian and 11 per cent of ESWI pupils, were highly rated. The most common form of behaviour difficulty for all groups was associated with learning behaviour problems – rather than aggression or anxiety (the three sub-scales which formed the overall behaviour scale). In all, nearly 14 per cent of the Caribbean, compared with only 5 per cent of Asian and 8 per cent of ESWI pupils, were rated highly on the learning-difficulties sub-scale.

Much of the relationship between ethnic background and behaviour was accounted for by other factors (analyses demonstrated that father's social class, pupil's sex and eligibility for free meals made a significant contribution to the statistical 'explanation' of variations in

232   *Sammons*

behaviour in school). Nonetheless, taking a combined measure of behaviour over three years, analyses at the individual level indicated that, when controlling for the influence of all other background factors, Caribbean pupils were assessed as having greater behaviour difficulties[5].

It is likely that the higher incidence of behaviour difficulties in school (as assessed by teachers) amongst Caribbean pupils, may be due, in part, to the significant link between attainment (especially reading) and behaviour. Analyses indicated that the Caribbean group had significantly lower attainments in reading at each assessment than ESWI pupils (though not in comparison with Asian pupils). Controlling for first-year reading attainment removed the relationship between race and behaviour ratings in later years. It thus appears that lower attainment was related to behaviour, especially learning behaviour difficulties, and that the higher incidence of behaviour difficulties identified amongst Caribbean pupils in the sample over a three-year period was possibly attributable to this factor, rather than to race[6]. Nonetheless, the link between attainment and behaviour is complex and no clear conclusions can be drawn.

Differences in attendance were identified during the junior years according to ethnic background. In each year, children of Caribbean background were present for a higher percentage of the time than the ESWI group whilst children of Asian backgrounds were, on average, absent for a higher percentage of time (see Table 2).

Table 2: *Average percentages of time absent in years one, two and three by ethnic background*

Ethnic Group	% time absent		
	Year 1	Year 2	Year 3
Asian	11.7	11.6	10.6
Caribbean	7.1	8.2	6.1
ESWI	9.1	9.5	9.0
Asian N=	112 year 1;	104 year 2;	89 year 3
Caribbean N=	230 year 1;	221 year 2;	212 year 3
ESWI N=	1 047 year 1;	990 year 2;	889 year 3

Taking into account all other background factors, sex and age, analyses at the level of the individual pupil indicated that these differences in attendance were highly statistically significant for the Caribbean group, and were largest in the third year. At this stage, Caribbean children were absent for 3.3 per cent less time than the average for the sample as a whole (8.3 per cent). This represents just over a week's extra attendance in the school year.

Although Asian children, as a group, tended to have the poorest attendance, this trend was not statistically significant when other background factors were taken into account.

Overall, very little of the variation in children's attitudes to school or to different school activities was accounted for by background factors, sex and age in any year. Nonetheless, there were a few statistically significant differences in the attitudes of children from different ethnic backgrounds. Asian children tended to have more favourable attitudes towards mathematics in the second and third years and towards school in the first and second years. For those of Caribbean backgrounds, more favourable attitudes towards mathematics were identified in the first year, and more favourable attitudes towards reading in the third year.

As with the measures of attitudes, only a small proportion of the variation in children's perceptions of themselves in school was accounted for by background factors, sex and age. Asian children rated themselves significantly more favourably at the end of their third year in junior school than other children. There was, however, no evidence to suggest that Caribbean children had poorer self-concepts in relation to the school environment. (This finding is in contrast to some earlier research which suggested that black children had poorer self-concepts than their white peers.)

The results of analysing differences in educational outcomes according to race indicate that there were significant differences in some areas of cognitive attainment (specifically reading and mathematics) both at entry to junior school and in later years. Moreover, there were small but significant differences in progress in reading, with the Caribbean group making poorer progress than predicted by first year attainment. Differences, however, were not identified for two other aspects of language work, writing or oral skills.

It also appears that the effects of ethnic background varied for the non-cognitive outcomes of education. The incidence of behaviour difficulties was higher (though it still recorded only for a minority) amongst Caribbean children, in their class teachers' assessments.

This relationship, however, was apparently due to poorer attainment (behaviour and attainment being closely linked). In contrast, the Caribbean group had better attendance and Asian pupils poorer attendance during the junior years. On the whole, attitudes varied little, but the Asian group tended to have more favourable attitudes to school and to mathematics, while Caribbean children had more favourable views of reading. There was no evidence that minority groups had less positive self-concepts than their white peers (the Asian children actually had more favourable views of themselves in school than others).

3.6 *Sex differences*
Sex was strongly associated with pupils' attainments in reading and writing, with girls achieving more highly than boys at each assessment. For example, at entry the mean raw score in reading for girls was 50.8, that for boys only 41.4. Analyses at the individual level, taking into account all other factors, indicated that this difference represented a gap of about five months in terms of reading age, in favour of girls. The average reading score of girls was consistently higher than that of boys, thus girls did not lose their initial superiority in reading. In the *London Reading Test* given to all pupils in their fourth year in junior school, prior to transfer to secondary school, only 19 per cent of girls compared with 32 per cent of boys scored below the cut-off recommended for special-needs screening. This cut-off was designed to identify children who might have difficulty in coping with the level of reading required by texts used in the first year curriculum of secondary school. However, when progress in reading (change in attainment over time) was examined, no sex difference was identified. In other words, the gap in achievement between the sexes did not increase during the junior years.

For writing, the results were very similar, girls attaining more highly in both the qualitative and technical assessments throughout the junior period. Interestingly, however, no sex differences were found in the oracy assessments in pupils' abilities to communicate effectively in different types of speaking activity.

For maths, a rather different picture emerged. There was little difference between the sexes in their attainment as measured by the two groups' average written maths scores. As a group, the girls' score was marginally above that of boys on each occasion, though differences did not reach statistical significance until towards the end of junior schooling. However, when progress in maths was examined, at the individual level, it was found that girls had made greater progress than boys during their junior schooling.

There were no sex differences in pupil attainment or progress in practical maths or visio-spatial skills, areas in which the common belief or stereotype is that boys have greater innate ability than girls. The study, therefore, provided no evidence that girls were under-achieving in maths during the junior period. This means that the later 'fall-off' in girls' mathematics achievement during secondary schooling should be a particular cause for concern.

Marked sex differences in teachers' assessments of pupil behaviour in school were also identified. Boys were much more likely to be rated as having difficulties. This may be because of the strong link between poor attainment and poor behaviour identified in the research. The finding of an association between sex and behaviour in school was supported by field officers' classroom observations. Boys were significantly more likely to be observed 'off-task' (not doing whatever work they were supposed to be doing) than girls in each year. Girls were also more likely to report favourable attitudes to school than boys.

It was found that teachers generally took into account children's attainment, particularly those in basic skill areas, when rating pupils' abilities. As would be predicted from their higher attainment in reading and writing, more girls were rated as above average in ability than boys. For example, in the second year 35 per cent of girls compared with under 27 per cent of boys were rated as above average, whereas less than 25 per cent of girls but over one-third of boys were rated as below average by their teachers. However, perhaps rather surprisingly, given their higher attainments, more favourable attitudes and better behaviour, there was no evidence that class teachers had higher expectations of girls than boys.

3.7 Interactions between the effects of sex and ethnic background

Analyses were conducted to test for the existence of interactions between the effects of sex and ethnic background. The results provided some evidence of interactions between ethnic background and sex for both reading and mathematics attainment when the Caribbean and ESWI groups were compared. However, the effects only reached significance on two of the four occasions on which pupil attainment in these basic skill areas was tested. From the results, it appears that the gap in attainment between Caribbean and ESWI pupils was greater for boys than for girls. When progress was analysed, ethnic and sex interactions were not found to reach statistical significance. This result may, in part, reflect the strong links between sex, ethnic group and behaviour which were all related to attainment.

3.8 School differences

From the two examples (of sex and ethnic differences) of the strong links between background factors and pupils' educational outcomes, it is clear that proper account needs to be taken of the impact of these and other background factors when studying school effectiveness. This is because schools differ markedly in the composition of their pupil intakes. For example, there were marked differences between schools in the percentage of pupils from families with a low income, as measured by eligibility for free school meals (see Table 3).

Table 3: Differences between schools in the percentage of pupils from low income families and in ethnic composition

	% pupils eligible for free school meals	% pupils from ESWI backgrounds
Highest % any school	59.4	95.6
Lowest % any school	3.3	22.0
Average % all schools	30.7	59.0

(N of schools = 50)

There were also marked differences in the ethnic composition of the pupil intakes. Table 3 gives the range in the percentage of ESWI pupils. In the case of children from Asian backgrounds, five schools had intakes with more than a fifth of pupils from this group, and in one instance the figure was 38 per cent. In contrast, in 16 of the schools none of the first year intake was of Asian origin. The average for the sample of schools was 6.8 per cent.

Similarly, there were marked variations in the distribution of children of Caribbean backgrounds. One of the schools received over half, and a further six schools had over a quarter of first year pupils from this group. In eight different schools, however, none of the pupils was of Caribbean background.

Children's attainment in any particular basic skill area (e.g. reading, maths, writing) at entry to junior school was found to be a good predictor of their attainment in that area several years later. This is as might be expected; those who are good readers at entry tend to remain good readers as they grow older (though some children made more or less progress than might be predicted, given their attainment at entry).

It was also found that, even at entry at age seven, there were very marked differences between individual children in their attainment in basic skills (well over a two-year gap in reading ages amongst the year group in the JSP sample, for example). Moreover, some schools received intakes which contained pupils who had a much higher average attainment than other schools (see Table 4).

Table 4: Differences between schools in pupils' attainment at entry

	Reading skills	Maths skills	Visio-spatial skills
Average raw score all schools	45.5	24.1	24.4
School with highest average raw score at entry	62.6	29.3	31.1
School with lowest average raw score	17.3	18.3	19.4
Maximum possible raw score in pupil assessment	91	42	40

These figures on differences in intake again demonstrate why to study school effectiveness it was necessary to focus on the amount of *progress* made by individual children (the change in their attainment over time). Even after controlling for pupils' initial attainment at entry and for background factors, however, the data show that the school made a substantial contribution to children's progress and development. In terms of the first question asked (Are some schools more effective at promoting pupils' learning and development, when account is taken of intake?), it was found that schools *did* make a substantial difference to their pupils' progress and development. In fact, for many of the educational outcomes – especially progress in cognitive areas – the school was very much more important than background factors in accounting for variations between individuals (see Table 5).

Interestingly, the impact of school on progress in written maths and writing was relatively stronger than that for reading. This is perhaps because parents are more likely to have an influence on children's reading in the home (reading stories to the child and listening to the child read) than on writing and maths activities. The analyses of

Table 5: Relative importance of school and home background factors for pupil progress

| | % Variation in Pupil Progress | |
	School	Background
Reading	23.6	6.1
Written maths	23.1	2.5
Writing quality	19.7	2.4

children's oracy (speaking skills) and of their social outcomes also confirmed the overriding importance of school.

The size of the effects of each of the sample schools on each of the measures of pupils' educational outcomes was calculated. The differences between the least and the most effective schools were striking. Taking reading as one example, the most effective school improved a pupil's third-year attainment by an average of 15 points above that predicted by that child's attainment when they started junior school, taking into account her or his background. But in the least effective school, each child's attainment was, on average, 10 points lower than predicted. This compares with an overall average reading score for all pupils of 54 points, and a maximum possible of 100. The differences are shown in percentage terms in Table 6.

Table 6: Differences between the most and the least effective schools for different outcomes

Outcome	Most Effective school %	Least Effective school %
Reading	+28	−19
Written maths	+21	−21
Writing	+27	−21
Oracy	+27	−23
Self-concept	+14	−12
Behaviour	+32	−15
Attendance	+5	−4
Attitude to school	+38	−41

N of schools = 50

It was also relevant to establish whether some schools were *generally more effective* in promoting a broad range of educational outcomes than others. The results showed that a sizeable number of schools (14 in all) had positive effects on children's progress and development in most of the cognitive and most of the non-cognitive outcomes. These can be seen as the generally effective schools. In contrast, five schools were rather ineffective in most areas. Many schools were effective in a few, but not all areas. However, there were very few schools that only had positive impacts on pupil learning in cognitive areas, but were unsuccessful at fostering their social (non-cognitive) development, or vice versa.

3.8 School effects on different groups

It was also possible to compare the effects of schools on the progress of different groups of children. This comparison was made in order to answer the second question addressed by the research (Are some schools more effective for particular groups of pupils?). The answer proved to be 'no'. Generally, it was found that schools which were effective in promoting the progress of one group of pupils were also effective for other groups, and those which were less effective for one group were also less effective for others. Thus, a school that was effective for boys was also effective for girls, one that was effective for a child from a non-manual worker's family was also effective for one from a working-class family. Similar results were found when school effects were compared for children of different ethnic backgrounds. The data showed that an effective school tends to 'jack up' the performance of *all* its pupils irrespective of their sex, social class origins or race. Moreover, the evidence indicates that, although overall differences in attainment were not removed, on average a pupil from a working-class family attending one of the more effective schools, ended up attaining more highly than one from a non-manual family background attending one of the least effective schools.

3.9 Understanding school effectiveness

The results of the JSP indicate that the particular school attended can make a substantial difference to the future educational prospects of individual children. Given this, the third question addressed by the Project is crucially important. What makes some schools more effective than others?

In order to answer the third question, analyses were undertaken to establish what *factors* and *processes* related to school and classroom organization were related to positive school effects. In other words, the aim was to identify the ways in which the more effective schools differed from those which were less effective.

From the extensive data collected it was possible to look at a wide variety of process variables related to the school as a whole, and ones specifically concerning individual classrooms. These were divided into 'givens' and 'policies'. The 'givens' are those aspects not directly under the control of the school (e.g. the size of its pupil roll, intake, stability of staff, pupil mobility). The policies, in contrast, are aspects which can be altered by the school (e.g. the headteacher's leadership, curriculum, rewards and punishment system, organization, staff involvement and conditions). At the level of the individual classroom there are also a variety of 'givens' not under the direct control of the teacher (e.g. the size of the class, the composition of pupils in terms of balance of age, sex or ability, the resources available). In addition, there are many policy factors under the class teacher's direct control (e.g. record keeping, system of rewards and punishments, use of praise, amount and type of communication with pupils, preparation and planning) which were included in the investigation.

Much of the variation between schools in their effects on pupils' progress and development was accounted for by differences between schools in their policies and practices. Furthermore, a number of the significant variables were themselves associated. By a detailed examination of the ways in which classroom and school processes were interrelated, it was possible to gain a greater understanding of some of the important *mechanisms* by which effective education is promoted. (For a full explanation of the findings and their implications see Mortimore et al., 1988. A discussion of some of the results of particular relevance to teachers' classroom practice is given in Mortimore et al., 1987.)

4. KEY FACTORS FOR EFFECTIVE JUNIOR SCHOOLING

From the analyses it was possible to identify a number of *key factors* which are important in accounting for the differential effectiveness of schools. We emphasize that these factors are not purely statistical constructs. They have not been obtained solely by means of quantitative analysis. Rather, they are derived from a combination of careful examination and discussion of the statistical findings, and the use of educational and research judgement. They represent the interpretation of the research results by an interdisciplinary team of researchers and teachers.

It was found that some schools were more advantaged in terms of some of the 'given' factors – their size, status, environment and stability of teaching staff. There was evidence that smaller schools (in terms of number of pupils on roll) tended to be more effective than larger ones. Class size was particularly relevant: smaller classes with less than 24 pupils (the average in our sample was 25, with a range of 16 to 34), had a positive association with pupils' progress in maths, attainment in speaking skills, children's behaviour, attitudes to school and self-concept. Class size was most closely associated with pupil progress in the earlier junior years.

Not surprisingly a good physical environment, as reflected in the school's amenities and decorative order creates a positive location in which progress and development can be fostered. The stability of the school's teaching force is important. Changes of head and deputy head, though inevitable in all schools at some stage, have an unsettling effect. Similarly, it was found that changes of class teacher *during* the school year had an adverse impact on pupils' progress and development.

Nonetheless, although these favourable 'given' characteristics contribute to effectiveness, they do not, by themselves, ensure it. They provide a supporting framework within which the headteacher and teachers can work to promote children's progress and development. However, it is the policies and processes within the control of the head and teachers that are crucial. These are the factors that can be changed and improved.

Twelve key factors of effectiveness have been identified by the research. These factors were not independent of each other but, as might be expected, were closely linked and interdependent.

4.1 Purposeful leadership of the staff by the headteacher

'Purposeful leadership' occurred where the head understood the needs of the school and was actively involved in the school's work, without exerting total control over the rest of the staff.

In effective schools, heads were involved in curriculum discussions and influenced the content of guidelines drawn up within the school. They also influenced the classroom strategies of teachers, but only selectively, where they judged it necessary. This leadership was also demonstrated by an emphasis on monitoring pupils' progress through the years, and discussing teachers' work plans and records of individual pupils' progress on a regular basis.

4.2 *The involvement of the deputy head*
The findings indicate that the deputy head can have a major role in the effectiveness of junior schools.

Where the deputy was absent frequently, or absent for a prolonged period (due to illness, attendance on long courses, or other commitments), this was detrimental to pupils' progress and development. The responsibilities undertaken by deputies also seemed to be important. Where the head generally involved him or her in policy-decisions, it assisted effectiveness. This was particularly true in terms of decisions about allocating teachers to classes. Overall, the deputy's role seems to be a neglected one in terms of research yet it can have a significant impact; in many schools it was the deputy's role to be in charge of the day-to-day running of the school.

4.3 *The involvement of teachers*
In successful schools, the teachers were involved in curriculum planning and played a major role in developing their own curriculum guidelines. As with the deputy head, teacher involvement in decisions concerning which classes they were to teach, was important. Similarly, discussion with teachers about decisions on resource spending contributed to greater school effectiveness. It appeared that schools in which teachers were consulted on issues affecting school policy, as well as those affecting them directly, were more successful.

4.4 *Consistency amongst teachers*
The data revealed that continuity of staffing had positive effects on pupils' educational outcomes. Not only, however, do children benefit from teacher continuity, but it is also clear that stability, or consistency, in teacher approach is important. For example, in schools where all teachers followed curriculum guidelines in the same way (whether closely or selectively), the impact on progress was positive. Variation between teachers in their usage of guidelines, had a negative effect. There was a link between teacher consistency and the purposeful leadership of the headteacher.

4.5 *Structured sessions*
Pupils appeared to benefit when their school day was structured in some way. In effective schools, work was organized by the teacher,

who ensured that there was always plenty for children to do, and they were *not* given unlimited responsibility for planning their own programme of work. (In some schools in the UK young children are expected to plan and organize their own programme of work over extended periods, such as a half day or even a whole day session. This was found to be a much less effective strategy.) In general, teachers who organized a framework within which pupils could work, and yet allowed them some freedom within this structure, were most successful.

4.6 Intellectually challenging teaching

Unsurprisingly, the quality of teaching was very important in promoting progress and development. The findings clearly show that, in classes where pupils were stimulated and challenged, progress was greater.

The content of teachers' communications was vitally important. Positive effects occurred where teachers used, what we termed, 'higher-order' questions and statements; that is, where their communications encouraged children to use creative imagination and powers of problem-solving. In classes where the teaching situation was challenging and stimulating, and where teachers communicated interest and enthusiasm to the children, greater progress occurred. It appeared, in fact, that teachers who more frequently directed children's work, without discussing it or explaining its purpose, had a negative impact.

Creating a challenge for pupils suggests that the teacher believes they are capable of responding to it. It was evident that such teachers had *high* expectations. This was further seen in the effectiveness of teachers who encouraged their pupils to take responsibility for managing individual pieces of work, but provided plenty of feedback on the task.

4.7 Work-centered environment

The work-centered environment was characterized by a high level of industry in the classroom. Pupils appeared to enjoy their work and were eager to commence new tasks. The noise level was also low, although this is not to say that there was silence in the classroom. Furthermore, pupil movement around the classroom was not excessive, and was generally work-related. In schools where teachers spent more of their time discussing the *content* of children's work, and less time on routine matters and the maintenance of work activity, the impact was positive. There was some indication that more time devoted to giving children feedback about their work was also beneficial. It was also found that more intellectually challenging teaching tended to occur in work-centred classrooms.

4.8 Limited focus within sessions
Our data showed that learning was facilitated when teachers devoted their energies to one particular curriculum area within a session (although, at times, work could be undertaken in two areas and also produce positive effects). However, where sessions were usually organized such that three or more curriculum areas were concurrent (mixed activity sessions), children's progress was marred, and their behaviour and attitudes were poorer. A focus upon one curriculum area did not imply that all pupils were doing exactly the same work. There was variation, both in terms of choice of topic and level of difficulty, and positive effects tended to occur where the teacher geared the level of work to individual needs.

It was found that in schools where all children were working in the same broad curriculum area, teachers spent more time communicating about work and pupils were more involved with their work.

4.9 Maximum communication between teachers and pupils
It was evident that children gained from having more communication with the teacher. Thus, those teachers who spent higher proportions of their time *not* interacting with the children were less successful in promoting progress and development. Our field officers observed quite notable differences between individual teachers in the amount of time they spent talking to pupils.

The time teachers spent on communications with the whole class was also important. Most teachers devoted the majority of their attention to speaking with individuals. Each child, therefore, could only expect to receive a fairly small number of individual contacts with their teacher (on average only 11 in a working day). When teachers spoke to the whole class, they increased the overall number of contacts with children. In particular, this enabled a greater number of 'higher-order' communications to be received by *all* pupils. Furthermore, where children worked in a single curriculum area within sessions, (even if they were engaged on individual or group tasks) it was easier for teachers to raise an intellectually challenging point with *all* pupils. It also helped teachers to maintain the attention of all members of the class and to keep pupils on task.

4.10 Record keeping
The value of record keeping has already been noted, in relation to the purposeful leadership of the headteacher. However, it was also an important aspect of teachers' planning and assessment. Where teachers reported that they kept written records of individuals' work, and used these as a tool for monitoring progress, the impact was positive. Keeping records of children's social development and behaviour was also associated with more effective practice.

4.11 Parental involvement
From the research it was clear that parental involvement is a positive influence upon children's progress and development. Parental involvement included help in classrooms and on educational visits, and attendance at meetings to discuss children's progress. The headteacher's accessibility to parents was also important, showing that schools with an informal, 'open door' policy were more effective. Parental involvement in children's educational development within the home was also beneficial. Parents who read to their children, heard them read, and provided them with access to books at home, took them to the library etc., had a positive effect upon their children's learning.

4.12 Positive climate
The study provides confirmation that an effective school has a positive climate, atmosphere, or ethos. Overall, the atmosphere was more pleasant in the effective schools, for a variety of reasons. Both around the school and within the classroom, less emphasis on punishment and critical control, and a greater emphasis on praise and rewarding children, had a positive impact. Where teachers actively encouraged self-control on the part of children, rather than emphasizing the negative aspects of their behaviour, progress and development increased. What appeared to be important was firm but fair classroom management.

The teacher's attitude to his or her class was also important. Good effects were found where teachers obviously enjoyed teaching and communicated this to their students. Their interest in the children as individuals was also valuable. Those who devoted some time to non-school discussion or 'small-talk' increased progress and development. Outside the classroom, evidence of a positive climate included: the organization of lunchtime and after-school clubs; teachers eating their lunch at the same tables as the children; organization of educational trips and visits; and the teacher's use of the local environment as a learning resource for children.

The working conditions of teachers contributed to the creation of a positive school climate. Where teachers had time allocated for preparation on a regular basis, the school's impact on pupil progress and development was positive. Thus, the climate created by the teachers for the pupils, and by the headteacher and the Local Education Authority for the teachers, was an important aspect of the school's effectiveness. Furthermore, this appeared to be reflected in effective schools by happy, well-behaved pupils who were friendly towards each other and outsiders, and by the absence of graffiti around the school.

From a detailed examination of the factors and the processes which were related to schools' effects on their students, a picture evolves of what constitutes effective junior education. In particular, 12 'key-factors' have been identified. These factors depend on specific behaviours and strategies employed by the headteacher and staff. It is essential to realize that the school and the classroom are in many ways interlocked: what the teacher can or cannot do often depends on what is happening in the school as a whole. It is easier to be an effective teacher in some schools than it is in others.

Thus, whilst the 12 factors do not constitute a 'recipe' for effective junior schooling, they do provide a vital *framework* within which the various partners in the life of the school – head and staff, parents and pupils, and the community – can operate and on which they can build towards improvement. Each of these partners has the capacity to foster the success of the school. When each participant plays a positive role, the result is an effective school.

5. CONCLUSIONS

The JSP research has important implications for the various partners involved in the resourcing and management of schools, including national government, Local Education Authorities, teacher trainers, governors, heads, classroom teachers and parents. The most important implication which stems from the study is that schools matter. They matter in two senses: because they can help pupils to change and develop, and also because their effects are not uniform. The findings also demonstrate that schools often vary in their effectiveness in different areas, and point to the importance of examining a broad range of pupils' educational outcomes in any national or regional monitoring and in comparisons of schools' performance.

The results of school effectiveness research demonstrate that schools *do* make a difference to pupils' educational outcomes, and that the difference can be substantial. They also indicate what factors about schools and about classroom practice help to make that difference. In other words, the research means we can go a long way towards explaining *why* some schools are more effective than others.

Elswhere the links between two major studies of school effectiveness have been examined, and it is clear that there are many areas of agreement (see Sammons, 1987b). This shows the extent to which school effectiveness research is able to further our understanding of the importance of school as the major influence on pupils' progress and development, and the ways that school processes affect pupils. The consistency in the findings suggests that they can be used to develop a useful framework for school self-evaluation and improvement.

It must be acknowledged that the findings of earlier school effectiveness research have sometimes been criticized, as just a matter of common-sense, and the value of such research has been questioned. Because school effectiveness research by its very nature sets out to identify the components of good practice which is already occurring in many schools, it is inevitable that some of the findings appear to be purely 'common-sense'. However, the fact that there are such striking variations in the performance or effectiveness of individual schools makes it clear that it is not just a matter of common-sense. If it were, and if all were agreed as to what *is* common-sense in education, all schools would be found to be equally effective!

Nonetheless the common-sense aspect is worth acknowledging. Renihan and colleagues (1986) have commented: "The effective schools literature did not tell us anything startlingly revolutionary about organizing the school environment. Its major impact lay in highlighting factors vital to school success." (p. 17.) Similarly Rutter et al. (1979) concluded: "Research into practical issues, such as schooling, rarely comes up with findings which are totally unexpected. On the other hand, it is helpful in showing which of the abundance of good ideas available are related to successful outcomes." (p. 204.)

In conclusion, therefore, attention is drawn to two important points about school effectiveness research. Firstly, that the findings are relevant to *all* schools, teachers and pupils, and can and should be considered by all concerned with promoting educational excellence. "The characteristics that describe effective schools are practical, obtainable, and if we are serious enough and systematic and thoughtful enough, can come to describe all of the schools that we work in." (Edmonds, 1981, quoted by Toews & Barker, 1985, p.15.) Secondly, that an increase in effectiveness is also possible for all. Here, the findings that effective schools tend to raise the performance of all pupils, irrespective of age, sex, race or social class is of particular significance. The pressure to improve must be accompanied by a perception that improvement is possible for all schools as well as for all learners.

The importance of school effectiveness research for improving the quality of children's learning relates to the message that schools matter. Such research increases our understanding of what happens in schools, and therefore provides an appropriate basis for school self-evaluation and the development of school improvement plans. Those responsible for administering the education service, and who are accountable for the quality of the service they provide, have an overarching interest in promoting effective education. The results of school effectiveness research can be used to assist the development of appropriate in-service training for heads and teachers. Advisory and inspectorate services can also examine the findings to assist in the monitoring of quality in the education service.

NOTES

1 On school improvement: A conversation with Ronald Edmonds, *Educational Leadership*, December 1982, Vol. 40, No. 3, p. 14.

2 The ILEA is the largest School Board in Europe. It has more than 1000 schools (primary and secondary) and over 280,000 students attend these.

3 Many analyses were undertaken to investigate the strength of relationships between family factors (family size, position in the family, parental language) and attainment and progress in cognitive and non-cognitive outcomes. These relationships (wherever they were found to be statistically significant) were taken into account in analyses of progress and school effects. Moreover, all background factors found to be important in previous studies were included when assessing the effects of age, sex, class or race on individual attainment and progress. Other home-based factors were also investigated for the sub-sample of pupils involved in the home interview study.

4 Because the numbers of Asian children in different language groups were often small (e.g. Gujerati = 14 in year 1, Punjabi = 10) results on differences *between* sub-groups of Asian children should be treated with caution.

5 This ethnic effect, though statistically highly significant, was nevertheless small in comparison with the effects of pupil's sex, father's social class, or eligibility for free meals.

6 Controlling for attainment, however, did not remove the significant relationship between sex, free meals, and father's social class and pupil's behaviour. These factors continued to have a statistically significant impact.

ACKNOWLEDGEMENTS

The Junior School Project was instituted and directed by Dr. Peter Mortimore. It would not have been possible to carry out the study without the continued support of all the heads, teachers, students and parents involved. Thanks are due to the members of the research team, especially Louise Stoll, David Lewis and Russell Ecob, as well as to a number of teachers who worked as field officers on the project - Mary Hunt, Jennifer Runham, Dick Cooper, Pamela Glanville and Cathy Bunch. Thanks must also be expressed to past and present colleagues, in particular Audrey Hind, Kate Foot, Andreas Varlaam, Brian Clover, Christine Mabey, Anne-Marie Hill and Colin Alston.

REFERENCES

AITKIN, M., BENNET, N. & HESKETH, J. (1981a). Teaching styles and pupil progress: A re-analysis. *British Journal of Educational Psychology, 51*, 170-186.

AITKIN, M., ANDERSON, D. & HINDE, J. (1981b). Statistical modelling of data on teaching styles. *Journal of the Royal Statistical Society, 144*, 419-461.

Assessment of Performance Unit (APU) (1981). *Language performance in schools. Primary Survey Report No. 1.* London: HMSO.

Assessment of Performance Unit (APU) (1982). *Language performance in schools. Primary Survey Report No. 2.* London: HMSO.

BROOKOVER, W.B., SCHWEITZER, J.H., SCHNEIDER, J.M., BEADY, C.H., FLOOD, P.K. & WISENBAKER, I.M. (1978). Elementary school climate and school achievement. *American Educational Research Journal, 15*, 2, 301-318.

BROOKOVER, W.B., BEADY, C., FLOOD, P.K. & SCHWEITZER, J.H. (1979). *School systems and student achievement: schools make a difference.* New York: Praeger.

BUNCH, C. (1984). *Attitudes revealed in children's stories.* Research and Statistics Branch ILEA.

COLEMAN, J.S., CAMPBELL, E., HOBSON, C, MCPARTLAND, J., MOOD, A., WEINFELD, F. & YORK, R. (1966). *Equality of education opportunity.* Washington: National Center for Educational Statistics.

EDMONDS, R.R. (1979a). Effective schools for the urban poor. *Educational Leadership, 37*, 15-27.

EDMONDS, R.R. (1979b). Some schools work and can more. *Social Policy, 12*, 56-60.

EDMONDS, R.R. (1982). Programs of school improvement; an overview. *Educational Leadership, 40*, December, 4-11.

EGGLESTON, S.J., DUNN, D.K. & AJJALI, M. (1985). *The educational and vocational experiences of 15-18 year old young people of ethnic minority groups*. Department of Education: University of Keele.

ELDERING, L. (1988). *Ethnic minority children in Dutch schools: underachievement and its explanations*. Paper presented to the International Workshop on 'Education and the cultural development of ethnic minority children'. Kerkrade, Netherlands, 12-14 September

ESSEN, J. & GHODSIAN, M. (1980). The children of immigrants: school performance. *New community, 7*, 442-429.

ESSEN, J. & WEDGE, P. (1982). *Continuities in childhood disadvantage*. London: Heinemann.

GOLDSTEIN, H. (1980). Fifteen thousand hours. A review of the statistical procedures. *Journal of Child Psychology and Psychiatry, 21*, 363-366.

GOLDSTEIN, H. (1984). The methodology of school comparisons. *Oxford Review of Education, 10*, 69-74.

Good, T. (1979). Teacher effectiveness in the elementary school, what do we know about it now? *Journal of Teacher Education, 30*, 52-64.

GOODLAD, J.I. et al. (1979). *A study of schooling*. Indiana: Phi Delta Kappa Inc.

GOODLAD, J.I. (1984). *A place called school*. New York: McGraw- Hill.

GORMAN, T. & HARGREAVES, M. (1985). *Talking together: NFER/ILEA oracy survey*. Slough: Department of Language NFER.

GRAY, J. (1981). A competitive edge. Examination results and the probable limits of secondary school effectiveness. *Educational Review, 33*, 25-35.

GRAY, J. & JONES, B. (1985). Combining quantitive and qualitive approaches to studies of school and teacher effectiveness. In D. Reynolds (Ed.), *Studying School Effectiveness*. London: Falmer Press.

HUNTER, J., KYSEL, F. & MORTIMORE, P. (1985). *Children in need: The growing needs of inner London school children*. London: Research and Statistics Branch Report RS 994/85, ILEA.

JENCKS, C.S., SMITH, M., ACKLAND, H., BANE, M.J., COHEN, D., GINTIS, H., HEYNS, B. & MICHOLSON, S. (1972). *Inequality. A reassessment of the effect of family and schooling in America*. New York: Basic Books.

MABEY, C. (1985). *Achievement of black pupils: reading competence as a predictor of exam success amongst Afro-Caribbean pupils in London*. Ph.D. Thesis. London: University of London.

MADAUS, G.F., KELLAGHAN, T., RAKOW, E.A. & KING, D.J. (1979). The sensitivity of measures of school effectivenes. *Harvard Educational Review, 49*, 207-230.

MARJORIEBANKS, K. (1979). *Families and their learning environments: an empirical analysis*. London: Routledge and Kegan Paul.

MORTIMORE, J. & BLACKSTONE, T. (1982). *Disadvantage in education*. London: Heinemann.

MORTIMORE, P. (1983). *Achievement in schools*. London: Research and Statistics Branch Report RS 829/82, ILEA.

MORTIMORE, P., SAMMONS, P., STOLL, L., LEWIS, D. & ECOB, R. *(1986). The Junior School Project Main Report, 4 volumes*, London: Research and Statistics Branch, ILEA.

MORTIMORE, P., SAMMONS, P., STOLL, L., LEWIS, D. & ECOB, R. (1987). For effective classroom practices. *Forum, 30*, 1, 8-11.

MORTIMORE, P., SAMMONS, P., STOLL, L., LEWIS, D. & ECOB, R. (1988). *School matters, the junior years*. Wells: Open Books.

PURKEY, S.C. & SMITH, M.S. (1983). Effective schools, a review. *Elementary School Journal*, 83, 427-452.

RAMPTON REPORT (1981). *West Indian children in our schools: interim report of the Committee of Inquiry into the education of children from ethnic minority groups*. London: HMSO.

RENIHAN, P.J., RENIHAN, F.I. & WALDRON, P. (1986). The common ingredients of successful school effectiveness projects. *Education Canada, Fall*, 16-21.

REYNOLDS, D. (1982). The search for effective schools. *School Organization*, 2, 215-237.

REYNOLDS, D. (Ed.) (1985). *Studying school effectiveness*. London: Falmer Press.

RUTTER, M. & MADGE, N. (1976). *Cycles of disadvantage*. London: Heinemann.

RUTTER, M., MAUGHAM, B., MORTIMORE, P. & OUSTON, J. (1979). *Fifteen thousand hours*. London: Open Books.

SAMMONS, P. (1987a). *School Climate. The key to fostering student progress and development?* Paper presented to the Annual Convention of the Prince Edward Island Teachers' Federation on 'school atmosphere, the barometer of success', October 29-30, 1987, Charlottetown, Prince Edward Island, Canada.

SAMMONS, P. (1987b). *Findings from school effectiveness research: A framework for school improvement*. Paper presented to the Annual Convention of the Prince Edward Island Teachers' Federation on 'school atmosphere, the barometer of success', October 29-30, 1987, Charlottetown, Prince Edward Island, Canada.

SAMMONS, P. (1983). Educational priority indices: a new perspective. *British Educational Research Journal*, 9, 27-40.

SAMMONS, P., MORTIMORE, P. & VARLAAM, H. (1985). *Socio-economic background, parental involvement and attitudes, and children's achievements in junior schools*. London: Research and Statistics Branch Report RS 982/85, ILEA.

STRACHAN, V. & SAMMONS, P. (1986). *ILEA Junior School Project: The assessment of creative writing*. London: Research and Statistics Branch, ILEA.

SUMMERS, A.A. & WOLFE, B.L. (1977). Do schools make a difference? *American Economic Review*, 64, 639-652.

Swann Report (1985). *Education for all: The report of the Committee of Inquiry into the education of children from ethnic minority groups*. London: HMSO.

TOEWS, J. & BARKER, D.M. (1985). *The Baz-attack: a school improvement experience utilizing effective schools research 1981- 1985*. Alberta: Ian Bazalgette Junior High School.

TOMLINSON, S. (1988). *Ethnicity and educational achievement in Britain*. Paper presented to the International Workshop 'Education and the cultural development of ethnic minority children'. Kerkrade, Netherlands, 12-14 September.

United States Department of Education (1986). *What works, research about teaching and learning*. Washington: United States Department of Education.

VARLAAM, A., WOODS, J. & MORTIMORE, P. (1985). *Parents and primary schools*. London: Research and Statistics Branch Report RS 987/85, ILEA.

Weber, G. (1971). *Inner city children can be taught to read, four successful schools*. Washington, D.C.: Council for Basic Education.

APPENDIX 1: THE CHARACTERISTICS OF THE PUPIL SAMPLE

In 1980, a sample of 50 schools was selected randomly from 636 ILEA primary schools containing junior pupils. Analyses have confirmed that the sample was representative of junior age pupils in the Authority as a whole. In comparison with children nationally, however, the sample was bound to reflect the characteristics of children in an inner city area. Thus, the percentage of children from one-parent families, ethnic minority groups, those using English as a second language, and those receiving free school meals, were probably higher than figures for the country as a whole. Unfortunately, it was not possible to compare the sample with national figures directly, except for the free meals factor. At the start of the study 30.5 per cent of the pupils received free school meals, compared with 20.7 per cent nationally (CIPFA figures for 1980/81).

The characteristics of the sample at the start of the Project in terms of sex, ethnic group, language, parental occupations, family size and eligibility for free school meals are shown in table A.

Table A: The characteristics of the sample of pupils at the start of the Project

Ethnic and Language Background		
		%*
Ethnic Group	African	2.9
	Asian	6.5
	Caribbean	12.9
	Chinese	1.0
	ESWI	60.6
	Greek	1.7
	Turkish	1.5
	Other	12.9
Child's First Language	English	84.4
	Not English	15.6
Fluency in English	Not fully fluent	7.7

Parental Occupations (Registrar General's Classification)

		Mother's	Father's
Non-manual	I	0.9	2.6
	II	5.8	13.9
	III	11.8	8.1
Manual	III	3.3	35.0
	IV	10.1	8.2
	V	5.7	7.3
Long Term Unemployed		0.8	6.1
Economically Inactive		59.2	2.1
Absent		2.3	16.8

Family Size and Structure

Family Size	Only child	15.8
	Two children	42.5
	Three children	23.6
	Four or more children	18.1
Child's Position in Family	First born	40.2
	Second born	32.5
	Third born	16.1
	Fourth born or later	11.3

Income

	Free meals received	30.5

N of pupils = 1823

* Pupils for whom information was not known were excluded in the calculation of percentages for the characteristic concerned.

11

Jo Kloprogge & Lotty Eldering

*Leiden University & Institute for Educational
Research in the Netherlands*

Outline for a
European Research Programme

The chapters in this volume are based on the papers presented at the
International workshop on "The educational and cultural development of ethnic minority children", held in Kerkrade, the Netherlands,
September 1988. They represent the views of experts in various academic fields and from several European countries on the current situation and prospects of ethnic minority children in education. The
themes that were discussed concerned:
- ethnic-cultural and socio-economic factors influencing the school
  careers of ethnic minority children
- second language acquisition
- school organization and school effectiveness.
Among the considerable variety of views, corresponding to the various scientific disciplines and theoretical standpoints of the participants and to the differences in the educational situation of ethnic
minority children in their countries, quite a few issues of common
concern and topics for further research were identified at the workshop.
Firstly the general idea that ethnic minority pupils lag behind their
majority classmates needs to be differentiated. In several chapters it
has been pointed out that the academic achievement of ethnic minority pupils has been improving slowly in recent years, although differences between various ethnic groups remain substantial. A com-

prehensive theory to explain this diversity is still lacking. One relevant question is : can the educational performance of children from these groups be explained by general theoretical models, or should it be explained by specific factors, related to immigration, minority position and ethnic/cultural/linguistic backgrounds?

The lack of knowledge about the preschool phase of ethnic minority children was stressed during the discussions as a second subject of concern that needs further attention in research. So far the preschool period of minority children has been neglected in research. A central question in this context is how to prepare children of preschool age better for school in order to prevent them from starting another cycle of failure. What can be expected of intervention programmes for children of this age?

Thirdly, it was generally agreed that parental involvement as a factor influencing the school career of children is underestimated. Research on this topic should not only focus on factors that encourage or hinder parental involvement, but should also pay attention to how ethnic minority parents themselves view the schooling of their children and more specifically how they define school success and failure.

The aforementioned topics all point out the importance of the ethnic-cultural backgrounds of the pupils. This is in line with the conclusions with regard to theme two, second language acquisition. It was emphasized that more insight in the second language acquisition process might be gained from – communication and ecology oriented – studies with a developmental perspective. This process should not only be studied in schools, but also within the family and the peer group. Research on the organization and effectiveness of schools indicates that the teacher plays a crucial role in realizing equal opportunities for all pupils. The way in which the teacher is involved in school affairs, teaches and structures the lessons, communicates with pupils and parents, is very important for the progress of the pupils. The outcome of a research project in Britain, which suggests that schools which are effective for majority pupils are also effective for ethnic minority pupils, in cognitive as well as in non-cognitive fields, was considered of great importance.

The very fact that so many problems and developments in the European countries are similar or at least comparable, indicates that an international research programme is desirable and feasible. What would be the advantages of such research, when compared to research on a national level?

First of all, the way in which immigrants are received and find a place in a specific country, partly depends on the attitudes and the behaviour of the residents and institutions in the host country. Research on a national level tends to disregard the influence of these factors because the national situation has to be taken as a fixed point of reference. In international comparative research the differences in national situations can be studied as an independent variable, which may give insights that are beyond the scope of national research.

Current research tends to stress the characteristics of minority groups and their members, such as educational level, length of stay in the country of residence and culture, language and religion. It tends to disregard the peculiarities and effects of the political and educational system of the host country. Several chapters in this volume show that the effects of these systems may be just as important to explain the educational disadvantages of minority groups as the characteristics of these groups themselves.

Secondly, in research on a national level there may be little variety in the minority groups that may be studied. Asiatic minority groups, for instance, comprise a large part of the total population of immigrants in Britain, but are hardly found in the Netherlands or in France. Besides the possibility to extend the variety of ethnic groups, research on an international level offers prospects for comparing groups from the same ethnic origins in different countries. The integration process of the first, second and third generation immigrants of the same origins may proceed differently in the various countries. Italian immigrants in Belgium, for instance, are in many ways different from Italians who are living in the Netherlands. These variations can only be studied adequately through internationally organized research.

Taken together, research transgressing national borders allows a much greater variety of dependent and independent variables to be studied. The results of research with such a wide scope can improve theory building and generate knowledge that is more useful in public policy making.

Most researchers will agree that educational problems with regard to minority groups are complex. They involve a great variety of groups speaking different languages and having different cultures. They also involve the indigenous population in the countries where these groups are living. They are complicated by the development of migrant cultures with specific characteristics, different from the dominating culture of the country of origin as well as from that of the host country. Research efforts should take account of the complexity of these problems.

Participants at the workshop agreed that this implies that research activities should have a long-term perspective and should be fundamental in nature. The use of longitudinal designs was considered the most appropriate approach to observe, compare and analyse developments in life styles, school careers and first and second language proficiency. Within these longitudinal designs, a combination of quantitative and qualitative research is considered necessary. The first kind of research should give broad information about the situation of immigrant groups, for instance with regard to socio-cultural and socio-linguistic factors, educational attainment and school careers, the second kind should provide insights into ongoing processes and help to formulate hypotheses.

Starting from these important, but still general notions, some priorities for international research can be suggested under the headings of the aforementioned themes.

1 *Ethnic-cultural and socio-economic factors which affect school careers*
a. A large-scale socio-cultural and socio-linguistic survey of the situation of ethnic minorities in several countries is needed. Such a survey should yield systematic information about the situation of ethnic minority groups in Europe and about factors that influence the educational opportunities of these groups positively or negatively.
b. A second priority is in-depth research, focusing on the first and last two years of primary education and on preschool-age children and their families. This research should give insight in the child-rearing practices of parents and the way they view and shape the (educational) future of their children. Within this project attention has to be paid to schoolcareers also.

2 *Second language acquisition*
a. A cross-cultural study of home language use of ethnic minorities and intergenerational patterns of shift within and between ethnic minority groups should be executed.
b. Longitudinal research into L1/L2 acquisition in several countries is needed.

Although it was generally felt that linguistic problems are to a large extent interwoven with social and educational problems and that linguistic models and solutions will not reach far enough to solve these social and educational problems too, the linguistic element in itself was considered of utmost importance in view of the challenges of a multicultural society. Nevertheless, there seems to be a gap between generally accepted views and insights of linguists with regard to L1/L2 learning on the one hand , and political views and educational practices on the other. A more intensive communication and exchange of ideas between linguistic experts, educationalists and policy makers was therefore recommended.

3 *School organization and effectiveness*
Studies in this field should concentrate on:
a. Ideas and perceptions of teachers about teaching children from ethnic minority groups and the relation between these ideas and actual teaching practice
b. The effects of different teaching styles and different pupil groupings on pupil achievement and interethnic relations
c. Effective strategies to support the teaching of ethnic minority pupils in mainstream education
d. Teacher-pupil interaction
e. Teaching of the first and second language

In-depth research in these fields may be more fruitful when there are opportunities for experiments and the evaluation of these experiments. Research findings should be incorporated in teacher training programmes that deal with ethnic minorities.

It is clear that designing an international research programme, based upon the ideas formulated during the conference at Kerkrade, will not be an easy task. The issues mentioned above will have to be elaborated. Funds will have to be acquired. Researchers from various scientific disciplines, working in different organizations, will have to cooperate.
As a first step, the *Dutch Institute for Educational Research* has agreed to support the development of the suggested research themes into more elaborate research proposals. Although there is still a long way to go, there are perspectives to realize an internationalization of some of the research efforts with regard to the education of ethnic minority children in European countries.

The presence of ethnic minority groups in these countries is not a temporary phenomenon. Due to the arrival of new groups of immigrants (such as political refugees) and the relatively high birth rates among minority communities, European countries will become more multicultural in the remaining part of this century and in the next. For education this is a problem as well as a challenge. Educational systems will have to change to be able to cope with pupils who seem to fall outside the categories of pupils they were used to in the past. Nearly all (Western) European countries find themselves in this situation. It is clear that research is an important means of finding a way to improve the educational situation of ethnic minority pupils. It is also clear that an international research programme offers better perspectives to find this way than does local or national research.

List of Contributors

PROF. DR. URSULA BOOS-NÜNNING   *Erziehungswissenschaften, University of Essen, Watelerstraße 54, 4050 Mönchengladbach 2 Rheijdt, Federal Republic of Germany*

DR. JACQUELINE COSTA-LASCOUX   *Centre National des Recherches Sociales, Université de Paris, 12 Place du Panthéon, 75005 Paris, France*

PROF. DR. LOTTY ELDERING   *Centre for Intercultural Pedagogics, Leiden University, Wassenaarseweg 52, 2300 RB Leiden, The Netherlands*

PROF. DR. GUUS EXTRA   *Department of Language and Minorities, Tilburg University, P.O. Box 90153, 5000 LE Tilburg, The Netherlands*

PROF. DR. MANFRED HOHMANN   *Erziehungswissenschaften, University of Essen, Watelerstraße 54, 4050 Mönchengladbach 2 Rheijdt, Federal Republic of Germany*

PROF. DR. ÇIGDEM KAGITÇIBAŞI   *Department of Psychology, Bogaziçi University, Bebek - Istanbul, Turkey*

DRS. JO KLOPROGGE   *Evaluator of the Dutch Educational Priority Programme, Dutch Institute for Educational Research, Sweelinckplein 14, 2517 GK The Hague, The Netherlands*

PROF. DR. EUGEEN ROOSSENS   *Centre for Social and Cultural Anthropology, Catholic University of Leuven, Tiensestraat 102, B-3000 Leuven, Belgium*

DR. PAMELA SAMMONS   *Research and Statistics Branch, Inner London Education Authority, Addington Street Annexe, The County Hall, London SE 1 - 7 UZ, Great Britain*

DR. SVEN STRÖMQVIST   *Department of Linguistics, University of Göteborg, Renströmparken, S-41298 Göteborg, Sweden*

PROF. DR. SALLY TOMLINSON   *Department of Educational Research, University of Lancaster, University House, Bailrigg Lancaster LA 14 YW, Great Britain*

DR. TON VALLEN   *Department of Language and Minorities, Tilburg University, P.O. Box 90153, 5000 LE Tilburg, The Netherlands*